Praise for ...

New Tools for New Times:
The Workflow Paradigm

"Great way to grasp quickly what workflow automation really means—from the top," Mike Sullivan, President, Tek-Tools Inc., California.

"The information contained in the appendices makes it a really useful reference book," Hugh Makgill, Makgill Project Management Ltd., New Zealand.

"This book provides a much-needed roadmap to the current state of the workflow world, going all the way from high-level descriptions on the need for workflow down to specific case studies and provides a way for the reader to grasp some of the impact of this new computing paradigm," Michael Squires, Senior Staff Architect, Sequent Computer Systems, Oregon.

"The Workflow Paradigm revolutionizes our whole understanding of the concept of work." Michael Wolff, Michael Wolff Associates, Scotland.

"This book is more concise and practical than the other 123 books and articles on BPR that I've read over the past several years," Ron Cannon, Management Consultant, New Jersey.

"We are very young in bpr at present and it is my job to push the concepts forward. To date I have found your book invaluable and have already put together a migration discussion document to take us forward." Graham Smith, Head of Systems and Methods, Materials Department, Brunei Shell Petroleum, Sudan.

"This book brings my students up to speed really quickly on BPR. It provides an excellent introduction to this new paradigm," Eldridge Huntington, Adjunct Professor, School of Management, California State University.

New Tools for New Times:

The

Workflow

Paradigm,

Second Edition

New Tools for New Times:

The

Workflow

Paradigm,

Second Edition

The Impact of Information Technology on
Business Process Reengineering

Edited by

Layna Fischer

Future Strategies Inc., Book Division
Lighthouse Point, Florida

For information:
Future Strategies Inc., Book Division
3640 North Federal Highway,
Lighthouse Point FL 33064 USA
Telephone: 305 .782 .3376 Fax: 305 .782 .6365
e-mail: waria@gate.net

Cover design by Author's Advantage, Chris Pearl.

Library of Congress Catalog Card No. 9472343
Publisher's Cataloging-in-Publication Data

New Tools for New Times: The Workflow Paradigm, Second Edition
/Edited by Layna Fischer
p. cm.
Includes bibliographical references, appendices and index.
ISBN 0-9640233-2-6

1. Organizational change. 2. Organizational effectiveness. 3. Quality control. 4. Information Technology. 5. Information resources management. 6. Management information systems. 7. Office practice — Automation.
Fischer, Layna J.

Do you want to be a positive influence in the world?
First, get your own life in order.
Ground yourself in the single principle so that your
behaviour is wholesome and effective.
If you do that, you will earn respect and be a powerful influence.
Your behaviour influences others through a ripple effect.
A ripple effect works because everyone influences everyone else.
Powerful people are powerful influences.
If your life works, you influence your family.
If your family works, your family influences the community.
If your community works, your community influences the nation.
If your nation works, your nation influences the world.
If your world works, the ripple effect spreads throughout the cosmos.
Remember that your influence begins with you and ripples outward.
So be sure that your influence is both potent and wholesome.
How do I know that this works?
All growth spreads outward from a fertile and potent nucleus.
You are a nucleus.
John Heider
The Tao of Leadership
Section 54

Table of Contents

Introduction

Layna Fischer, President & CEO, Future Strategies Inc.
Chair, Workflow And Reengineering International Association (WARIA)

This is the second edition of *New Tools for New Times: The Workflow Paradigm*. It has been reengineered in keeping with the philosophy we expound. The first edition was a tremendous success—the best-seller in its field—but successes need to be examined. Both books and companies need to be reinvented on a continual basis in order to remain successful.

Several important new chapters have been added: Process-Driven Workflow, Workflow and Electronic Commerce, Workflow Management Standards and Interoperability, and a Three-Step Process to Workflow Automation. Other chapters have been updated and revised. The Vendor Directory has been verified, expanded and updated.

The first edition of this book was a valuable resource (and, to date, the only one of its kind available), not only for thousands of practitioners and users in our industry, but also for hundreds of university and graduate students around the world.

Tremendous confusion still exists about business process reengineering (BPR) however, and how to use it most effectively. Despite the growing numbers of related titles on the bookshelves, there is still insufficient data to meet informational needs.

Some authors argue that reengineering should entail a radical rethink of the whole business, not parts of it. Others say that BPR requires new information systems and incremental process change. Some business and industry media writers suggest that BPR is yet another management fad.

Reengineering has to do with reviewing how a business works in order to achieve dramatic performance improvement and be more responsive to the customer. Grasping that much puts you into the right ballpark—only to discover vast confusion about the game in progress.

Is BPR the same as business process improvement, workflow redesign and management? How close are they, in turn, to incremental process improvement, business transformation or core process redesign? How does workflow automation fit into all this? What tools are at my command?

So, the question remains: What does workflow automation and BPR mean to *me, the user?*

To find answers, we turned to people whose experience, knowledge and insights we trusted. This anthology is the result. The authors represent as many different backgrounds and disciplines as there are BPR interpretations and workflow methodologies. One benefit of an anthology is the breadth of experience and talent that the contributing authors bring to the subject, like musicians to a symphony. You are presented with a more balanced presentation than available from a single author beating a solo drum. Here, you are able to weigh the ideas and approaches from leading academics, consultants, users and vendors in the workflow and BPR industry. Several detailed case studies complete the book.

With or without new paradigms, it is inevitable that information combined with high technology will launch new products and services. Before we can reach the critical task of bringing new products and services to market, we have to examine the underlying paradigms and their differing natures as they relate to products, categories and competition.

While every company and consultant has its own understanding of workflow-enabled business processes, most agree that reengineering is about an organization's processes—any activity or group of activities that takes an input, adds value to it and provides an output to an internal or external customer. As we researched further, some clear definitions emerged. BPR is the conscious reshaping of an organization behind a new corporate vision, the marketplace and the customer.

Using a holistic, innovative approach, BPR reviews all business activities across the enterprise. This may result in a redefinition of workflow processes, organizational structures and technology to allow the company to streamline, change or delete the way in which work is done. The ultimate objective is to yield sustainable improvements in profitability, productivity, customer satisfaction and quality while maximizing the potential of the individual and the team.

> **using a holistic, innovative approach, BPR reviews all business activities across the enterprise**

For most companies, this means change. Big-time change. The next immediate question is: How do I manage change? Changing the way we do things means changing the organizational culture. With reengineering, as with any change, comes upheaval, rebuilding, retraining, restructuring and, frequently, redundancy as the reengineered companies find that they can do the same work with fewer employees. Jobs may be eliminated, but the work is not.

How do we manage change? The key to the change effort is not attending to each piece in isolation, but connecting and balancing all the pieces. In managing change, the critical task is understanding how the pieces balance off one another, how changing one element changes the rest, how sequencing and rhythm affect the whole structure. It means managing the communication between those who are expected to implement the new strategies, managing the organizational context in which change can occur and managing the emotional connections that are essential for any transformation. We discovered that the primary responsibilities for the change management architects include:

- Establish the context for change and provide leadership
- Stimulate clear apolitical communication
- Provide committed resources

The most important aspect of workflow redesign is its holistic nature: Strategy, process, technology and people are aligned to achieve outstanding results. When an organization wholly commits itself to redesign, the most significant impact is on its employees and its customers. Stalled or failed efforts are mostly caused by failure to manage the organizational side of the process.

The ongoing success of a reengineered organization is its ability to continue to evolve, to reinvent itself on a regular basis to keep up with the rapid change local and global competition. Organizations learn to see beyond their current mindsets and challenge themselves to learn and generate new processes that support continual improvement. Reinvention is not changing *what is*, but creating what *is not*. The key term is reconfigurable. To make this sort of agility possible, leaders are honing such techniques as rapid product development, flexible production systems and team-based incentives.

> **reinvention is not changing *what is*, but creating what *is not***

How do you go about reengineering your organization? Here, again, it depends who you ask. There is a consensus, however, that certain steps need to be taken to ensure that rethinking is accomplished before the redoing begins. Each of the following areas needs to be scrutinized before reengineering can happen.

- Education, training and retraining of workers
- Assessment of the business processes
- Vision statement by the leaders
- Resources available for commitment
- Cost/benefit analysis
- Performance metrics of current performance

Before implementing any strategy, however, it is necessary to return to the basics and understand profit, productivity and effectiveness. Executives need new skills to create an environment for qualitative decision-making—decision-making that is both effective (satisfying the customer) and efficient (doing things right, not just the right things). Efficient in the short run is to make the process recurrent, in the long run it involves transforming the organization from mechanistic behaviors to an organic, integrated team.

Because this book is intended to be a valuable resource, we include a Vendor Directory wherein most companies provide short profiles of their product offerings. Because we realize that new products are constantly being developed in this area, we welcome submissions from companies not listed here to be included in the next edition of the book.

Workflow technology and business process reengineering have far-reaching implications. As your personal guide, we hope this book offers you insight into planning, development and implementation of a reengineering strategy.

When asked what single event was the most helpful in developing the theory of relativity, Albert Einstein was reported to have answered, "Figuring out how to think about the problem."

I agree.

Layna Fischer
May, 1995

Process-Driven Workflow

Stowe Boyd, President
Work Media

Workflow in transition

The nature of the workflow industry, and the very concept of workflow it-self, have undergone a major shift in the last few years. What is the nature of the change, what are the forces driving it, and what impacts will it have on the future course of workflow?

First, let us start by listing some of the things that the workflow transition is not.

- It is not a linear extrapolation of trends that were foreseen in the '80s, such as client/server application development (although that has rippled through the industry in predictable fashion), object-oriented databases (ditto), or the increased power and lowered cost of computers (likewise). These have changed the industry in very small fashion, relative to other pressures.

- It is not the result of a clear winner emerging from the pack of workflow vendors. The market is still divided among the top ten or twenty vendors, with a few coming and a few going in the past few years.

- It is not the outgrowth of workflow being discovered as the next "killer app" or "killer metaphor." If anything, workflow systems have stayed too close-to-home, and too conservative in their basic premises to pose a radical alternative to other modern information management and application development environments.

- It is not the reward of diligent marketing by the vendors, finally persuading the market of the utility and importance of workflow. On the contrary, the workflow community has faced an unabated uphill struggle in getting across the message of the benefits that come from automating business work through the agency of computers.

What, then, is driving the change in the workflow industry?

The rise of process

Much of the recent interest in workflow is a direct effect of the explosion in business process activities. As more and more companies adopt business process techniques as the cornerstone of their business strategy, they work to build a process-centered information technology infrastructure.

In particular, process practitioners eagerly investigate any technologies that appear to offer even moderate leverage in narrowing the process gap: the lag between drawing process diagrams on a clean sheet of paper, and the ultimate realization of the process in the factory assembly line, front office, or field sales force.

Helping to close the process gap from what might be called the process modeling or Business Process Reengineering (BPR) design side is a large and tantalizing market; one vendor of a well-known process drawing tool sold over 125,000 copies in 1994, at an average price of over $100. This product supports no real analysis, and no automation, and has pulled in over $15,000,000 in one year.

Workflow sits at the other end of the process gap. The technology seems to offer leverage to business analysts, and the growing ranks of business process adherents evaluating workflow is driving several transitions:

• Workflow vendors have quickly accommodated the mind set and interests of their new prospective clients, leading to superficial changes — such as revamped marketing literature — and in some cases, significant efforts to investigate and respond to the different needs of process-centered business.

• The user of workflow is changing. The day of the MIS programmer, or the programmer/consultant, as the primary customer for workflow is passing. Now, Fortune 1000 firms are developing a cadre of business analysts, trained in the application of business process thinking. These are the new market, the next wave for the workflow sales curve.

• The basis of competition is shifting. In recent years, the level of integration of a workflow system with image and document management was the principal metric for product evaluation and selection.

Historically, all the generally applied matrices for product evaluation, such as those of BIS Strategic Decisions and IDC, were skewed toward canonization of "production" workflow, basically distributing products along a single dimension, where "best" equates to "highest throughput of the application system." And the most challenging systems for testing throughput were those involving the most complex imagery and the most complex automation.

This is changing, because the business analyst is involved in revamping the processes of the entire firm, not just cranking up the efficiency of image and document intensive operations in the back room. As Michael Hammer put it, "Reengineering is ripping the guts out of a business, and putting it back together to compete in a new business context."

Process-driven workflow

Today in the electric age we feel free to invent non-linear logics as we do to make non-Euclidean geometries. Even the assembly line, as the method of analytic sequence for mechanizing every kind making and production, is nowadays yeilding to new forms.

Marshall McLuhan, Understanding Media — The Extensions of Man. 1964

Today's telephones, ovens, and lamps are so different in form and operation from their ancestors that a time traveler from the early part of the century would be hard-pressed even to recognize them for what they are. In similar fashion, the next wave of technology that will carry the name workflow may appear so different from its namesake as to be unrelated in other than name. The premises that have motivated workflow up to the present time are being replaced by a new set of ideas, and these will rapidly spawn new products, technological hybridization, and a shift in the boundaries for the workflow market.

Workflow was, and still is, a seductive approach to modeling the automation of work. As McLuhan's quote above suggests, and as we have witnessed in the thirty years since his landmark work was published, linear industrialism is being obsoleted by the non-linear information age. We are standing just inside the border of this new age, having used the tools of the previous era to get us there.

What are the areas where the greatest changes are likely? Where we will see these technologies applied? And what non-linear logics will replace the central paradigm of workflow: the assembly-line sequence of repetitive tasks?

First-order approximations

It is already clear to most workflow vendors that systems devised to support heads-down, high-volume electronic paper pushing ("clerkware," as Action Technologies' Rodrigo Flores calls it) are not a priori suitable to assist heads-up, high-variability coordination of information, people, and other resources (what we call knowledgeware).

To be used by business analysts as a process calculus, the representation of process must be rich; one result of the new scrutiny on workflow is a growing appreciation of the need for richer formalisms than the simple flowcharts that dominate in the industry. While these process algebras may be profitably applied to many processes, the most challenging process areas remain outside their reach.

This is motivating the traditional workflow vendors to extend their process modeling tools, allowing business analysts to decorate the flowcharts with more information, and different forms of information, than formerly possible. For example, process modeling tools very commonly support a higher degree of information at the process diagram level than workflow systems: in particular, a richer representation of time and people's relationships to each other is often present.

In many cases, workflow representations are too low level to be easily raised to the level where business analysts want to operate. This has driven workflow vendors to consider developing or integrating high-level BPR-style design tools, with translation or export to the workflow level.

17

Dimensional analysis

During the course of a 1995 workflow study performed in partnership with Bruce Silver, and managed by BIS Strategic Decisions, I determined a set of dimensions along which workflow systems could be arrayed. The dimensions are strongly skewed toward process, and do not focus on performance per se, in the sense of images/hour. They are intended, on the contrary, as a means to evaluate workflow products (and other related technologies) relative to the requirements of process design, analysis, simulation, realization (or automation), and evolution (or maintenance).

The dimensions are nicknamed after various physical characteristics of real-world objects, such as height, depth, and mass, mainly to make them seem less abstract. In the following table these dimensions are described, and various questions presented which may be directed toward a particular product.

At Work Media, we are applying the dimensions in a series of BPR tool evaluations we plan to publish in the latter part of the year; abbreviated product reviews applying the dimensions have appeared in industry magazines, such as *Enterprise Reengineering*.

Dimension	Description/Questions
Depth	Richness of representation, completeness of tool or method What are the primary forms of information? Are tasks, roles, processes, and relationships between them represented? What other information about the primary forms are supported? Can the representation be extended for specific domains of use, to make it more industry or company specific?
Height	Scalability of representation, support for modeling complex processes and process interactions Does the tool/method support both decomposition [top-down approach] and composition [bottom-up approach? What forms of interactions between processes are supportable?
Width	Representation of time and the movement of information in the process How is time represented? Is it an explicit, basic kind of information, or is it implicit, or hidden away? How is the possibility of two events occurring in parallel handled? Is parallelism the norm, or the exception? How are time-based events — such as deadlines — treated? Do the relationships between process steps represent time sequence, or information flow, or both?

Area	Representation of distribution of processes and process components
	How (if at all) does the tool/method allow for modeling physically or organizationally distributed aspects of process, such as two parts of a process, one which takes place in New York and the other in DC, or in two locations in one city? How does 'Area' interact with other dimensions?
Mass	Level of knowledge required to use the tool/method for modeling process
	What level of training or understanding is necessary for minimal proficiency in the tool/method? How 'heavy' is the formalism used? Is it an intuitive approach, with cues derived from everyday work experience, like calendars, timelines, flow charts, or does it employ novel forms of representation?

Successive approximations

Extending the dimensions to their logical conclusions leads to some interesting conjectures about what we are likely to see in new workflow implementations, as the market pressures of process-driven workflow begin to be felt.

Height: Relation, Not Sequence

The industrial assembly-line model forces attention to the precise sequencing of events, and makes the relationships of people participating in the work secondary. What we have learned in the past twenty years — in manufacturing, in service industries, in financial sectors — is that the relationships between the participants are more critical to success than the speed of the line.

This is exactly the rethinking of business premises that motivated Just-In-Time manufacturing: shortening the purchase order cycle and the delivery response time of suppliers (focus on the sequence) cannot provide the next tier of productivity. Rewriting the relationship between supplier and producer to eliminate delays and waste is the key.

So, the natural consequence should be process formalisms which support a rich representation of interactions and relationships between the agents involved in processes. These are emerging, but they have yet to have any great impact on workflow.

We have also heard from visionaries like Prahalad/Hamel and Drucker that the most important factor in corporate success may be (r)evolutionary adaptation to changes in the business context.

Adaptation to change is problematic with today's workflow systems for several reasons. First, they are seldom integrated with any well-engineered solution for managing change across the life of a process specification. Without a change management approach, the reasons for changes are lost, and the nature of differences across versions and variants is not conserved. This, too, is a form of process knowledge that needs to be saved, if in fact workflow systems are to provide the enterprise-wide payoff that has been discussed for so many years. However, even the most farsighted vendors support only an external approach to version control and configuration management.

Depth: Agents — Not Roles, Not Processes

Until quite recently, a supposed fundamental distinction between data and function in programming languages dominated the overwhelming majority of application development. The new object-oriented paradigm for programming, which has been around since the '60s, in effect dissolves the distinction, with tremendous conceptual benefits.

Similarly, workflow was held with a hard boundary between people and processes. People, characterized by roles, authorizations, passwords, and user ids, are thought of as sitting at the computer, picking work from queues or in baskets, applying gray matter, and shuttling the work packages along. Workflow processes are thought of as application frameworks into which business rules, user interactions, and external applications are channeled, and which respond to the various stimuli impinging on them by moving from one state to the next.

> adaptation to change is problematic with today's workflow systems for several reasons

Generalizing the behavior of people and processes is already at work in other related technologies, where the term "agent" is in use. An agent is an active, responsive, and self-directed participant in goal-directed, purposeful activity. This is clearly what we ascribe to people (at least in principle); however, processes are not generally imbued with enough agency to be thought of in the same fashion.

Still, this is the direction in which things are going. Consider various vendor-support for processes which simply monitor state in the workflow server, and modify environment variables to direct the logic of other workflows. Likewise, at least one vendor supports multi-entrant processes, so that a single workflow may be directed to perform multiple tasks during its lifetime. Also consider that several vendors have devised products where workflows may modify their own maps; this truly borders on a form of adaptive control, or even limited learning.

What we can anticipate, then, are process formalisms which treat people and processes as agents of two different flavors. These interact in the context provided by other processes, and so on. This is the depth of representation that will allow for the same sort of conceptual breakthrough for process modeling and workflow development as object-oriented development has ushered in for application development. Workflow vendors will soup up their systems, revamp their graphical editors, and begin to operate in the context of a more powerful concept.

Note that the convergence of agent-based workflow with other agent-based technologies, notably telecommunications and electronic commerce, is exactly the sort of innovative pressure that dissolves boundaries between industries and markets.

Width: Knowledge, Not Data

As we shift to agent-based workflow, the concept of workflow data changes. Folder variables, folders, documents, all managed and passed around from task to task, become subsumed as state information managed by agents.

Today, a workflow standardizes a set of data items which are shared by the tasks in the process, external programs, and displayed to people. Agents, however, share a body of knowledge about process and interaction at a higher level than data structures. At the very least, we can anticipate the transition to a message-based paradigm, where agents publish the messages they are capable of responding to, so that others may come along, read the published list, and send an appropriate message.

> the overwhelmingly most critical factor is investment in core competence of the firm

This is an area of intense research in the industry, and one which promises the best form of integration with other knowledge-based applications.

Width: Time Invested, Not Time Spent

The well-known business process visionaries, Keen and Knapp, have made a strong case for the primacy of process investment in process-centered management. The basis of their arguments are that success in process reengineering come from "putting all the wood behind the arrow": investing key resources — money, time, management attention, technology — into key processes.

As for the first factor, only the minority of process tools — and functionally no workflow products — support a true mechanism to predict, analyze, and monitor process investment. There are mechanisms to measure costs associated with time spent performing work in a process. However, the most critical factors — training, process rework, mentoring, and development of core competencies away from the process — are not associated in any discernible way with the process formalism. These higher-order processes need to be linked in some identifiable way with their charges, so that knowledge about process investment can be captured, and managed.

Overwhelmingly, today's workflows are tied to keeping track of time on the assembly-line level: how much time elapsed for a work packet through the workflow, how much time in each participant's work queue, average time to handle certain forms of transactions, and the like. While this information has its place, to help tune or improve a process, it will not lead to process insight or radical improvements. And it will certainly not help in deciding if the process should be done at all.

> a workflow standardizes a set of data items which are shared by the tasks in the process, external programs, and displayed to people

More important are the soft metrics, such as time spent in training and improving the process. It has been demonstrated in any number of contexts and studies that improving or revamping a process generally pays better dividends than attempting to reward (or punish) process participants based on the throughput of the process. Focusing on the hard metrics is a natural consequence of the structure of most workflow products.

Area: Interprise, Not Enterprise

There is an anecdote about the drunkard who searches for his keys under a street lamp, rather than in the bushes where he lost them because "the light is better out there." In a similar fashion, workflow has tended to focus on automating process within a single organization, or organizational unit, rather than the more challenging issues involved in processes that span organizations.

Today's workflows have only minimal support for modeling geographically or economically distributed processes. What is missing is a simple and direct means to split a process into pieces, where one "chunk" will run, for example, at a client's system, a second chunk will run on a supplier's systems, and the remainder will run on the company's server.

There is a growing appreciation of the enormous benefits to come from electronic commerce. Workflow has traditionally limited its scope to the enterprise, and has been directed toward handling workflow within the walls. In a sense, the end of the workflow map has represented the end of the organizational unit, and interaction with other groups with the process are not on the map.

The area of most benefit, however, is interprise: clearly, companies succeed by managing their relationships with customers, suppliers, and partners wisely, not through finely-tuned internal processes. Consider the benefits when a product's manufacture encloses a workflow disk in the box, so that customer support can be handled by the user installing the workflow, and transacting a customer support process without having to call "1-800-GoAway."

22

We see that the largest pay-off from process-driven workflow will come from a shift in emphasis toward this end of the spectrum, and that those vendors who move into this space will likely propel workflow into general use, on a par with spreadsheets.

Mass: Processwise, Not Processed

Charlie Chaplin's landmark film, *Modern Times*, was a chilling indictment of the dehumanizing influence of industrialism. Who can forget the incredibly funny, but frightening image of Chaplin's Little Fellow madly tightening bolts with wrenches in both hands, while the foreman relentlessly speeds the line.

There is an echo of the assembly-line clangor in workflow systems; the basic orientation toward Taylor-style repetitive tasks is evident, and difficult to counter. No one who has watched credit card clerks processing hundreds of applications per day can fail to see the parallels.

The shift to the information age is a shift to a new competitive basis, a new currency for success. That shift is from low-cost, high volume production or services to high-information, narrow volume production. To win in this new economy we must reinvent our beliefs about products, business, work, and success.

The overwhelmingly most critical factor is investment in core competence of the firm; this means investing time, money, and attention toward training company staff. And, increasingly, this will mean educating people about process: how to conceptualize and to talk about processes, how to improve process, how to redesign processes radically , and how to organize and manage through process structures.

New workflow will focus very strongly on these areas, and will incorporate the capability to train process participants automatically, allowing them to gain mastery interactively. These lessons have already been painfully learned in manufacturing. Processwise staff are the critical success factor in process-centered business. Workflow will need to extend the current level of guidance and help systems into training, mastery, and on-line review.

Last words

Today's workflow systems have reached a level of utility and sophistication that allows complex departmental processes to be described in linear step-by-step fashion, and effectively automated as working client/server application systems. This is a great step forward, is widely applicable, and is truly the outgrowth of an industrial age vision of top-down control imposing efficiency and order.

Process-centered management is at its core a rejection of top-down control, and an acceptance of the inherent messiness arising from constant change in pursuit of competitive advantage. Static management structures, organizational boundaries, and hierarchical reporting become less central, or may fall away altogether.

In a sense, the framework in which today's workflow was designed to fit has been scrapped. The new framework, process-centered management, requires redrawing the blueprints for workflow, and coming up with new approaches.

Process-driven workflow, incorporating some or all of the features discussed above, will emerge over the next few years. This may arrive in an uneven, market-oriented fashion, or could be accelerated by the entry of a new innovative product, currently unknown. Paradoxically, for workflow to become a common-place application development paradigm, this inside-out shift in its underlying premises must take place. Just as we move forward in business — rethinking organization structure, reengineering processes, and reworking the concept of work — we will need to remodel workflow to play a larger, and more central role in the new economy we have just entered.

Workflow Management Standards and Interoperability

Workflow Management Coalition
Keith D. Swenson, Architect
Fujitsu OSSI

Introduction

Workflow Management (WfM) is evolving quickly and exploited increasingly by businesses in a variety of industries. Its primary characteristic is the automation of processes involving combinations of human and machine-based activities, particularly those involving interaction with IT applications and tools. Although its most prevalent use is within the office environment in staff intensive operations such as insurance, banking, legal and general administration, etc., it is also applicable to some classes of industrial and manufacturing applications.

Many software vendors now have WfM products available and there is a continual introduction of more products into the market. The availability of a wide range of products within the market has allowed individual product vendors to focus on particular functional capabilities and users have adopted particular products to meet specific application needs. However, there are, as yet, no standards defined to enable different WfM products to work together, resulting in incompatible "islands" of process automation.

The Workflow Management Coalition (WfMC) is a grouping of companies who have joined together to address the above situation. Most WfM products have some common characteristics, enabling them potentially to achieve a level of interoperability through the use of common standards for various functions.

The WfMC was established to identify these functional areas and develop appropriate specifications for implementation in workflow products. It is intended that such specifications will enable interoperability between heterogeneous workflow products and improved integration of workflow applications with other IT services such as electronic mail and document management, thereby improving the opportunities for the effective use of workflow technology within the IT market, to the benefit of both vendors and users of such technology.

Workflow systems overview

Despite the tremendous variety in WfM systems available, they all exhibit certain common characteristics, which provide a basis for developing integration and interoperability capability between different products. All WfM systems may be characterized as providing support in three functional areas:

- Build-time functions, concerned with defining, and possibly modeling, the workflow process and its constituent activities

- Run-time control functions concerned with managing the workflow processes in an operational environment and sequencing the various activities to be handled as part of each process

- Run-time interactions with human users and IT application tools for processing the various activity steps

These components exchange information in a variety of ways, which leads the WfMC to standardize five main interfaces:

1. specifications for process definition data and its interchange

2. interfaces to support interoperability between different workflow systems

3. interfaces to support interaction with a variety of IT application types

4. interfaces to support interaction with user interface desktop functions

5. interfaces to provide system monitoring and metric functions to facilitate the management of composite workflow application environments

Product Implementation Model

The **Process Definition Tool** is used to create the process description in a computer-processable form. This may be based on a formal process definition language, an object relationship model, or in simpler systems, a script or a set of routing commands to transfer information between participating users. The definition tool may be supplied as part of a specific workflow product or may be part of a business process analysis product, which has other components to handle analysis or modeling of business operations. In the latter case there must be a compatible interchange format to transfer the process definitions to and from the run-time workflow software.

The **Workflow Enactment Software** interprets the process description and controls the instantiation of processes and sequencing of activities, adding work items to the user work lists and invoking application tools as necessary. This is done through one or more co-operating workflow management engines, which manage(s) the execution of individual instances of the various processes. The workflow enactment service maintains internal control data either centralized or distributed across a set of workflow engines. This workflow control data includes the internal state information associated with the various process and activity instances under execution and may also include checkpointing and recovery/restart information used by the workflow engines to co-ordinate and recover from failure conditions.

The workflow engines also include some form of application tool invocation capability to activate applications necessary to execute particular activities. The generality of such mechanisms may vary greatly, with some simple systems offering support only of a single fixed tool such as a form or document editor, whereas others may provide methods for the invocation of a wider range of tools, both local and remote to the Workflow engine.

Where process navigation decisions, or other control operations within the workflow engine, are based on data generated or updated by workflow application programs, such data is accessible to the workflow engine and termed **workflow relevant data** (also known as "case data"); this is the only type of application data accessible to the workflow engine. **Workflow application data** is manipulated directly (and only) by the invoked applications, although the workflow engines may be responsible for transferring such data between applications (if necessary), as different applications are invoked at different activity points within the workflow process.

Where user interactions are necessary within the process execution, the workflow engine(s) place items on to **worklists** for attention by the worklist handler, which manages the interactions with the workflow participants. The worklist handler is a software component which manages the interaction between workflow participants and the workflow enactment service. It is responsible for progressing work requiring user attention and interacts with the workflow enactment software via the worklist.

> within a workflow system there are a number of supervisory functions

Within a workflow system there are a number of supervisory functions which are normally provided; these are typically supported on the basis of supervisory privilege to a particular workstation or user(s). These functions may enable supervisors to alter work allocation rules, to identify participants for specific organizational roles within a process, to track alerts for missed deadlines or other forms of event, to trace the history of a particular process instance, to inquire about work throughput or other statistics, etc. Where distributed workflow engines are used there may need to be specific commands to transfer such control operations or (partial) responses between different workflow engines to provide a single administrative interface.

In a concrete product implementation the structure of implementation may be realized in a variety of different ways; among the main alternatives considered are:

- centralised or distributed workflow enactment service

- worklist handler location(s) and distribution mechanism

The approach taken by the Coalition is to define a boundary around the workflow enactment service, which exhibits various standard functional attributes accessible via a set of common APIs. The internal mechanisms by which the enactment service delivers this capability are not defined and may include one or more homogenous workflow engines, communicating in a variety of ways.

To support interworking between different products, interfaces are defined for specific co-operative functions between different enactment services so that a composite multi-vendor workflow application may execute parts of a particular process on different enactment services (each comprising one or more specific vendors workflow engines). This is considered a more realistic approach (except perhaps in the long term) than attempting to standardize the internal interfaces

> ## to support interworking between different products, interfaces are defined for specific co-operative functions

There are various possible product implementations of this worklist interaction model depending upon the nature of the product implementation and, in particular, on the type of infrastructure used to support the distribution of worklist handling. The four example scenarios are as follows:

- Host based Model—the client worklist handler application is host based and communicates with the worklist via a local interface at the workflow engine. In this case the user interface function may be driven via a terminal or a remote workstation.

- Shared filestore model—the worklist handler application is implemented as a client function and communication is via a shared filestore, which lies on the boundary between host and client platform environments and is accessible to both.

- Electronic mail model—communication is via electronic mail, which supports the distribution of work items to individual participants for local processing. In this scenario the worklist would normally lie at the client.

- Procedure Call or Message Passing model—communication is via procedure call, or other message passing mechanism. In this scenario the worklist may be physically located on the workflow engine or at the worklist handler according to the particular implementation characteristics.

In each case it is feasible to construct a common API, which supports worklist handler access to the worklist and workflow engine functions, but which is located behind a specific worklist access function appropriate to the product implementation style.

The Five Interfaces

The figure below illustrates the major components and interfaces within the workflow architecture.

The **workflow enactment service** provides the run-time environment in which process instantiation and activation occurs, utilizing one or more workflow management engines, responsible for interpreting and activating part, or all, of the process definition and interacting with the external resources necessary to process the various activities. A **workflow engine** is responsible for part (or all) of the runtime control environment within an enactment service.

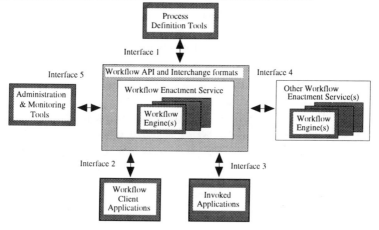

The Workflow Application Programming Interface (WAPI) may be regarded as a set of API calls and interchange functions supported by a workflow enactment service at its boundary for interaction with other resources and applications. Although this architecture refers to five "interfaces" within WAPI, a number of the functions within each of these interfaces are common (for example process status calls may be issued from the client application interface or the administration interface). The WAPI is thus being defined as a common core of API calls /interchange formats with specific extensions where necessary to cater individually for each of the five functional areas.

A variety of different tools may be used to analyze, model, describe and document a business process. Where a workflow product provides its own process definition tool, the resultant process definitions will normally be held within the workflow product domain and may, or may not, be accessible via a programming interface for reading and writing information. Where separate products are used for defining and executing the process, the process definitions may be transferred between the products as and when required or may be stored in a separate repository, accessible to both products (and possibly other development tools).

The interface between the modeling and definition tools and the runtime workflow management software is termed the **process definition import/export interface**. The nature of the interface is an interchange format and API calls, which can support the exchange of process definition information over a variety of physical or electronic interchange media. The interface may support the exchange of a complete process definition or a subset—for example a set of process definition changes or the attributes of a particular activity within the process definition.

There are two aspects to the Coalition's work in this area:

1. derivation of a meta-model which can be used to express the objects, their relationships and attributes within a process definition and which can form the basis for a set of interchange formats to exchange this information between products

2. API calls (within the WAPI) between workflow systems or between a workflow system and process definition product, providing a common way to access workflow process definitions. Access may be read, read/write or write only and may manipulate the set of standard objects defined within the meta-model or a product-specific set (for example defined in a product type register).

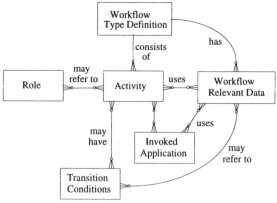

A set of API commands within WAPI is under development to support ac-
~rocess definition data. It is expected that such specifications will cover a

number of functions of the following general types. Commands are expected to be provided which operate on a list, or on individual objects or attributes.

Interface 2 provides general access for workflow enabled applications. The functions provided by interface 2 include session establishment, process starting and termination, actions on process instances, such as state changes, process instance status, worklist retrieval, retrieval/update of workflow relevant or application data, and administrative functions.

Interface 3 provides a standard way for a WfM system to invoke an external application. It is intended to be applicable to application agents and (longer term) applications which have been designed to be "workflow enabled" (i.e. to interact directly with a workflow engine). In the simple case, application invocation is handled locally to a workflow engine, using information within the process definition to identify the nature of the activity, the type of application to be invoked and any data requirements.

The invoked application may be local to the workflow engine, co-resident on the same platform or located on a separate, network accessible platform; the process definition contains sufficient application type and addressing information (specific to the needs of the workflow engine) to invoke the application. In this case the conventions for application naming and addressing are local between the process definition and the workflow engine.

> the Workflow Management Coalition is moving forward on providing a reference model architecture

A key objective of the coalition is to define standards that will allow workflow systems produced by different vendors to pass work items seamlessly between one another. This is the job of interface 4.

Interface 5 defines a common interface standard for administration and monitoring functions which will allow one vendor's management application to work with another's engine(s). This will provide a common interface which enables several workflow services to share a range of common administration and system monitoring functions.

Interoperability Scenarios

Workflow products are diverse in nature ranging from those used for more ad-hoc routing of tasks or data to those aimed at highly regularized production processes. The work of the Coalition has therefore focused on developing a variety of interoperability scenarios which can operate at a number of levels from simple task passing through to full workflow application interoperability with complete interchange of process definition, workflow relevant data and a common look and feel. In this area it is expected that relatively simple interoperability scenarios will be supported initially, with the more complex situations requiring further work on interoperability definitions. Four possible interoperability models has been identified, covering various (increasing) levels of capability.

The **Connected Discrete (Chained) Scenario** allows a connection point in one process to connect to another point in another process. It is useful to think of these connection points as being the terminus and starting points of the processes, but for full generality it is presumed that the connection points can be anywhere within the processes. This model supports the transfer of a single item of work (a process instance or activity) between the two workflow environments.

The **Hierarchical Scenario** allows a process executed in a particular workflow domain to be completely encapsulated as a single task within a (superior) process executed in a different workflow domain. A hierarchic relationship exists between the superior process and the encapsulated process, which in effect forms a sub-process of the superior. The hierarchic relationship may be continued across several levels, forming a set of nested sub-processes. Recursion within this scenario may, or may not, be permitted by individual product implementations.

The **Connected Indiscrete (Peer-to-Peer) Scenario** allows a fully mixed environment; for example, one process might include activities which may be executed across multiple workflow services, forming a shared domain. In this scenario, the process would progress transparently from task to task, without any specific actions by users or administrators, with interactions between the individual workflow engines taking place as necessary.

The **Parallel Synchronized Scenario** allows two processes to operate essentially independently, possibly across separate enactment services, but requires that synchronization points exist between the two processes. Synchronization requires that once the processes each reach a predefined point within their respective execution sequences, a common event is generated. This type of mechanism may be used to facilitate functions such as process scheduling across parallel execution threads, checkpointing of recovery data or the transfer of workflow relevant data between different process instances.

There are two major aspects to the necessary interoperability:

- the extent to which common interpretation of the process definition (or a subset) is necessary and can be achieved

- runtime support for the interchange of various types of control information and to transfer workflow relevant and/or application data between the different enactment services

Where both enactment services can interpret a common process definition, for example, generated from a common build tool, this enables both environments to share a single view of the process definition objects and their attributes. This would include activity, application, organization and role names, navigation conditions, etc. This potentially enables individual workflow engines to transfer execution of activities or sub-processes to heterogeneous workflow engines within the context of a common naming and object model. This approach is particularly applicable to interoperability scenario 3, where several systems are co-operating at peer level, although can also be employed in simpler scenarios.

Summary

The Workflow Management Coalition is moving forward on providing a reference model architecture as a framework for comparing and integrating systems from different vendors. Fujitsu is an active participant in this coalition with the aim that Regatta Technology, Fujitsu's workflow offering, can interoperate with other systems, regardless of the vendor. This is the goal of the Coalition, and one that should be very welcome to end users. Those evaluating workflow systems should ask the vendor whether the system is "open" by supporting these common interfaces and models. Such a system has a far higher chance of being extended and customized in the future.

Acknowledgments

This document was the joint effort of many individuals of the Workflow Management Coalition. Most significantly David Hollingsworth from ICL who served as the chairman of the Reference Model working group for the development of the first version of the reference model, from which most of this information was taken. It could not have been completed without the hard work and dedication of many individuals including Gene Pierce, Dave Shorter, Mike Grabert, Raul Medina-Mora, Robin Maxwell, Jon Pyke, Kurt Ogris and many more people, too many to mention here.

WfMC contact information

Workflow Management Coalition
Avenue Marcel Thiry 204
1200 Brussels, Belgium
Tel: +32 2 774 96 33
Fax: +32 2 774 96 90
100113.1555@compuserve.com

Appendix—terminology

Below is an abbreviated glossary of terms that are being standardized by the WfMC. The WfMC Glossary document, available from the secretariat in Brussels, includes an expanded explanation and the usage of these terms, including synonyms.

AND-Join: When two or more parallel executing activities converge into a single thread of control.

AND-Split: When a single thread of control splits into two of more threads in order to execute activities in parallel.

Application Data: Data that is application specific and not accessible by the workflow management system.

Audit Trail: A historical record of the state transitions of a workflow process instance from start to completion or termination.

Business Process: A kind of process that supports and/or is relevant to business organizational structure and policy for the purpose of achieving business objectives.

Iteration: A workflow process activity cycle involving the repetitive execution of workflow process activity(s) until a condition is met.

Manual Process Activity: The manual process steps that contribute toward the completion of a process.

Manual Process Definition: The component of a process definition that cannot be automated using a workflow management system.

Manual Process Execution: The duration in time when a human participant and/or some non-computer means executes the manual process instance.

Manual Process Instance: Represents an instance of a manual process definition which includes all manual or non-computerized activities of a process instance.

Organizational Role: A synergistic collection of defined attributes, qualifications and/or skills that can be assumed and performed by a workflow participant for the purpose of achieving organizational objectives.

OR_Join: When two or more workflow process activities physically connect or converge to a single activity. In this case there is no synchronization of the threads of control from each of the two or more workflow process activities to the single activity.

OR_Split: When a single thread of control makes a decision upon which branch to take when encountered with multiple branch(es) to workflow process activities.

Parallel Routing: A segment of a workflow process instance where workflow process activity instances are executing in parallel and there are multiple threads of control.

Process: A coordinated (parallel and/or serial) set of process activities that are connected in order to achieve a common goal. A process activity may be a manual process activity and/or a workflow process activity.

Process Activity: A logical step or description of a piece of work that contributes toward the accomplishment of a process. A process activity may be a manual process activity and/or an automate workflow process activity.

Process Activity Instance: An instance of a process activity that is defined as a part of a process instance. Such an instance may be a manual process activity instance and/or a workflow process activity instance.

Process Definition: A computerized representation or model of a process that defines both the manual process and the automatable workflow process.

Process Definition More: The time period when manual process and/or automated (workflow process) descriptions of a process are defined and/or modified electronically using a process definition tool.

Process Execution: The duration in time when manual process and workflow process execution takes place in support of a process.

Process Instance: Represents an instance of a process definition which includes the manual process and the automated (workflow process).

Process Role: A synergistic collection of workflow process activities that can be assumed and performed by a workflow participant for the purpose of achieving process objectives.

Sequential Routing: A segment of a workflow process instance where workflow process activities are executed in sequence.

Sub Process Definition: A process that is called from another process or sub process that includes the manual process and the automated (workflow process) components of the process.

Tool: A workflow application that interfaces to or is invoked by the workflow management system via the workflow application programming interchange/interface.

Transition Condition: Criteria for moving, or state transitioning, from the current workflow process activity to the next workflow process activities in a workflow process.

WAPI: The application programming interface/interchange for client workflow applications and tools in order to be able to interface to the Workflow Enactment System. WAPI is the acronym for Workflow Application Programming Interface/Interchange.

Work Item: Representation of work to be processed in the context of a workflow process activity in a workflow process instance.

Work Item Pool: A space that represents all accessible work items.

Workflow Application: A software program that will either completely or partially support the processing of work items in order to accomplish the objective of workflow process activity instances.

Workflow Enactment Service: A software service that may consist of one or more workflow process engines in order to create, manage, and execute workflow process instances. Client workflow applications/tools interface to this service through the WAPI.

Workflow Interoperability: The ability for two or more workflow engines to communication and interoperate in order to coordinate and execute workflow process instances across those engines.

Workflow Management System: A system that completely defines manages and executes workflow processes through the execution of software whose order of execution is driven by a computer representation of the workflow process logic.

Workflow Participant: A resource which performs partial or in full the work represented by a workflow process activity instance.

Workflow Process: The computerized facilitation of automated component of a process.

Workflow Process Activity: The computer automation of a logical step that contributes toward the completion of a workflow process.

Workflow Process Activity Instance: An instance of a workflow process activity that is defined as part of a workflow process instance.

Workflow Process Control Data: Data that is managed by the Workflow Management System.

Workflow Process Definition: The component of a process definition that can be automated using a workflow management system.

Workflow Process Engine: A software service of "engine" that provides part of all of the run time execution environment for a workflow process instance.

Workflow Process Execution: The duration in time when a workflow process instance is created and managed by a Workflow Management System based on a workflow process definition.

Workflow Process Instance: Represents an instance of a workflow process definition which includes the automated aspects of a process instance.

Workflow process Monitoring: The ability to track workflow process events during workflow process execution.

Workflow Process Relevant Data: Data that is used by a Workflow Management System to determine the state transition of a workflow process instance.

Worklist: A list of work items retrieved from a workflow management system.

Worklist Handler: A software component that manages and formulated a request to the workflow management system in order to obtain a list of work items.

Reengineering the Business Process

Michael F. Parry, Vice President, Strategic Alliances
Integris Inc.

Any process can be changed and the goal of reengineering is to improve — more to the point, to *strive* — for maximum improvement possible to levels that have been called dramatic. A rational review of a process can always find ways of improving it; we would rather strive for fundamental, dramatic improvements that are achievable, sustainable and easily expanded upon as new opportunities present themselves. Only in this way are American companies going to be able to compete effectively in the global market in which we now find ourselves. In the next few years, world trade accords are going to further blur the lines that once distinguished us from all other world economies. Now we must exploit what we do best, innovation, to maintain our leadership positions in this newly expanded marketplace. Innovation in our business processes appears to have the biggest payoff of all classes of investment, with the possible exception of education.

Michael Hammer, James Champy, Thomas Davenport and others have made effective arguments for the efficacy of process reengineering and we will not try to encourage you any further. This chapter explores how to go about capturing the often phenomenal benefits that process reengineering appears to promise while minimizing the false starts and the risks of business disruptions during reengineering. The methods described are general in nature, but more likely to be readily applicable to office processes where the stock in trade is typically information. In this context, process reengineering capitalizes on the rapidly expanding information technology capabilities that are impacting our lives and businesses more and more each day. If any further incentive is needed to embrace the principles of process reengineering, we should all remember that the concepts are likely being embraced by the businesses of our competitors as well.

Knowing when to consider reengineering business processes is just the beginning and methods for testing existing organizations and their processes as candidates for change will be explored. Once confirmed that a process will respond to reengineering and that it is likely to be economical to effect the change, it's yet another challenge to figure out what to change and how to change it. This chapter will go through the steps that identify which parts of the process could change, how to identify the productivity benefits that can be achieved as a result and what impact, in a variety of areas, both good and bad, can be expected. A range of technological and non-technological methods will be summarized as approaches to implementing process reengineering. This will not be a description of a methodology, rather, it will comprise a study of the principles, a checklist, if you will, of the things that must be considered to effect successful process reengineering. From these, you will be able to formulate the methodology that best suits your situation, organization and objectives.

1.　Define Which Organizations can Benefit from Reengineering

Commitment to change is universally agreed as the most critical prerequisite to successful process reengineering. Without active, demonstrable commitment from the top, organizational stamina quickly wanes as the complexities of reengineering become evident. Advocates of process reengineering would have you believe that any part of an organization can benefit from not just change, but dramatic — some would even proffer cataclysmic — change. While this may be true in the absolute sense, sound business judgment requires a more measured approach to ensure the maximum return on investment while minimizing risk. Because we do not have the luxury of tossing out all our processes, relying on achieving greater goals by starting over, we have to establish a more rational means to distinguish the low from the high potential opportunities and the low from the high risk opportunities.

Focus on objectives

Whatever you end up reengineering, to be acknowledged as effective, the results must roll up to the enterprise goals. Because reengineering can, and likely will, have a dramatic influence on virtually all aspects of an enterprise, we need a focus, a set of principles, that can be referenced continually to determine whether the changes we are likely to bring about are truly desired in the grand scheme of things. The best place to start is by understanding the enterprise objectives — and they had better relate, in some significant way, to your relationships with your customers. Two critically important reasons for clarifying and documenting enterprise objectives are: 1) they will form the basis for understanding and validating why you are reengineering at all and 2) they can be used as a measuring stick for all other reengineering actions and consequences.

> objectives should concisely reflect clear business directions

Understanding and documenting enterprise objectives may seem like a trivial task until you convene the executive group that is, in essence, the keeper of these resolutions. Most organizations will demonstrate a wide variety of interpretations, depending on whom you ask, about what the overall objectives are. It is even more interesting, when you delve down deeper into the management structure and discover that, just as rumors often do, objectives, too, change their definition as you move throughout the organization. Obviously, the simple solution is to document the enterprise objectives from the top and to map them to the fundamental purpose of the enterprise: to serve its customers.

What the objectives state is yet another matter, perhaps better left to the management science specialists. For now, suffice it to say that objectives should concisely reflect clear business directions that can be subscribed to by all in the organization, certainly all in the management layers of the hierarchy. Unlike goals, objectives need not necessarily be achievable, indeed, many proponents of "always slightly out of reach" objectives have made compelling cases in the annals of management science. However, objectives should be at least believable and measurable progress should be evident and recognized to encourage further progress.

Once the objectives are defined from the top of the enterprise, document them to serve as a recurring reminder. Then have each department formulate its own set of objectives that roll up to the enterprise level objectives. Each manager and worker in each organization must understand how their job helps achieve their respective departmental objectives and hence the enterprise objectives. Document them, make them part of individual performance reviews, make them visible and above all, make them relate to serving the organization's customers.

> the benefits of reengineering mission-critical systems can be leveraged through a larger business base

Now, armed with a clear set of objectives, you have the map for reengineering — you can find your way through all of the redirections that are going to come your way. You can distinguish the worthwhile from the unprofitable. You can sort through alternatives rationally and, in general, keep your efforts focused on the objectives that must be addressed.

Focus on mission-critical systems

The benefits of reengineering mission-critical systems can be leveraged through a larger business base. The temptation of any new reengineering venture is to start in some safe part of the enterprise where errors have a small impact and can be easily contained and dealt with. While this may be intuitively true, it falls far short of the potential for reengineering. Much better results are almost always obtained by reengineering the more visible parts of an organization. Adequate returns on investment are much more difficult to achieve unless your reengineering takes place at or near the mission of the organization. Fundamentally, that mission is to serve its customers — to add value better than your competition. Reengineering records management, for example, will not deliver any dramatic improvements for an insurance company, but will be quite rewarding for a reference library. The trick, of course, is not to destroy a mission critical part of your business in an attempt to improve it. To avoid that, we will describe later a number of ways to minimize the risk inherent in change, as effected through process reengineering.

Once you have identified the mission critical operations, consider the impact of information technology on the essential mission of the candidate organizations. An organization that primarily uses information to perform its objectives is much more likely to derive benefits from reengineering than a machine shop (although the point is easily debatable). This is especially true today with the wide array of information technologies available and emerging each week. One technology in particular, workflow, is particularly adept at managing the coordination of information and information processing resources while being flexible enough to adapt to your ever-changing business environment. Indeed, reengineering for process efficiency is largely missing the mark. Unless your new processes give you the ability to adapt to your customer changing needs, you will find yourself constantly facing the need to reengineer — a daunting prospect, known only to those who have reengineered.

Consider also the proximity of the operations you are considering for reengineering to your company's customers. We are, after all, in the customer service business regardless of our industry in the broad sense. Anything you can improve upon which is visible to your customers will be beneficial to you. Of course, a careful assessment of what your customers consider improvements is always worthwhile.

An obvious example is Customer Service (in the traditional definition of that function). Customers contact this organization to get either information or action that depends on timely, accurate information. Whether the task of customer service is correcting billing errors, finding waylaid shipments, taking orders or handling complaints, good and complete information is the essential ingredient necessary for successful customer interactions. Some of the benefits that can be achieved through reengineering customer service organizations are faster resolutions, more accurate and complete information, less personnel time spent per customer satisfaction and more personalized responses. Each of these benefits achieves the prime objective of reengineering:

Make it easier to service customers better

Making it easier implies that your costs go down. Servicing customers is what your organization is all about. Servicing them better is what will keep them from looking to your competition for that better service. Ed Crego and Peter Schiffrin in their book, Customer-Centered Reengineering, state that unless your customers are more than satisfied - actually delighted - they are at risk to move to your competition. That means you constantly have to exceed your customers' expectations — which, in today marketplace, are constantly changing as customers become more sophisticated about their options. The need for adaptable new processes becomes evident.

Many other opportunities exist in today's businesses, even in organizations where reengineering has already happened. Reengineering, incidentally, should be a continual process, a cultural mode that pervades the organization, especially as new technologies emerge to support information management processes. Below is a far from complete list of functional organizations that have benefited from reengineering:

Order entry — Instead of putting customers on hold while records are retrieved, customer records and incoming telephone calls are automatically directed to available order takers in under five seconds, providing complete order history and full on-line catalog indexed by item number, description text words, order history, color matches to other products, etc. New orders, shipment information, item descriptions and comparisons, billing information and prior order history are all available to respond to customer inquiries immediately.

Insurance Application/Renewal — Automobile underwriting and commitment can be accomplished in one day. Agencies get paid quickly, increasing incentives to bring in more business. Customers get faster service and (where allowed) the benefit of lower costs.

Mortgage Processing — Origination to commitment can take place in less than one week, a powerful incentive to attract new customers without lowering mortgage interest rates or points.

Accounts Receivable — Lower costs allow closer scrutiny of a lower level of potential write-offs. Discrepancies are more likely to be favorably resolved because more complete information is readily available.

Hospital Admissions — Admissions verification and effective patient tracking results in dramatically lower write-offs for uncollectable accounts. A major urban hospital can save tens of millions per year per hospital, easily paying for the systems to effect these savings!

Claims Processing — Medical claims can be processed in one to three days, encouraging group plan subscriptions because of improved service levels. An important side benefit: the cost to process claims goes down also, further improving profitability.

Magazine Publication — Rapid nationwide exchange of issue information results in regional publishing centers that enable regionally focused issues and quicker distribution. The results again: lower costs and better customer acceptance (higher sales).

This list is but a small sample of the possibilities for reengineering processes. These candidates all have two things in common: they use information as their major resource and they noticeably impact the relationship with the end customer.

Establish an analytic champion

Once the possibilities have been identified, you will need a champion, a person who can take the reengineering effort forward and make it happen. This person will have to have first hand knowledge about the operation of the organization(s) about to be reengineered. He or she will also have to be analytic in nature, understanding the intricacies of the reasoning that is part of the alternative evaluation process that ultimately leads to new process designs for the organization. The role of the champion needs to include the analysis of the processes and assist the inevitable refinement process that takes place as a continual byproduct of reengineering. This person will need to enlist the active participation of all who will be affected by the reengineered process so that the ultimate solution is "owned" by those who will have to live with it once it goes into operation.

Within the organization that will be the target of reengineering efforts, the champion will need to focus activities on all of the issues that will be affected, and are addressed in the remainder of this chapter. The primary role of the champion is to provide local leadership. Reengineering is often viewed as an external effort that will threaten the *status quo* and human nature tends to resist change. The local champion will be viewed as a protector of all of the agendas threatened with disruptions by reengineering and needs to actively and enthusiastically step up to that role.

> anytime your customer sees you doing something better, you win

2. Identifying procedural elements that can be effectively redesigned

In any organization, a number of inefficiencies exist that, once identified, can usually be easily corrected. Reengineering is not correcting inefficient operations; instead, it is fundamentally changing them so the results are dramatically better. In many cases, inefficient operations can be eliminated or replaced by other resources. In this section, we will explore how to recognize these opportunities and what can be done about them.

Independent sequential processes

These represent opportunities to design parallel systems that dramatically reduce cycle times and the resultant operational and competitive costs. An independent operation is one that does not depend on the results of a predecessor. While it's probably true that no operation other than brainstorming is completely independent of anything that occurred in the past, this discussion is about operations that unnecessarily occur sequentially.

An example comes from the mortgage industry. A mortgage folder typically contains 100-175 pages by the time closing has taken place. After closing, called post-closing in mortgage institutions, mortgages are prepared for servicing (collecting money) and reselling to other investors. Because the folders are so large, the five to eight different post-closing processes were typically done sequentially, the process consuming two or more months. Most of the processes are, in fact, independent of one another; ensuring that sufficient hazard insurance coverage exists, setting up customer accounts for collections, acquire VA or FHA certification to improve resale options, etc. A quick survey of these processes reveals their relative independence. Workflow can now effectively manage these processes as they occur in parallel. Using this approach, a typical bank can complete much, if not all, of its post-closing operations in a month or less. That month translates to higher cash flow, lower asset risk — greater profits that can be turned into investor or customer value.

Redundant processes

A little research into the processes of any modest size organization will often reveal redundancies. These exist for a variety of reasons and can almost always be eliminated (some redundancies are deliberate to provide a measure of reliability). They result from the natural reduced communications that occurs among departments as organizations grow — it becomes harder and harder to exchange views effectively with an increasing number of people. Duplicated processes are relatively easy to spot; usually though, the redundancies are subtle and their identification is often a result of some detective work on the part of the business process analyst.

Competitively visible processes

Anytime your customer sees you doing something better, you win. The message is, of course, to identify those parts of your processes that are visible to your customers and earmark them for reengineering. Even modest performance improvement to your internal operations can have a dramatic impact on your business bottom line if your customers believe that your efforts have been performed on their behalf.

The same thinking that reduced processing times for mortgage post-closing has also resulted in significantly reduced cycle times for the part of mortgage processing that happens before closing, mortgage origination and underwriting. While post-closing was a process essentially invisible to the mortgage customer, he or she is vitally interested in the time it takes to get a mortgage commitment and when they can move into their new home (boat, vacation villa, etc.)

Time-sensitive information

Define the timeliness of the information you need and ensure that you get it. A typical example of the use of obsolete information is found in most 401K plans. Status reports that form the basis of investment decisions are often months late, frequently invalidating changes in investment choices employees make with them. Recent reengineering efforts for some 401K plans now have voice response accesses which provide up-to-date information and investment change options in near-real-time.

Make sure that the information used to support your processes is, in fact, timely enough to make your processes worthwhile. Otherwise, you run the risk of having needless (another form of redundant) processes. In other words, if no one is taking action on the results of a process because to do so will either not have the desired effect or worse, have a negative effect, it is likely that the process is using information that is obsolete or otherwise inappropriate.

Conflicting policies

Don't undo what you have spent resources to do elsewhere. If you discover that one of your processes transforms information from format A to format B and that somewhere downstream it's reformatted back to A, you can, of course eliminate the second transformation.

Usually these conditions occur in larger organizations when individuals have stimulated the development of systems for particular purposes without adequately considering whether the satisfaction of these purposes existed elsewhere.

Decision support

Let machine makes decisions whenever possible. Let people do what they do best: think and judge. Let machines do the mechanical work of moving information. People are better at reviewing boring work than doing it. Decision support systems typically allow you to incorporate decision criteria into information systems. The systems make the decisions while humans review those decisions and have override capabilities with which to manage unusual circumstances. That clever Italian mathematician, Pareto, suggested the current maxim: 20 percent of the effort produces 80 percent of the results. Allowing machines to process all of the "normal" work will probably mean that humans can do a much more effective job of processing the exceptions or complex work. In a typical large American city, city retirement programs involve about a half dozen different types of transactions. So-called normal or routine transactions represent about 60 percent of the transaction volume. However, most cities today still have a single process to handle all transaction types. Routine transactions take about 30-40 minutes to process yet consume 2-3 weeks of elapsed time because their processes are burdened by the more complex minority of transactions. Reengineering in its simplest form would produce two processes, one for normal work, another to handle the unusual or complex work.

Workflow systems, a new class of information management tools, are particularly good for implementing decision support systems at a relatively low cost. Indeed, workflow technology is rapidly changing the role of today's information worker from that of information transcriber and mover to that of a true knowledge worker, namely an information user. This represents a dramatic shift in the characteristics of our workforces. Later, we will address the issues surrounding employee retraining after reengineering.

Data entry replacement

Eliminate data entry if at all possible; it's expensive and error prone: most replacement technologies easily pay for themselves. The present state-of-the-art in OCR (optical character recognition) technology is rapidly becoming as good as human data transcription. For certain kinds of data such as machine printed text, OCR easily surpasses human data entry in speed and accuracy. A clear opportunity for reengineering is a situation that has people keying in data from computer-generated paper. This information was already in machine readable form and the challenge is to acquire in that form instead of paper.

Imaging can be an effective way of quickly capturing information from paper, but it will always be better to access the data before it has been put onto paper, if it is available electronically. If the electronic version is not accessible or the paper can not be avoided, then put the sheets into a scanner and manage the data from the image. Consider though, that imaging is but another data form, nothing more. In fact, it is the data form of last resort for textual information, only to be used if the original text is not available electronically.

That previous discourse should not be viewed as a tirade against paper-based information. Paper, in our present culture is still an incredibly flexible medium for containing and sharing information. It is readily available, easily packaged and modified, high portable in small quantities and, in many legal environments, the only acceptable form. If those qualities characterize your mode of satisfying your customers, then paper is clearly your medium of choice until another ubiquitous medium becomes available.

Inefficient information sources

Get information in a form easiest for you to use. In our discussion about data entry replacement, above, we suggested accessing the data before it reached paper. The key to successful reengineering is to get the information you need in the form you need it. With minimal data reformatting (reformatting is used here in the sense of media conversion), fewer people are needed to get it where it's needed. For each of the processes you are considering reengineering, describe what your ideal information format is and define the sources for it and costs of obtaining it in that format.

3.   The Technology Factor

Process reengineering is not likely to provide the improvements desired without the application of new technologies. Indeed, process reengineering makes it possible to exploit the capabilities of new technologies and it is exactly this characteristic that makes it necessary to understand how technologies can influence the outcome of any reengineering effort. While technology companies extol their products to have certain benefits, they are also widely known for putting a great deal of positive (sometimes even to excess) spin on their claims. It is not necessarily the fault of the technologists; many of them have little appreciation for how you intend to use their creations. More still have much more engineering experience than business experience and cannot fully comprehend all of the factors that distinguish successful technology from functional (the message here, for technologists, is that to be functional does not guarantee success). User interfaces are vitally important, even more important than performance in some instances. Consider the automatic transmission, for example: clearly a triumph of user interface over performance. What really matters, in the long run, is whether the technology can efficiently support the processes that are designed to add value for your customers.

The paragraphs below highlight some of the key points about technology that you must consider during a reengineering effort. To ignore them is to guarantee surprises, often unwanted ones.

Know what the technology can (and can't) do

It is vitally important to know what available technologies are capable of before you start to reengineer a set of processes. To do otherwise is akin to starting to design a house without a good knowledge of available materials, their standard sizes, strengths, etc. The objective in reengineering is not to create a new process at any cost, but to create a new process in an economical manner, reusing existing resources whenever possible without compromising process efficiency. Recall the earlier premise: to strive for maximum improvement with a minimal investment

If your organization does not have the technical breadth to appreciate the full range of available technologies, consider hiring organizations who do. These can be consulting firms who perform feasibility studies for proposed processes, often using simulation tools to obtain quick answers at low cost. Another source is to ask prospective vendors to demonstrate their products or provide you with evaluation units for short term pilot operations.

> the reengineering team is made up of representatives from the organization

The ideal mix, derived from many years of systems integration experience, seems to be the teaming approach. The reengineering team is made up of representatives from the candidate organization who have a solid understanding of the processes, the company, its customers and the industry in which they operate and representatives who bring process reengineering skills and knowledge about information processing technologies. The team members can then feed off of their collective knowledge about all of the importance aspects of a reengineering project. Indeed, many state and local government agencies are realizing that their normal mode of defining requirements and issuing RFPs is highly inefficient because the requirements were developed in a reengineering and technology vacuum. More often than not, the requirements have to be modified as the project gets underway, especially when detailed designs start to emerge. This translates into added costs or project delays or both. A better solution is to form client/technologist teams to assess the full range of options before the project is committed.

Understand how process change be impacted by technologies

It is not sufficient to design a new process without an extensive investigation into the effects the new process will have on interfacing process and internal operations. Often processes in organizations are balanced to one another, either deliberately or they simply evolve that way, so that the output volume from one approximately matches the processing capacity of its recipient process. Were the predecessor process to be significantly improved so that the throughput doubled, for example, its output would swamp the successor process. The problem is that without forethought, doubling the throughput of the successor process could be expensive, relying on overtime or other extraordinary applications of resources and could, potentially negate any benefits gained by improving the first process.

A comprehensive reengineering effort should consider the potential impact on all of the interface points to that process. We have seen many times that a reengineering effort tends to grow to include many of the neighboring processes. This not unwelcome as the benefits from reengineering now extend to other parts of the organization and profit from the economies of scale at the same time (some of the technology components, for example, can be shared by more than one process).

One side-note: do not assume that the mere application of technology will have the desired effect. Certainly imaging, for example can improve the productivity of some processes, but applying imaging technology without totally reviewing the information requirements of a process, is, to borrow a concept from Michael Hammer, paving a cowpath — the cows are going to take just about as much time getting back to the barn as when it was unpaved. It always surprises us how many prospective clients issue RFPs that say, in effect, we want imaging and workflow technology to improve the efficiency of our (enter any description) process.

Keep an eye on costs

Technology can be expensive to buy and to operate, but done right, it does pay off. Knowing what the technologies can do is only one prerequisite; knowing their costs is another. The costs of technology are threefold: acquisition, operation and maintenance. Acquisition includes all of the costs associated with getting the technology: buying, licensing, installing, training, connecting to legacy systems, replacing obsolete equipment, etc. Operation costs are those which are variable according to the use of the technology. Supplies and the need for human involvement make up the bulk of the operations costs. In this category, a difficult user interface or an inefficient data format is going to be more expensive to operate than an easy one. Maintenance costs are those incurred to keep the technology current and functioning. There is an interesting trade-off in maintenance costs: should you accept off-the-shelf systems with relatively low maintenance costs and absorb the high operational costs because they do not do exactly what you need? Or should you opt for a customize solution that exactly meets your needs and is operationally very efficient, but has high maintenance costs? These are questions that need to be answered during the financial analysis of any reengineering project you are considering.

Verify capabilities

Most new technologies have many problems as well as very interesting capabilities, but the risks can be minimized to acceptable levels. Obviously, seeing the technology in action doing your business process is ideal, but often it is not practical to verify in this fashion, especially if yours are processes that require some degree of customized technology.

Other means include pilot programs where a small version of your process is tested and the results extrapolated to the full-sized version. While this works well, extrapolating is not always linear and results can be surprising once full operations are started. This is especially true when multiple, sequential processes are piloted with buffers between them. Another problem with pilot operations is the cost of the investment in equipment and people to run the pilot.

Parallel operations have long been used to verify new process effectiveness, but these tend to be very costly in terms of the people resources needed to staff them.

One low-cost technique to overcome this is to use simulation tools to model the new process and assess its potential performance. This provides a set of results at very low cost with inputs that can be readily altered to test alternate hypotheses about efficiency assumptions, processing rates, workloads, etc. Most modeling and simulation tools require a well-trained simulation analyst to successfully implement, but the results are usually well worth the effort.

Consider verification costs as part of the transition costs to a reengineered process. As we will explain in the discussion about Return on Investment (ROI), below, these costs need to be factored into the equation that explains the value of the reengineering effort.

4.   The Human Resources Factor

The pragmatic issues like productivity and redeploying people are often separated in reengineering efforts, especially during the early phases. As stated above, creating more value for your customers should be your prime motivator for any reengineering project, done in good times when you can best afford to do a good job. If the organization is growing or expects to, excess people can usually be absorbed by the growth of demand for people. Of course, that assumes that the skill sets are going to be required in the new process (or somewhere else in the organization) and that retraining is an economic and realistic alternative.

If, on the other hand, the purpose of reengineering is to reduce costs while maintaining capacity with little or no growth expected in the near future, the problem of redeploying staffs becomes one of staff reduction, always an unpleasant alternative. Here, we explore these issues.

Growth supports excess staff absorption

Your deployment options for excess staff become much easier when you are anticipating growth. In fact, even if reduced business activity is your prime stimulus for reengineering, the results of reengineering could result in increased productivity to point of stimulating increased sales through lower prices or better service. This condition is especially likely to be true if you have thoroughly explored your relationship with your customers and, as a result, understand what really matters to them. With that understanding, you will be able to devise means of better serving your customers (and perhaps use excess staff to do so) even if you do not reengineer any processes.

Reengineering is rarely a quick fix to a cash flow problem and therefore not a good candidate to solve business downturns. Indeed, reengineering often requires a sizable investment and from that perspective, business growth periods are the times when most companies undertake reengineering projects, simply because they can afford them. Another good reason to reengineer in good times is to avoid what has been termed "victory disease." Very successful companies, especially those that have been successful for a long time, often view themselves as infallible — a deadly

> very successful companies, often view themselves as infallible

notion in today's marketplace. In 1993, Fortune magazine explained the concept of corporate dinosaurs: previous giants in the corporate world who could not (or chose not to) adapt to new market conditions. IBM, Sears and General Motors are presently recovering from that state — through reengineering.

The bottom line on staffing, though, is that reengineered processes will raise productivity (require fewer people per unit of output) and we must understand all of our options for redeploying these people. As mentioned above, normal or better growth often absorbs the excess headcounts, but absent that growth, imaginative methods have to be devised to appropriately utilize the people skills freed up. Apart from the distaste of layoffs, business leaders should consider that released people have knowledge about your operations that your competitors would like to know.

Retraining is viable but a sometimes limited option

You mostly have to work with the staff you have or face replacing them. Since reducing or replacing staff is at least an unpleasant if not also expensive option, we recommend incorporating retraining as one of your options. Retraining staff can be accomplished successfully if you start with a set of rational expectations. It is not prudent, for example to expect stock clerks to become customer service managers without very extensive training. Training costs and the time it takes newly trained employees to become fully productive also needs to be factored in to the transition costs mentioned below in the discussion about ROI. Recall that education and process innovation are two of the highest ROI investments you can make in a business. Obviously, for education to pay off, you must have a sound business plan in place that defines how you intend to use the newly educated.

Change forthrightly

The fear and uncertainty of change can have a major negative impact on people and therefore productivity. Unfortunately, we find that reengineering is often thought of as synonymous with downsizing or the even lamer euphemism, rightsizing. Dragging out a major process change can have a devastating impact on the outcome. People, driven by their uncertainty (and the need to pay their mortgages), can become noticeably less productive or, worse, leave. Competitors can find out about your planned changes (perhaps by hiring some of your ex-employees) and adopt countermeasures that could partially or complete negate any benefits you anticipated.

Extreme secrecy is not necessarily the answer either because much valuable risk-mitigating information will come from your employees. The answer lies in applying the right resources to get the job done right and forthrightly. Get experts to help you sort through the myriad technical details, the cultural and organizational issues. Strive to understand fully and quickly all aspects of the project before committing to proceed.

> your objective is to maximize your benefits while minimizing your risk

Do not start with solutions, start with objectives, specifically objectives tied to serving your customers better and let the solutions address the objectives. The alternative is to find yourself constantly in search of a sufficiently important problem to apply your solution to so that the "numbers" come out right. There is no quicker way to lose credibility, time and support from your superiors and subordinates than to start with a solution without first clearly understanding what goals you are striving to achieve.

5. Defining Expected Return on Investment

Return on Investment (ROI) must be known for any organization to justify changes to its processes. Calculating ROI is hard enough, but even harder in some organizations is defining what a good ROI should be. Here, we look at two points: 1) how to select decision criteria (objectives) to determine whether a proposed reengineering is worthwhile, and 2) what to document for costs and benefits that lead to an ROI figure.

The prime consideration is how to express the "goodness" of an investment. ROI is essentially the interest rate you might expect if you put the funds necessary to achieve process reengineering into a bank account that produces the same funds flow annually. In most spreadsheet systems, ROI is usually expressed as Internal Rate of Return (IRR). Most IRRs greater than twice the best one can expect from the best monetary investments (with variations that are a function of a number of factors, see below) are generally considered worthwhile. Alternatively, some organizations prefer to look at payback period as the metric to assess the value of potential investment. This is the time after the start of the reengineering investment when the accumulated benefits equal the accumulated investment, in other words, the break-even point. Generally, payback periods of two years of less are considered worthwhile investments for many businesses, with significantly different times depending on a number of factors such as growth potential, confidence in forecasts, etc. Highly effective reengineering projects (those with strong commitment, good methodologies, focused on customer value, etc.) should expect payback periods under one year.

> pilot operations allow you to start with a small subset of the work

Changes must achieve a desired objective

The objective need not be financial to have business significance, it can be educational (pilot projects), or for publicity (we have the latest and greatest), etc. The important thing is to understand and select what objective(s) you want to achieve by reengineering. With a clear understanding of quantifiable objectives, you will be able to measure performance against objectives. This, in turn, will allow you to plan a phased approach to implementing the reengineered processes based on how well your expectations are met at various stages.

Quantify value

Clearly defined objectives also make the task of determining ROI easier because quantifiable benefits can be readily incorporated into the calculations. Cash flow, competitive impact, etc., are all well understood and readily identifiable values that can be quantified for the purpose of establishing ROI. The value of a reengineered process is much more than the productivity improvements gained, although these may be one of your objectives and the major component of value.

Consider the value of transferring some of your variable costs into fixed costs through mechanizing parts of your processes. Consider the value of using workflow to give the flexibility to adapt to changing market conditions faster than your competition. Consider the value of lowering your overhead to provide you with the means for riding out economic hard times with less drain on cash positions. Consider the reduced reliance on cash flow from operations, freeing up cash for productivity investments in other areas. In general, the fewer of your resources you need to serve your customers, the better your organization will be able to serve those very same and other (new) customers.

6. Minimize Disruption Costs

Defining a new process through reengineering is an exciting prospect until you realize that someone actually has to implement the new system. A myriad of new problems suddenly confronts you: what to order, how to put it together, retraining, cutover from legacy systems to new systems, interfacing with legacy systems, etc. Adequate planning, of course, is intended to solve these problems, but no amount of planning can foresee all of the possible occurrences from a significant reengineering project. Therefore, one of the considerations for any reengineering effort is to choose approaches that minimize disruption costs.

Think big, start small

While it may be tempting to try to capture the benefits from reengineering a large part of the organization, we strongly urge you to "think big, start small." Understand the enterprise impact, but pick a manageable first pilot. Know what the possibilities are by extending your reengineering efforts throughout the enterprise, but set milestones that will allow your management teams to gauge progress against plans, to assess the achievement of benefits against expectations. Once you are satisfied that your plans were well founded and, indeed coming to fruition as expected, expand the scope of your efforts to wider and wider parts of the organization.

Plan for operational cutover

The combination of new technologies and procedures can coexist with legacy systems, but only if well planned. Running parallel systems as was common twenty years ago no longer seems practical in light of the leaner organizations we all seem to be running in the nineties. With the exception of highly critical processes (airline flight operations, wire transfers, long distance switching, etc.), we just do not have the staff levels to do duplicate work for the purpose of checking out new systems. Other, more efficient methods are needed.

Pilot operations allow you to start with a small subset of the work that can be isolated easily and corrected if things go wrong during the initial phases. Another approach is to use simulators, as mentioned above, to refine the processes without committing real work or disrupting operations. Only when you are satisfied that you fully understand the impact of startup and cutover should you start the new processes in real operational environments. While this may seem like an exceedingly stringent requirement, consider that many in other parts of the organization are not going to believe in process reengineering as you do and will exploit and perhaps even aggravate or exaggerate every real and perceived failure.

Factor in transition costs in ROI analysis

There is a cost to change; minimize it by understanding it and simplifying it. But above all, do not ignore these costs. Someone will surely want to know about these costs and any equivocation on your part will prolong the acceptance of the project and with that, the capture of the potential benefits.

7. Protect Yourself from and Prepare for Emerging Technologies

It is now obvious that technology, especially workflow, can have a profound impact on the success of reengineering efforts. What is perhaps not so obvious is that technology is going to change constantly and with it the equations that define risk and reward.

> ### *Constant Change is Here to Stay*

Here we suggest some guidelines for you to improve your chances of exploiting emerging technologies to their fullest.

By the time you use it, technology will be obsolete

At the rate that new technology is emerging and promising new capabilities, it is often a major dilemma whether to acquire it now and reap the benefits or wait only a short time until something better comes along. If that is your only decision, then our recommendation is clear: buy it now. It does not matter whether in six months something better is going to be available; your objective is to maximize your benefits while minimizing your risk. Waiting for another, yet untested, product is simply delaying the time when you can capture the advantages from the technology that you already know. It's not necessary to strive incessantly for the latest and greatest to get the best bang for the buck (to use a couple of well-worn clichés). The caveat is, of course, build your systems such that you always have the options of inserting new technologies when they make sense.

Leave architectural attachment points for new technologies

When you do decide to upgrade, make it simple by planning ahead and using open architectures. It is not necessary to design API's (application program interfaces) into your systems to be ready for the next wave of technology. It is, however, essential to configure your systems around widely used communications protocols so that new systems will be relatively easy to integrate and can exchange data with one another and legacy systems. It is also vital to separate services from users with client-server architectures.

The client-server environment is an architecture that lends itself well to providing the modularity needed to accommodate diverse components that are required to interoperate. In this architecture, services such as databases, connectivity to external systems and shared resources are provided through servers. Servers can use any operating system that provides the service levels needed and can move information within the local area networking system. Routers are provided to communicate with other network protocols. Workstations are tuned to provide an efficient user interface independent of the services needed.

> the potential benefits are enormous, not just for the present, but into the foreseeable future

Standards are particularly useful at strategic points in a client-server configuration. Certainly all components have to be able to access all others through the networking scheme including that accessible through routers. The information contained on various network-wide repositories such as a jukebox should be in a format that is usable by all components needing it. The database accesses should be available from any component of the system. Printers should be usable by all components needing print services, etc.

Institutionalize reengineering

Always have an easy way to evaluate the potential impact of new technologies. Whether you subscribe to TQM (Total Quality Management) or Continuous Improvement, it is not the label that is important; it is the concept that there is always room for improvement and you should be constantly striving for it. Encourage your employees to question why things are done the way they are. Inform them of the business objectives that they are charged with supporting (instill in them a sense of process ownership). Invite suggestions and never dismiss any as too ridiculous without first analyzing its merit. Before Ford adopted an invoiceless payment system, who would have believed that vendors could be properly paid without first submitting invoices?

8. The Impact of Standards (or Lack Thereof) on Reengineering

Standards are always going to lag emerging technologies and, in essence, define the risks associated with new technologies. That does not mean that standards ought to be adhered to rigidly, excluding technologies that do not comply; nor does it mean that standards ought to be ignored in favor of capturing the advantages of state-of-the-art technologies. Some reasonable compromise is called for that both captures the performance level promises of new technologies and protects mission critical systems from incompatibilities between components and growth options. This is especially true in an environment of constant process reviews which is strongly advocated by all proponents of process reengineering. As new capabilities emerge, it is often desirable to take advantage of them, but without an assurance that they will successfully coexist with other parts of your information systems, it is difficult and risky to exploit them fully, if at all.

Standards will help and hurt

Interface consistency is desirable, but standards, by their very nature, almost always lag new technologies, limiting access to the capabilities these technologies promise. Obviously, standards exist to ensure interoperability and, as has been discussed already, interoperability among system components is crucial to the success of modern information management systems where information *sharing* has become at least as important as information *processing*. As important, however, is the ability to exploit the offerings of state-of-the-art technology, often unhampered by the shackles of standards. The dilemma is to find ways to get the protection of standards and the functionality of new technology.

The solution lies in a thorough assessment of your willingness to take risks and an adherence to a minimum set of standards that ensure adequate information exchange. In other words, it is not the risks, it is the surprises that count. More and more system integrators are considering some form of risk sharing options in their fee structures. Another version of this same concept is benefit sharing, effectively royalty payments in lieu of fixed fees for system performance or operational milestones. What makes sense for your organization will depend on your assessment of risks and the capabilities of new technology.

The key to a successful compromise lies in establishing open architectures for information repositories. SQL (structured query language), for example, is a *de facto* standard for database access that crosses many popular databases. SQL provides access to information for any component that can formulate its request in this well-defined format. SQL as a standard is, therefore, one we do not recommend compromising without extensive justification. However, having said that, it should be pointed out that many of the popular SQL databases (Oracle, Informix, Sybase, etc.) all have extensions that provide added functionality that make them more competitive. This added functionality, by design, means that they are not fully interchangeable.

Enterprise information management architectures are vital

The issue is not what hardware or operating system you should standardize on, but how do you want your data to be available to all who need it? The operative concept here is "when you need it." It is, therefore, vital to establish an information strategy that defines what information is essential to your business operations and how you want to make that information available to those parts of the organization that need it.

Consider also that networking and collaborative computing will increase the need (and potential) for information sharing and with that, the vulnerability of your information from sources that could threaten your business. Client-server architectures are deliberately designed to share information in a highly efficient manner. Sharing implies that people can access it. The challenge here is to institute sufficient protection to safeguard the information, but not so many that the legitimate sharing becomes difficult.

Operational consistency solves many organizational issues

Retraining, career paths, cross-training all become readily achievable with an effective client-server information management system. Adherence to standards that enable efficient information sharing makes it relatively easy to provide network based training programs, parallel processing of independent tasks, remote monitoring of work progress and backlogs, manufacturing scheduling with very early data about backlogs and many other previously difficult tasks. Workflow is the glue that can make all of this happen.

Summary

While some of the advice given here might seem to some to be contradictory, as in any well-controlled system, there are going to be forces working at odds with one another that keep the system from going out of control. The premise of reengineering is not, in this author's opinion, an option to institute cataclysmic change; instead we view it as an application of three important ingredients:

> *Imagination, Tempered by Business Acumen, Supported by Technology*

In process reengineering, each of these ingredients has both a tempering and stimulating effect on the other two. We have described a number of areas that need attention before, during and after process reengineering and suggest that the risks of change and the use of advanced technologies can be appropriately minimized as a result of attention to these areas. A constant customer focus cannot be overemphasized. The potential benefits are enormous, not just for the present, but into the foreseeable future. Much of the data processing and communications infrastructure being contemplated today is with reengineering in mind. The so-called information highway, workflow and collaborative computing environments are but three of many important technologies that will support and encourage process reengineering for remainder of this and well into the 21st century.

The mere fact that we are all going to reengineer our processes in some significant way in the next few years is going to become a self fulfilling prophecy. Competitive pressures thus generated will continue to apply pressures on us to improve our abilities to serve our customers even further. As they become more and more sophisticated about the value of information and the capabilities of the technologies, it's going to be our customers who will provide all the stimuli.

Case Study: George Mason University

Peter J. Denning, Associate Dean for Computing

Chair, Computer Science Department

George Mason University

and Raúl Medina-Mora, Senior Vice President and

Chief Scientist

Action Technologies Inc.

Business process reengineering has emerged as an important practice but is not yet a discipline. The molecular element of all business processes is the workflow loop, an interaction between two people in which one (the performer) fulfills a commitment to the satisfaction of the other (the client). A process is a network of loops. The satisfaction of external clients and of internal workers is connected directly to recurrent completions of loops throughout the process. A process, however dysfunctional, is held in place by the tacit agreement of the participants; reengineering comprises providing technology to support the new process and in reorganizing the practices of the participants. Mapping the business process with loop notation is the basis of a discipline. All these points are illustrated with a case study of a complex, major university process; curriculum management.

Introduction

Many organizations are considering business process reengineering as a possible entrée to a new era of productivity and effectiveness. Hammer and Champy talk about replacing the command-and-control structure with fluid, project-oriented teams, a radical shift in the interpretation of communication in organizations (Hammer 93). Drucker says that the old ways of improving productivity are not effective for knowledge work and emphasizes the need for effective communication of information among workers (Drucker 93).

Well before these realizations became popular, Fernando Flores proposed a new interpretation of work: the making and fulfilling of commitments (Flores 79, Winograd and Flores 87). He claimed that effective coordination of action was the same as effective communication and that the flow of work could be traced by watching "speech acts" in the communications of those coordinating.

We will explore Flores' interpretation by showing it at work in a case study of course scheduling at George Mason University. Flores' interpretation produces a new method called business process analysis that can allow its practitioners to see the sources of the breakdowns in work, reveal the connection to moods and trust, show how information technology can support work, and guide the redesign of work processes toward greater productivity and satisfaction. One of the main lessons is that redesigning the process is not sufficient to produce the change in people's habits, for the current "culture" of the organization provides a context in which the current "way of doing business" makes sense. To effect organizational change, it is necessary not only to reveal the processes and propose a redesign, but to reveal the main assumptions of the common sense, to work toward a new social contract among those involved, and to provide technology that easily supports their new practices.

What is Work?

A hundred years ago, Frederick Taylor introduced the principle of "scientific management," a view that sees the organization's work as a collection of tasks, each of which can be described by a precise procedure whose steps are particular motions and activities of a worker; the job of management is to spell out and optimize the tasks and to supervise the workers in carrying them out.

> time-and-motion and information-processing concepts of work are no longer sufficient

According to Drucker, Taylor averted a class war because the increased productivity of manufacturing operations under Taylor's principles raised the economic standing of every worker. So great was the improvement of productivity that unions were forced to accede to new work practices despite their initial resistance. According to Drucker, Taylor's principles permitted the US to win World War II by rapidly becoming the most productive maker of weapons, planes, and ships eventually building them faster than all enemies were able to destroy them.

In the 1940s, those versed in computer design began to interpret the motions and activities of workers as flows and transformations of information; the individual worker could be viewed as a function that processes input information into output information. The separate algorithms describing individual worker functions, when joined together, constitute an overall algorithm for the organization. These views were reinforced in the 1950s when Hebert Simon described management as decision-making by evaluating alternatives, and in the 1960s when Jay Forrester analyzed organizations as non-linear feedback signal-processing systems. In effect, these views have made it attractive to think that Taylor's principles can be extended to knowledge work.

The problem is that these information-interpretations have been not helped much with knowledge work in practice. According to Dertouzos white collar productivity declined in the US by several percentage points during the 1980s;

blue-collar productivity did rise during the same period, but blue-collar work is a shrinking percentage of the total (Dertouzos 89). These input-process-output models of organizations do not and cannot represent human commitments. They are blind to the human processes in which people request work and agree on what will be done, who will do it, and when it will be done; they do not provide a mechanism for making sure that the customer is satisfied. In recent years this has turned from an annoyance into a crisis. It is now apparent that the time-and-motion and information-processing concepts of work are no longer sufficient to describe what is going on in many organizations.

Workflows

In Flores' interpretation, work is initiated and completed in the business processes, the processes that deal with requests for work to be done, agreements about when and what will be done, who is responsible for doing it, and whether the parties are satisfied with the outcome. The movement of information and material is the consequence of work, and supports work, but is not the work itself.

The atomic unit of work is a "loop" (also called a workflow), a closed cycle in which a "fulfiller" completes action leading to the satisfaction of a request by a "requester." In carrying out an agreement, a fulfiller becomes, in turn, the requester of others for pieces of the work, and thus a whole network of requesters, loops, and fulfillers comes into play for the completion of the original request. The resulting interconnection of loops depicts the social network in which a group of people, filling various roles, carry out an organizational process that renders service to the customers.

In the business world, the requester and fulfiller are called, respectively, customer and performer, or sometimes consumer and producer. In the professional world, these two roles are often called client and professional. We will use the terminology client and performer. A loop refers to a cycle of recurrent transactions between particular roles of clients and performers. The same person can be the performer in one loop and the client in another. An organizational (or business) process refers to a particular network of loops. Satisfaction means that the client declares that the agreement (implied contract) between client and performer has been fulfilled; satisfaction does not mean gratification and it is not a report on the psychological state of the client. Satisfaction often means mutual satisfaction because many loops are, in fact, exchange transactions, in which both parties expect something from the other.

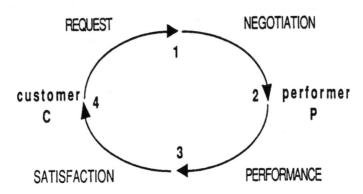

Figure 1

Figure 1 depicts the familiar workflow loop, which consists of four segments connecting four events. The loop begins with the formulation of a client's request, culminating in its delivery to the performer. The second segment is negotiation on the mutual conditions of satisfaction, culminating in an agreement between client and performer. The third segment is performance, culminating in the performer's declaration that the work is done. The final segment is acceptance, culminating in the customer's declaration of satisfaction or the pair's declaration of mutual satisfaction. (The loop notation and structural elements are the copyright of Action Technologies and Business Design Associates.)

> these problems will not be resolved until organizational practices (people's habits) change

Every one of us engages in tens or hundreds of loops a day. Every request or offer opens a loop, and every fulfillment to our satisfaction closes a loop. In organizations, there are certain kinds of requests, such as placing orders or processing engineering trouble reports, that recur over and over again. The processes for fulfilling them are the business processes of the organization.

Figure 2 illustrates a process for procuring material. The main loop (procure equipment) connects to several secondary loops (verify status, get bids, place order) in which the main-loop performer is the client. Flows of information associated with an accounting data system are shown in gray. In many organizations, the main loop is missing the fourth segment. This can happen when the procurement office does not follow up with the client to see if the materiel has been delivered and is satisfactory. To deal with the consequent complaints and inquiries, a new loop (resolve complaints) must be set up; the time and effort spent on this loop is mostly waste because it could be eliminated by organizing the main loop for completion.

Incomplete workflows invariably cause breakdowns, and persistent incompletions give rise to waste, delay, and complaints that interfere with the ultimate purpose of work client satisfaction. Human beings are remarkably inventive about finding ways to break loops.

Here are examples in each of the four segments:

Request: The requester can fail to make clear that a request is being made, thinking that the hint or suggestion has been heard as a request. The form of request may not be as expected by performer.

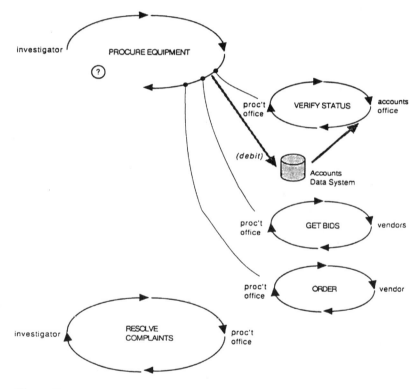

Figure 2

Negotiation: The intended performer can fail to clearly decline a request, leaving the client to expect something that will not happen. The performer can ignore the request, leaving the client frustrated with no response at all. The two parties can emerge from a negotiation without suspecting that they have different understandings of the conditions of satisfaction.

Performance: The performer can stop work without telling the client. The performer can deliver shabby results. The performer can begin work gratuitously, without the beneficiary requesting it.

Satisfaction: The client can fail to acknowledge receipt of the results. The performer can fail to find out if the client is satisfied.

the first step was to construct the map of the workflows *as they are actually performed*

A fifth source of breakdown is lack of awareness of the workflows themselves. An example is the use of in-boxes and out-boxes exclusively for communication between clients and performers; the client never knows whether a performer is working on the task and the performer never knows who submitted the request. It is important to note that all five types of breakdowns are never completely avoidable because the parties are never completely explicit and rely on assumptions that they have the same understandings of the basic language in which workflow acts are phrased.

If the incompletions persist long enough, the performers of their loops will no longer be trusted by others, and eventually management will be distrusted for allowing the situation to persist. Distrust can seed other bad moods such as frustration, inconsistency, misunderstanding, resentment, resignation and dissatisfaction. Outside the organization, the same persistent incompletion can produce more distrust, lowered reputation, lack of credibility, loss of market position, lowering of quality and dissatisfied customers. In contrast, if everyone in the organization is conscientious about completing the loops of which he or she is a part, the overall sense of mutual trust and satisfaction will be high, as will the ability to complete on time and satisfy customers.

Evidently, many of the problems that trouble organizations are connected with persistently incomplete workflows. These problems will not be resolved until organizational practices (people's habits) change and the workflows are consistently completed. Redesigning workflows to make them complete or organizational processes to make them more productive is not simply a problem of deploying information technology in the right places. An organizational process, however dysfunctional, is held in place by a set of shared, often unspoken agreements among the participants, sometimes called the "company culture" or "common sense." Technology can help facilitate changes, but not unless the participants understand the nature of work and how incompletions can cause problems, and even then not unless they agree to the changes.

Case Study

OBSERVATION FOR WORKFLOW MAPS
Client:
Who makes requests or accepts offers
Who must be satisfied with the outcome
Who must distinguish roles from individuals

Performer:
Who makes offers or receives requests
Who does the work
Who must distinguish roles from individuals

Phase	Client Act	Performer Act
Request	Initiate Request	
Negotiation	Counter Decline counteroffer Accept Counteroffer	Counteroffer Agree Decline
Performance		Report Completion Revoke
Satisfaction	Decline to accept Declare satisfaction	
Any phase	Cancel Comment	Comment

In the spring of 1991, a group of faculty and administrators of George Mason University formed a working group to investigate the university processes that were producing the most complaints, and to recommend changes in the design of those processes and the information technology supporting them. The first author of this chapter (Denning) was a member of that group. The group found that the notations discussed above were very powerful and enabled them to see exactly the organizational processes that were incomplete or needlessly complex and thus to recommend specific actions to relieve the problems. The study also enabled the group to see the kinds of technology that would be useful to support a proposed new process.

Investigative Process

Curriculum management is the single largest process in any university. At George Mason University, it affects 21,000 students, 650 faculty, and many administrators daily. It encompasses advising, career counseling, plans of study, curriculum planning and course scheduling. Breakdowns anywhere in this network of subprocesses produce unmet expectations, leading to dissatisfied clients (students) and performers (faculty). Because curriculum planning is a long-term process, breakdowns can significantly delay student graduation. As it is in many universities, this process is the subject of endless complaints from all participants. We chose it as the subject of our investigation.

The first step was to construct the map of the workflows *as they are actually performed*. The investigation was conducted by interviewing people from the student records (registrar's) office and from each of the schools. In each case, we sought to identify who makes what kinds of requests of whom, how those requests are conveyed, how the participants reach agreements, what steps are done to carry out typical agreements, of whom the performer makes subsidiary requests, how the final results are conveyed, and how the loop is closed or not closed. (*Figure 2* shows what we look for during interviews.)

As an interview proceeded, we sketched the loops and showed the unfolding map to those we were interviewing. As they began to see their own process unfold before their eyes, they were able to validate the map or tell us how to alter it. The ActionWorkflow Analyst tool can significantly accelerate the map-making process (Action 93).

The second step, conducted as part of the same interview, was to ask the participants to describe the breakdowns they were routinely encountering in their own processes and in the interactions with others on whom they depended. We asked them about their principal concerns. We also asked them to discuss the most important constraints they felt they had to live with, both in terms of rules and of values. From these questions, we were able to deduce the breakdowns that were the most irritating, the cultural common sense they had, and the changes that would be most valued.

The third step was undertaken only after the entire map was completed. We sought a new process that would produce the same overall result with significantly less complexity, notably the elimination of wasteful loops created to resolve breakdowns in the basic process. We asked what would have to change, both in terms of social agreements and technology, for people to accept the new process and begin practicing it.

In summary, the steps of the investigation were:
a. Map existing work process using loop notation
b. Identify breakdowns perceived by stakeholders (including frustration and anguish they experience)
c. Reveal background cultural and other assumptions that underlie the process
d. Propose new assumptions that would reduce waste and remove breakdowns
e. Reengineer the work process based on the new assumptions;
f. Evaluate the information technology required to support the new process

g.   Evaluate the cultural changes (points of the "social contract" requiring rene-
     gotiation) needed to effect the new process.
     As a helpful guide in the redesign stages (e) above, we asked, "Who is al-
ready doing it in a way that produces the results we want?" We can then learn
from that group.

Case Details

     The major complaints about the curriculum management process were:
1.   Approximately 10 percent of students applying for graduation have not met
     requirements due to unavailability of courses, closed sections, or inaccurate
     information about degree requirements.
2.   Many students cannot graduate in the four-year span because courses they
     need as prerequisites are offered infrequently or are full.
3.   Many students request and receive special exceptions and waivers to substi-
     tute courses for others that are not available. Processing these requests oc-
     cupies much faculty and staff time.
4.   Students' graduation records often do not reflect the coherence advertised in
     the catalog; students often take significantly more coursework than required
     for their majors.

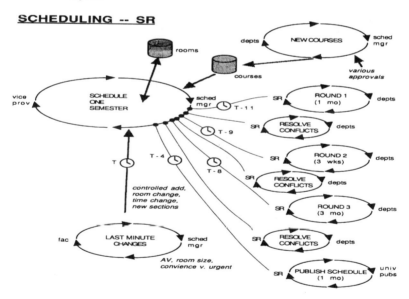

Figure 3

5. Approximately 20 percent of the classes in the published schedule are changed after students have registered, requiring cancellation and reregistration.
6. On the first day of classes, many faculty find themselves confronted with students who could not register because the class was full and who request special permission to register.
7. Many departments do not provide adequately for advising. Faculty say they receive little reward or recognition for time spent advising.

To discover the loops of the work process, a subset of the working group met individually with the persons responsible for course scheduling in the Schools of Education (SED), Business Administration (SBA), Information Technology and Engineering (SITE), Nursing (SN) and in the Student Records (SR) office. The workflow maps constructed during these interviews are shown in the accompanying charts.

The first of these charts shows the main loop in the SR (Registrar's) office (Figure 3). Beginning 11 months prior to the start of the semester being scheduled, this office sends a request to all departments to draft an initial schedule. Two more drafts are sent to the departments for further comment and refinement. Between each of these "rounds," SR office personnel must work with individual departments to resolve conflicts—for example, when the demand for MWF 10 a.m. classes exceeds available rooms. The "final" schedule is published in the preceding semester in time for students to register. (Information flows between workflows and databases are shown as gray arrows in the figure.)

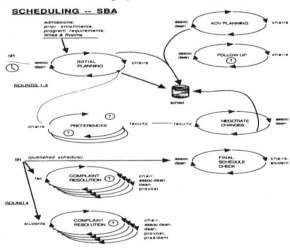

Figure 4

The remaining charts show what happens inside the schools when these requests arrive. Figure 4 is typical; it shows the process within the school of business, which is similar to those within engineering and education. The seeds of the complexity can be seen in the early incomplete loop during which the department chairs ask faculty to state their preferences for courses to teach and times to hold classes. It is not clear that all faculty have agreed to state their preferences or that the department chairs are satisfied with their responses.

The complexity reaches full bloom later, after the final published schedule is issued. Many faculty experience reactions from annoyance to outrage on seeing this schedule; they immediately enter into negotiations with the nearest "person of authority" (chair, dean, provost) to have the schedule corrected to reflect their preferences and needs, and they often do this without consulting with the person officially responsible for the schedule.

What is striking about the course-scheduling process is its complexity. It takes many pages of maps to display all the loops that sprawl over many units of the university. Many of the loops seem to provide only incremental improvements over the previous iterations. There are many special loops in which complaints are resolved. Given the lengthy cycle time of the process (eleven months) it is little surprise that there are so many last-minute changes.

> **it takes many pages of maps to display all the loops that sprawl over many units of the university**

In discussing with stakeholders the reason this process has evolved into its present form, we discovered the following assumptions that are part of the unspoken background tacitly agreed to by everyone:

1. *Scheduling is performer driven.* The first three rounds of course scheduling are rooted in negotiations with faculty. Student demands are incorporated late and in some cases, not at all, and are often not known accurately. While the faculty get several months to react to the draft schedules, the students get only a few days. Department chairs, deans, the provost and sometimes even the president are seen as appropriate authorities for faculty to call upon for changes if the published schedule does not meet their preferences. Workflows for resolving complaints are disconnected with the Registrar. In effect, the real client—the student—is lost.

2. *Students have little responsibility.* Their only job is to check with advisors to make sure they are fulfilling requirements and to register for the coming semester during the prescribed registration periods.

3. *SR office assigns all the rooms.* This office is responsible for finding rooms to meet departmental requests. It must negotiate with various parties for changes when rooms are not available. It is a bottleneck. Few blocks of rooms are assigned to schools for local scheduling.

4. *There are three patterns for classes*: Monday-Wednesday-Friday for 1 hour each, Tuesday-Thursday for 1.5 hours each, or any evening for 3 hours each. Patterns that include Saturday classes are excluded.

5. *The summer schedule is independent.* Summer budgets and summer FTE formulae are different from academic year budgets and FTE formulae. Summer schedules offer much less than the actual demand.

6. *In some schools, graduate schedules are determined separately from undergraduate.* This increases the effort to construct a complete schedule.

7. *The published schedule is a mini-catalog.* This adds delay to the assembly and publication of the schedule.

> redesigning those processes is not simply a matter of drawing new maps

These assumptions constitute the terms of a "social contract" that keeps the current course-scheduling process in place. They are the starting point for reengineering.

The most important assumptions are the first and the second. These assumptions appear to arise from the traditional assumption that faculty are responsible for determining the curriculum and know best what constitutes a good education for the students. What new assumptions would lead to a simplification of this process, possibly to its theoretical minimum of a single loop? What changes of habits would be needed to bring about these assumptions? How might the "social contract" be renegotiated to accomplish this? How might the conditions of satisfaction of students and faculty be made explicit?

To arrive at a simpler process, the group stated the result sought: Design a schedule that accommodates most student demand (operationally, 95 percent of students get a schedule that includes the courses they need each semester), requires minimal faculty effort to formulate (operationally, one round), and requires few last-minute changes (operationally, less than one percent). We asked of any group is already achieving these results. The School of Nursing (SN) is. Their process can be used as a blueprint by everyone in the university.

The SN approach is based on a distinction between two distinct responsibilities of the faculty: 1) to determine the curriculum, and 2) to cooperate with the students in delivering the curriculum effectively. The SN's success derives from the way they approach the second responsibility: The process of delivery is driven by student demand for courses to fulfill degree requirements.

The last chart (Figure 5) shows a possible revised process that incorporates the assumptions of the SN process. The entire process map is expressed in one page rather than the many in the current map. This simplicity is achieved by transforming the basic assumptions to these:

1. *Students are given responsibility for working with advisors to determine and file plans of study.* A plan of study is an agreement between student and advisor about the courses the student will take each semester to fulfill the degree requirements and prepare the student for a chosen career. The filed plans are interpreted as requests by the students, who, in turn, would be guaranteed to find classes corresponding to their plans. About 75 percent of the demand could be learned from filed plans.

2. *The schedule is generated in one round after departments are given their demand data.* Early in the semester before the one being scheduled, each department would confer with its faculty about the demand data and would commit to a schedule for the following semester.

The lead time to publish a schedule based in these assumptions would be much shorter than the current 11 months. The schedule could be published late in the semester prior to the one in which the courses are taught. The SN process is already built on these two assumptions.

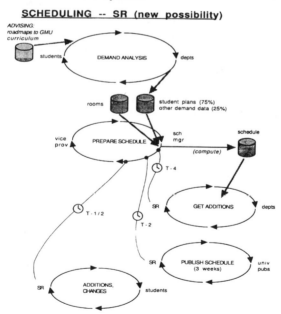

SCHEDULING -- SR (new possibility)

Figure 5

In contrast, SN shows the least complexity; their highly structured program has limited options.

A key enabling technology here is one that supports the formulation and storage of student plans of study. This would require computer systems in each department that would allow students to fill in template plans and confer with their advisors before filing or modifying them. It would require a distributed database system that could construct a unified view of all the department and school databases to estimate demand for each course and would allow each department to determine the demand for its courses. The presence of such technology would not suffice to produce greater satisfaction with curriculum management: the entire process must be redesigned.

Conclusions

We have shown, with examples of work processes of the university, how it is possible to observe and map large processes in a way that creates the possibility of redesign, not only for greater efficiency and lower waste, but more importantly for greater satisfaction of everyone involved in or with the processes. With these maps it is possible to connect negative organizational moods such as poor morale, distrust, resentment, waste, excessive cycle time, and low public satisfaction with breakdowns in workflow loops or with excessive complexity of the process. The Young & Rubicam study demonstrates clearly that redesigned processes in which the loops are regularly completed produce significant, measurable improvements in employee satisfaction (Marshak 93).

We have also shown that the existing process, no matter how dysfunctional or unsatisfactory, is held in place by its participants' habits, by organizational "culture," and everyone's shared sense of what is "right." Redesigning those processes is not simply a matter of drawing new maps and introducing new technology. It is also a matter of reorganizing people's practices and self-interest— shifting their conditions of satisfaction. For this reason, we speculate that extraordinarily complex processes involving many departments and many people will be difficult to modify without providing technology that allows the participants to see significant personal gains in productivity within the new process.

With such technologies, it will be possible to manage organizational processes to systematically produce client satisfaction, to reduce cycle time, to increase productivity, and to quickly redesign the process to meet new conditions of satisfaction.

Notes

Action Technologies. 1993. *User's Manual for ActionWorkflow Analyst.* Action Technologies, 1301 Marina Village Parkway, Alameda, CA 94501.

Peter Denning. 1992. "Work is a closed loop process." *American Scientist 80,* 4 (July-August). 314-317.

Michael Dertouzos, Richard Lester, Robert Solow. 1989. *Made in America.* The MIT Press.

Peter Drucker. 1993. *Post Capitalist Society.* Harper Business.

Fernando Flores. 1979. *Management and communication in the office of the future.* Ph.D. Thesis, Department of Philosophy, University of California at Berkeley.

Fernando Flores. 1991. "Designing new principles for a shifting business world." Business Design Associates, 2200 Powell Street, Suite 400, Emeryville, CA 94608.

Michael Hammer and James Champy. 1993. *Reengineering the Corporation.* Harper Business.

Raúl Medina-Mora, Terry Winograd, Rodrigo Flores, and Fernando Flores. 1992. "The Action Workflow approach to workflow management technology." *Proceedings. ACM Conference on Computer Supported Cooperative Work* (November).

Ronni Marshak. 1993. "Young & Rubicam improves productivity with workflow." *Workgroup Computing Report 16,* 5 (May), 12-20. Published by Patricia Seybold Group, 148 State Street, Boston, MA 02109.

Terry Winograd and Fernando Flores. 1987. *Understanding Computers and Cognition.* Addison-Wesley.

Acknowledgment

Peter Denning would like to thank his colleagues on the *George Mason University Working Group on Service Improvement,* which met during Spring 1992:

Kees DeKluyver (chair), Deborah Boehm-Davis, Julia Boyd, Art Chickering, James Finkelstein, Menas Kafatos, Catherine Malloy, David Rossell, Frederick Siff and Suzanne Swope.

Growing the Smart Organization

Professor Nicholas Imparato
McLaren School of Business, University of San Francisco

This chapter is adapted from "Jumping The Curve: Innovation and Strategic Choice in an Age of Transition," *published Fall, 1994 by Jossey-Bass Publishers and co-authored with Oren Harari. The basic theme is that epochal changes in the economic and social environment require organizations to reinvent their structure and processes. Companies need to find a substitute for the function-based and bureaucratic orientation that has served as a way of organizing work since the rise of the Industrial Revolution. In the book four methods or organizing principles are presented.*

In this chapter, Imparato outlines the first principle and ways it can be implemented.

Epochal changes in the economic and social environment are requiring organizations to reinvent their structure and processes.

Organizations designed as machines are basically designed to do the same thing over and over again. They are not designed to be innovative. The circumstances that require adaptiveness make the case for alternatives to the mechanistic approach. The circumstances include changes in the world economic structure and availability of new communication tools.

The alternative is some kind of organic approach. To have practical value, it must efficiently tie together the ideas of constant change, flux, interconnectivity and permeable boundaries, as well as the importance of intangibles and information. Trying to build a set of organizational structures and procedures that do this while simultaneously attending to today's business demands can be difficult. For many the sensation is like trying to build an airplane while they are flying it. Experimentation is everywhere; no one is certain about how to get from here to there, safely.

One approach is to begin with a process. The process in this case deals with how information moves and communication takes place. The intention is to build the organization around some fundamental ideas about how it should operate before determining how it should look. The recommended organizing principle is: *Build the company around the software and build the software around the customer.* The goal is to establish a process as the source of integration for the company.

Software means more than just technology and programming code. The term refers to the firm's processes and methodologies that enable it to respond quickly to a changing mix of customer needs and wants. Building the company around software means organizing production and work around the knowledge the organization has about its business environment. It means using technology to bring flexibility and adaptation, not rigid procedures, to the firm's capabilities. Building the software around the customer means that when the customer is the central focus of these efforts, the market, the world beyond the inward-looking bureaucracy, determines the roles that need to be played, the strategies that need to be pursued and the goals that need to be set. All in all the organizing principle suggests the need to constantly recreate the organization.

There is an underlying philosophy or point of view that the principle reflects, namely that organizations are restless. Whereas paper-based organizations, for example, deal with assumptions of static processes (a detailed job description is expected to have a lifetime of several years), organizations built around dynamic software assume fluidity and evolution. Nor is it assumed that the world "outside" the organization is still. Demographics and customer tastes change. Competitors find opportunities. Trade rules disappear. Databases that document the turmoil of the market are valuable; databases that can fashion data in a way that employees can use immediately are more so. The challenge becomes how to create organizations that are flexible and that permit an easy use of information. This eventually entails determining on an ongoing basis the scope of information provided to people, the number of locations, the most useful format and the conditions of information exchange (for example, security, privacy).

> build the company around the software and build the software around the customer

A strategy of this kind helps us redefine the organization. It is no longer a collection of bodies, capital, buildings and other resources. Indeed, a company's home office-bricks, mortar and two-by-fours contribute less added value than the competence and market awareness of its workforce. The diffusion of information technology helps knowledge-based activities and organizational intelligence attain strategic importance. In this environment, the company becomes something more intangible, a knowledge reservoir for the entire community that holds the collective wisdom of everyone associated with it; a brain of sorts.

As a derivation of the organic model, the idea of the organization-as-brain focuses on the role of information and the way information is used for self-management. The underlying premise is that responsibility for thinking, judgment and creativity exists everywhere in the organization. The capacity for renewal is seen as a function of intelligence and openness that characterizes all levels of the organization, not just a few people in the president's suite. The metaphor suggests that an organization can regulate itself by constantly monitoring the environment, by coordinating multiple parts to perform as a whole and by absorbing negative feedback to correct actions. The implication is that the organization can learn.

In this setting one shared purpose is to make the brain smarter, quicker acting and more customer sensitive. By the same token, the purpose of the brain is to enable all workers, from shipping dock to the executive suite, to do their jobs better. We measure success not only by achieving certain productivity goals for a day or a quarter or a year but also by growing the intelligence and capabilities of the brain.

> collaboration means more than one individual sharing an insight with co-workers

A major value of the brains metaphor is that it alludes to what needs to be done. It helps prescribe activities that should take place, and leads easily to the organizing principle. Using the organizing principle, in turn, to establish structure and processes means that an organization aggressively employs the use of information technology in four distinct but related ways.

These are:

- A drive to leverage knowledge across the organization
- An acceleration and facilitation of collaborative work within the organization and between the organization and "others"
- Strenuous efforts at mass customization, slenderized marketing and individualizing customer sets
- Liberation from the constraints of the paper-dependent environment.
- Each of these initiatives is in one way or another related to the others. They are different attributes of the same strategy. What they have in common is the application of the brain metaphor in a way that energizes the organization around processes that are driven by the customer environment rather than by bureaucratic tradition.

1. A drive to leverage knowledge across the organization

Mrs. Fields Cookies has had substantial success in using information technology to advise store managers in conducting daily operations. What Randy Fields envisioned and eventually architected was a software system that captured the ideas that co-founder Debbi Fields and other experts had about every aspect of how to run the business, from baking to selling, from people management to production schedules. The goal was to collect their ideas and incorporate them as a set of recommendations that anyone in the field could call up on a computer and utilize immediately. These suggestions were included within modules for sales reports, scheduling of daily activities, inventory control, financial reporting and an assortment of other functions. In short, a whole array of traditional management activities were automated at the same time advice and coaching were available using instruction sets from the "best and brightest." The underlying premise in such a system is that every successful business person has a knowledge about her job that is part derived from a common sense shared by many and part derived from a unique set of insights and instincts. The trick is to capture those insights in a way that other people in the organization can use them.

For example, the same pattern of problems might occur across a number of stores during the same week. Then one store manger in Topeka, let's say, experiments with a solution that has not been tried before. The results are superb. Sales go up. Customers appear delighted. Cost ratios stay in line. Noted by an expert at homebase or at the district level, the new wisdom is quickly spread electronically throughout the system. The e-mail component of the network becomes more than form or data transmission; it is about coaching and education using live performance information. Because a solution comes from the field, it is more likely driven by customer input than driven by administrative necessity.

> **the challenge becomes how to create organizations that are flexible**

Telecommunications networks allow peer to peer communication so that the idea can be elaborated and polished right away by those who are face-to-face with the customer. Thus, a new alternative, another solution, can be brought to the repertoire of activities other mangers can engage to be effective. Over time it will be tested by different locations and evaluated for its appropriateness in specific conditions. At some point the insight, assuming its continued validity, is included in revised standards and procedures. What has happened is that one employee's business learning not only affects the performance of her store and operations, but also through the computerized brain, assists others in the pursuit of their objectives.

To use such an approach means that every facet of the business would be affected. If one were to build an organization around such a system from the beginning, the way it would conduct business would be radically different from the way business is typically managed. For one thing, recruitment would change. In effect, the organization would look to hire a different kind of person to run stores than the kind of person that is normally hired today. Administrative skills would be less important than communication skills. The machine would do a lot of the information processing and administrative grunt work, freeing the store manager to spend more time coaching employees and being with customers. Listening, communication and judgment become more important. The technology would aid the search for ideas and suggestions that might facilitate operations for the day; it would also encourage the creation of solutions and ideas. In short, a different kind of skills hierarchy would be supported by the technology, one that is more outward looking in its orientation. Increasingly, the emphasis would be on innovation, not on managing a list of administrative "to do's."

When everyone has access to the collected intelligence of the organization and can input data so that the activity of all other workers will be affected, it is possible to say that strategy can begin anywhere in the company. It is no longer the preserve of just the top three or four people in the organization. MTV sales personnel discovered during customer visits that resistance was due in many cases to a competitor's low price (Turner Broadcasting System). The news was transmitted electronically and shared quickly among other sales personnel. Executives were apprised; they were able to respond rapidly with a new pricing strategy that saved deals for MTV. Although some organizations are dominated by strong leaders who get similar results when they make site visits (the late Sam Walton comes to mind), they cannot visit all the stores at the same moment. This system is "on" 24 hours a day everywhere in the world. The power to make a difference becomes tangible on a moment-to-moment basis. Randy Fields has said that this is the one true value of all information technology. The intended outcome, he reported in an interview, is making it "normal for every employee, but especially those who are dealing directly with the customers, a player when it comes to deciding the way things should work."

> performance comes from finding the optimum set of niches

2. An acceleration and facilitation of collaborative work within the organization and between the organization and "others"

Collaboration means more than one individual sharing an insight with co-workers. E-mail might be a necessary component of collaborative procedures in a wired community, but it is not sufficient. Joint effort on a common project is at the heart of collaborative work.

Groupware used by Young and Rubicam, for example, constructs a software map of workloops among members of that organization and its clients. The process defines the combination of commitments and agreements made in connection with a project. Commentary and annotation, questions and data sharing are part and parcel of the communication that takes place. In short, feedback is not attached at the end of a process; it is built in from the beginning as an integral part of the workflow. From the start, it is assumed that the organization—in this case a project organization—is going to learn its way through the task at hand, prevailing upon all the wisdom past and present it can muster.

As it becomes clear who is supposed to do what, for whom and why, roles are distinguished and identified. Priorities are better understood and therefore easier to maintain. Knowledge about the customer's needs and objectives is brought directly to people who are doing the work with the greatest impact on customer satisfaction. A client, for example, could look at production estimates or at the first pass of the creative team and provide feedback almost immediately. Without additional labor, the system brings the customer inside the organization by facilitating and clarifying communication.

Such an approach generates an egalitarian atmosphere that encourages creativity and risk taking. People begin to genuinely understand what it is that they are paid for: high knowledge activities such as judgment and innovation. In the end, they feel more self-fulfilled at the same time they become more sensitive to the larger needs of the community.

In one study across a varied set of customers, Young and Rubicam found that the use of technology in this way could increase the number of jobs completed on time by 63 percent and completed on budget by 19 percent. The agency decreased overtime and duplication of effort. Most significantly, it reduced re-do's caused by miscoordination by 64 percent.

Nonetheless, it is important to note the crucial role of the non-technical factors that are at play in applications of this sort. There is a need, say both Nick Rudd of Young and Rubicam and Action Technologies, the software provider, "to accommodate the realities of how people work together." Software which does not accommodate such realities becomes much like other bureaucratic mechanisms that are counter-productive — in the end huge amounts of time and energy would be spent trying to find ways "around the system."

3. A focus on mass customization and slenderized markets

The decline of the mass production economy is driven by a number of factors. Demographic patterns and lifestyle factors, as just one example, have altered dramatically. Whereas the typical household in the 1950s had father at work, mother at home and the children at school, now about one in four households consists of one person living alone. Close to 60 percent of women work outside the home. Differences in expectations are bound to result, creating the opportunity to do target, niche and database marketing. The common element in these approaches is that they are dependent on using information that is external to the company or information that is attained, directly or indirectly, by close and systematic observation of customer behavior.

Success becomes a function of the application of knowledge to a greater number of smaller and smaller markets. As one entrepreneur put it: performance comes from finding the optimum set of niches. The trend toward individualization, moreover, places greater demands on linking the different parts of the organization so that its response can be flexible and error-free.

American Airlines reconfigures databases to generate a pricing matrix (massaging discounts, promotions, and previous purchasing data) that includes a large number of fares for any flight. By anticipating what price can be charged for what type of customer for what package of variables (length of advance purchase, for example) the company raises its revenue per seat. Coopers and Lybrand's Tax News Network offers clients information about local, state, federal and international tax law and related items. Customers get reports customized to their interests. The same information can be used repeatedly for different clients in different ways.

Information technology permits innovations that would have been impossible just a decade ago. McGraw Hill, for example, lets college professors create their own individually designed textbooks by selecting and combining chapters, depending on personal need and interest, from other books under the publisher's banner. If Blockbusters has its way, customized videos will not be far behind.

When organizations customize, every aspect of their operations is affected. Large amounts of information moving quickly around the organization create a demand for flexibility not needed before. Flexible manufacturing, adaptive supplier arrangements, responsive advertising and sales programs, contingent compensation systems and other areas are all shaped by the drive to customize.

4. Liberation from the restraints of the paper dependent environment

Paper consumption doubles about every four years. The problem is not paper but paper-based management systems. Paper-based systems demand considerable time and energy to coordinate and conduct the collection, tabulation and distribution of information. Despite often monumental efforts to prevent it, the greater the amount of paper that has to be handled, the greater the number of errors that occur. The errors cause re-work and less time to go beyond an administrative function. Generally, quality and customer satisfaction are hurt.

When such activities are computer-based, mistakes are reduced. The leader's attention can be directed to asking the "what if" questions and to searching for underlying trends. Authorities are pushed lower and lower as approval processes appear less and less relevant to creating added value. The business expertise of everyone in the company matures. Managers have the energy and time to pursue how they can develop the business for tomorrow.

Bill Macfarlane, the vice president of information services at the Disney Stores, the 170 location retail operation for the Disney enterprise, has automated all the organization's manuals. Revising an on-line manual is economical, requiring very little time for placing the revisions in the existing text and then distributing the new information across the system. The duplication costs associated with a paper-based system, in contrast, can be a formidable expense. More significantly, the same information can be used by everyone in the system at the same time. An electronic management system can reinforce a clarity in directions and priorities in a way that is simply impractical in a paper-based system. The focus, as the organizing principle suggests, can stay on the customer.

The real "kick," says Macfarlane, is in the longer term application of paperless management systems to the redesign of work processes. For example, when a company looks at putting paper forms in electronic format, a whole set of questions arises. These are: What forms should stay and which should go? What information is needed and what is not? Where is the information system adding value? Where is it losing opportunities to add value? And so on. In effect, the effort to answer these questions puts the organization in a reengineering mode. If the activity is one that continually takes place, then the company has stepped toward institutionalizing the reengineering process itself.

Other ways that one can use paperless management systems include applications for interviewing, scheduling labor and work assignments, and managing financial and inventory systems. In each case the focus is not to simply replace the paper system with electronic communication but to alter the way business is conducted. Once again, every aspect of the enterprise from performance expectations to human resource strategy to cooperative alliances is affected. The software harnesses the talent of the enterprise so that customer needs own "top of mind" position for every manager every day.

Considerations

As indicated, growing the smart organization or building the organization around the software and the software around the customer is obviously about more than the selection of the proper software product, the application package with the most attractive functionality or price. The problems that confront an organization today are socio-technical; the solutions have to be as well.

Technology can be used to reinforce a command and control environment just as it can be used to flatten hierarchy. Privacy can be invaded. Supervision can be drawn tighter around a work group. Access to information can be restricted. Processes can be made inflexible. To avoid such outcomes a fundamental truth needs to be acknowledged: The direction that an organization takes is a function of leadership, values and culture more than it is a function of processing speed and elegant protocols.

Similarly, the technology can be used to create the perception that the organization has been remade just when it needs to be unusually vigilant about the changes still needed. Reengineering, for example, is a double-edged sword. On the one hand, it has value in removing cumbersome and wasteful processes. On the other, it can mesmerize people around the enterprise into thinking that some kind of permanent solution has been achieved. It might imply a promise of sta-bility ("once we get things right") at a time when things are unlikely to settle down. Positioned as a technological effort, reengineering does not go far enough. Ultimately, the boom in productivity comes from a commitment to renew the organization every day.

In this context, business decisions should drive implementation, not the al-lure of some technology. All the initiatives should start outside the technology with the demands of the customer. This means that delegation of key decisions to the technocrats is unfair to them and to the organization, besides being unwise. Even technicians who have mastered the business skills necessary for an industry cannot bring the same perspective as those who deal with the customer every day. Alertness for key opportunities more likely resides with those who are most intimately involved with competitor and customer information. Time and time again we have seen good intentions stalled at the starting gate as technicians were intimidated by questions posed by other managers. They recognized that the questions were only superficially about technology and really about funda-mental strategic choices the company could make, choices they felt ill-prepared to decide. In short, the organizing principle sets a precondition: the active en-gagement of leaders in the revitalization of their organizations.

Finally, sharing information needs to be recognized for the social activity that it is. Technology can only produce change that the enterprise is ready to accept. If a culture diminishes team efforts, groupware that facilitates collabora-tion will not be of much help. Distributive computing not only permits empow-erment, as another example, but also creates the need for companies to ensure that people know how to use that power and newly found decision-making op-portunities for the benefit all stakeholders.

Summing up, customer needs and expectations are constantly changing. The organization needs a way to effectively address those changes in order to do well. By organizing work around software, a way of coordinating a fluid and dynamic set of work processes, the enterprise creates flexibility and order simul-taneously. If it builds the software around the customer, the firm organizes itself so that the market, and not out-of-date bureaucratic requirements, determines strategies, priorities and goals. There are four ways of implementing the organiz-ing principle; each reflects the centrality of knowledge in creating structures and processes. Nevertheless, the promise that information technology has for creat-ing a world of unprecedented prosperity begins with resolving age old concerns about human relationships and personal responsibility.

Human and Organizational Issues

Dr. Helene Roos and Lois Bruss, Co-founders and Principals
HDA Consulting

Workflow technology is both a symptom and a tool of radical change in the workplace. A child of its time, workflow technology has emerged from stresses on productivity exerted by business globalization and the impact of microtechnologies. As it matures, the future success of workflow technology depends on its coupling with other significant non-technological strategies for organizational improvement.

Old paradigms for improved performance

The future of workflow technology is unfolding before us. Its development reflects changing mores in the work environment. These changes include the emergence of new management values and practices. The changes also are part of the gradual demise of a set of management strategies, called the Control Paradigm, that no longer work. See Figure 1.

Traditional Assumptions:

- The nature of business is in the mechanical age
- The business environment is relatively placid and changes in a slow, predictable manner
- Control is central to effective management

Emerging Assumptions:

- The nature of future business as it unfolds in the information age
- The business environment is changing at a phenomenal rate and in ways that are often difficult to predict
- Adaptation to change is central to effective management

Figure 1.

The Control Paradigm worked very well in its time. It developed while the economic climate of the United States was either stable or expanding from the 1900s until the 1980s. This country was the great manufacturing Goliath of the world, inhaling raw materials and exhaling consumer goods, transportation equipment, vehicles, machinery and other manufactured goods.

During the early part of the century, the United State's legendary status as the land of opportunity grew. Immigrants poured in, looking for new lives and jobs. Most of them did not speak English. They had limited understanding of words spoken by American managers, and they often could not communicate much with their polyglot co-workers.

The rise of Taylorism

In this environment, a set of assumptions about the nature of business management took root. In 1903, an American, Frederick Winslow Taylor, began writing about "scientific management."

> workflow technology has emerged from stresses on productivity

He believed that by breaking down work into simple tasks, productivity, quality and managerial control over outcomes would increase. He further suggested that through careful scientific analysis—which later became known as time and motion studies—a single best way for performing any job could be identified.

It was, in his view, the role of management to identify the best methods for performing work, and then dictate these to the workforce. This ensured that management always maintained control over the means and speed of production.

These ideas were well suited to the manufacturing environment of the early 20th century, reinforcing the concept of assembly line workflow, providing a rationale for segmenting job functions. Assigned narrow, repetitive tasks, unskilled or non-English speaking workers could be trained or replaced quickly.

Postwar prosperity introduces age of automation

Taylorism also reinforced the hierarchical structures that were cultural and economic norms. A key assumption was that management's role was to control the actions of the workforce. Management was considered most effective when it had carefully devised mechanisms to control as many aspects of the employee's worklife as possible—thus, the emphasis on work standards, labor reporting and time clocks. This method of work management was so effective in its time that it quickly spread to non-manufacturing work environments, such as office and backroom operations.

Although the economy stumbled during the Depression, the period following World War II saw the U.S. triumphing in technological innovation, standard of living and balance of payments for more than two decades. Both Europe and the Pacific Rim were rebuilding after the devastation of war. The U.S. faced no competition.

During the second half of the century, the Control Paradigm welcomed new technological advances as a way of driving productivity while increasing control. The watchword of the 1950s through the 1970s was "automation," and the challenge was to convert repetitive, definable, non-exceptional tasks into a combination of machine labor and machine intelligence.

Mainframe computers linked to "dumb terminals" managed huge transaction processing tasks. The dumb terminals themselves were a metaphor for the data entry positions they created, pushing alphanumeric gibberish into batches, bites big enough for the machine to gobble them efficiently.

But automation had built-in limits. For example, bank check-processing shops, highly automated and, whittled to the bone by efficiency initiatives, hit the productivity wall a few years ago. When attempts were made to drive up production, errors rose as well. The humans in the system could not meet higher benchmarks for the same set of tasks.

Decentralization of data processing, by desktop computers and midrange servers, brought automation to all parts of an organization. While the mainframe was still the workhorse transaction processor, an explosion of new software opened the door to personal and departmental productivity gains. Enabling technologies like e-mail and document image processing began to promise revolutionary access to information and a real possibility of reducing paper shuffling.

New technologies force a new look at work

Among the new enabling technologies, document image processing, in particular, encouraged businesses to view how work flowed through an office. The technology dramatically altered the way documents were transferred from one place to another. As a result, people began thinking about the process of work.

> the commitment and participation of every employee is of paramount importance

This hardware/software mélange offered an almost unthinkable workplace revolution— replacing paper documents with electronic images. These images were stored in electronic archives, available within seconds to users. Suddenly, paper-based work processes were no longer tied to the sequential progress of sheets of paper, traveling from hand to hand. Imaging offered the revolutionary opportunity to process one document in multiple locations at the same time.

The cost was high, largely due to the platform requirements for instantaneously moving bulky graphics files around a network. It was obvious that the potential benefits were extraordinary. Just as clearly, the hard-dollar payoff of simply replacing paper files and their cabinets with digital archives on optical disks barely covered the investment, if at all. More value had to be extracted from the system.

Imaging brought other management challenges to light. A seldom discussed, but long-standing problem with technological conversions became exacerbated with imaging. The hierarchical, here-is-how-you-do-it approach became exposed as a retardant to change. Employees resisted a new technology that made their expertise as file managers obsolete and clearly would eliminate many of their jobs.

Finally, it was obvious that the need to rethink the workflow was not only a matter of document flow, but all information that moved through business processes. Dramatic technological advances offered the opportunity not only to automate work, but to change the way work processes were approached. This was a major factor in the renaissance of reengineering in white collar environments, and the development of workflow technology.

Workflow as a discipline, not as a technological tool

The definition of "workflow" today branches in two directions. One is a study and analysis of *work processes*, composed of tasks, events or interactions, that create or add value in business environments. The other, when compounded into *workflow technology*, generally refers to software components that either analyze or manage components in business processes.

> dramatic technological advances offered the opportunity not only to automate work, but to change the way work processes were approached

In the case of imaging technology, workflow software was an early component of these systems, because something was needed to manage the movement of image files and relate them to data folders and work in process. This software, which is based on e-mail technology that moves data and messages according to preset criteria, does not force any investment in workflow analysis. As mentioned previously, workflow software supports any set of tasks, automates various approaches to management, and develops reports for many purposes. The tool is neutral.

The discipline, however, is not. For several years, consultants and researchers have been urging users of new technology to explore the interface between technology and people, and the process. Awareness and response to the challenges raised in this interface, they argued, differentiated those who derived bottom line improvements from those who experienced disappointing results.

Emerging paradigm for improved organization performance

The initiatives that are linking together technology, people and processes are reengineering, cultural transformation and workflow technology. Today many industry experts are recognizing the power of these initiatives to transform the workplace.

"The 21st century organization arises at the confluence of three streams. One is described by the term 'high involvement workplace,' meaning operations with self-managing teams and other devices for empowering employees," said Thomas A. Stewart in an article on management practices.

Control paradigm

- There is a single best way to perform any given job.
- Jobs are highly specialized, narrowly defined to assure optimal performance of the function.
- Management sets goals, controls schedules, dictates work design, and handles administration.
- Training is focused on technical skill development.
- Technical imperative: Technology and process flow are designed for optimal performance and then workers are fit into jobs.
- Rewards are based on individual performance against "scientifically set" standards.
- Controls are external.
- Job alienation is an accepted phenomenon.
- Organizational structure is highly bureaucratic.
- Employees are isolated from one another to minimize distractions
  © 1991 Belgard Fisher Rayner Inc..

Figure 2

"A second productivity turbocharger is a new emphasis on managing business processes. Third is the evolution of information technology to the point where knowledge, accountability, and results can be distributed rapidly anywhere in the organization. The trick is to put them together in a coherent, practical design."

In order to achieve Stewart's vision of the organization of the future, we need to transform organizational cultures from the paradigm of control to one characterized by commitment. See Figures 2 and 3. In the technological revolution, as in any other, the commitment and participation of every employee is of paramount importance.

Commitment paradigm

- There are many ways to achieve the same level of performance.
- Jobs are broadly defined and skill sets diverse to assure quick adaptation to change and effective resource utilization.
- Work teams set goals, determine schedule trade-offs, control work design and handle administration, while management provides longer term strategic planning and direction, identifies and removes barriers, and works directly with customers and vendors.

- Joint optimization: The social and technical systems are designed to assume that the human/machine interface is optimal.
- Training is focused on total employee development.
- Rewards are based on contributions made to the effectiveness of the team.
- Controls are internal.
- Job alienation is considered detrimental to organizational performance.
- Organizational structure is highly flexible.
- Groups are formed to ensure continual interaction and problem-solving among employees.

© *1991 Belgard Fisher Rayner Inc.*

Figure 3

A fundamental redesign of business processes, jobs and work structures is necessary for optimal integration of existing resources with new technologies. Workflow technologies provide the means to accomplish transformation in work process and culture. They also provide the distributed access to information that fuels transformation.

A new paradigm for technological implementation

In the traditional model of Taylorism, change was managed by "experts." They came, they measured, they pronounced, and the employees were expected to follow. Today, despite lip service to new management models, much change is still managed in the same way. The experts may be management consultants, MIS programmers, or local managers. It is still unusual when expertise is drawn from among the users.

New technology implementations fail for predictable reasons. Most of them reflect an attitude that the technology components, rather than the organization, are the subject of the change. See Figure 4. Most of these factors operate on assumptions from the old Control Paradigm.

Automation projects fail when...

- The projects automate mistakes—redundant, obsolete or otherwise expendable tasks.
- The projects fail to implement essential non-technical solutions, such as training, workflow redesign, or new organizational structures.
- The projects alienate the people who have to make it work, causing slow adoption or even sabotage.
- The projects create organizational chaos, rather than improved productivity.

- The projects are implemented only at the departmental level, rather than at the enterprise level where exists the greatest opportunity for gain.
- The projects are the wrong solutions to address the issues of the environment.

Figure 4

Today, however, these old assumptions no longer work. As a result of increasing global competition, American business is required to continuously improve and innovate at a rate of speed that prevents competitors from catching up or overtaking them. Managers can no longer know, let alone dictate the best way to do each and every task.

If implemented successfully, new technologies, such as workflow software, offer a means to effective completion. Individual or work-teams can shepherd a process—whether an insurance claim or a car assembly—from initiation to conclusion. The potential result is more control over quality, more ability to correct the source of errors, and more employee satisfaction and commitment to do a high quality job.

New technologies implementation: elements of success

In today's business environment, rapid and often unpredictable changes are occurring both internally and externally. Internally, many of these changes are initiated by implementing new technology. It is precisely this adaptation that is central to organizational effectiveness.

Because technology investments are largely made up of "things," (i.e., hardware and software) it is easy to make the mistake of believing the technology is "implemented" by buying it and installing it. In fact, nothing works without people. Organizations who give short shrift to the human factor often find that their costs are doubled—the communication and training that should have been done first, and the cleanup of the chaos created because it was not done in timely fashion.

These human issues become magnified in the process of redesigning work processes. Nevertheless, many work process redesign projects focus exclusively on technology, thereby failing to address human and organizational aspects of work. In these instances, organizations fail to explore non-technical solutions to improving business processes, such as training or changes to structure, procedure, and management practices.

Successful projects are characterized by a concurrent focus in four distinct areas. They are technology, readiness, operations and culture. See Figure 5.

Employee readiness

The readiness of employees for change must be fostered so that the potential of both the technology and human resources can be realized. Managing the natural resistance to change and helping to convert that resistance into commitment and enthusiasm is a planned process. This process requires an understanding of the following:

Past history: the extent to which past experiences have been positive or negative. For example, employees at two different insurance companies had vastly different expectations of their EIM systems; one company had very positive experiences with previous information system implementation; the other company had a history of failures. The company with a history of failures had a significant level of employee resistance.

Adaptability: the degree of flexibility or rigidity toward change. Organizations that frequently undergo change and have developed the skills to manage change tend to be better able to manage and optimize technological initiatives.

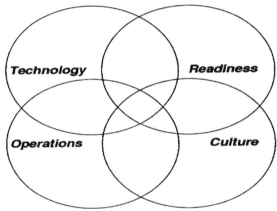

Figure 5

Goal congruence: the degree to which the project's goals match the individual's goals. Frequently the goals of redesign projects are unclear, leaving employees wondering why they are being subjected to meaningless change and confused about how the system will benefit them. In other instances, goals regarding downsizing are unclear or unspoken, leaving employees to assume that the system will eliminate their jobs.

Level of control: the extent to which individuals perceive themselves to have some control and involvement in the change process. The greater the level of control experienced by the employees, the greater their willingness to accept change.

Operations

The transformation of inputs and outputs requires substantial analysis and redesign. The most powerful technology cannot fix a poorly conceived work process; nor can it create motivating jobs to increase employee productivity.

For example, a recent Nolan Norton study of imaging technology experiences of 200 organizations was described in *Computerworld*. "Most people aren't succeeding at their efforts to exploit the technology," the study found. "The vast majority of imaging users are stuck in a rut, unable to expand the technology beyond a pilot project or a single department. How can that be? It's because imaging turns out to be much more thigned jobsan a new technology; it's a new way of doing business. And users who fail to recognize that are doomed to get stuck in first gear."

Business operations redesign, also known as reengineering, must be conceived as a two-pronged approach: the redesign of the work process and of jobs. One without the other diminishes the impact of any redesign effort. And job design is often the forgotten component.

> **effectively designed jobs support the success of redesigned work processes**

In their work on job design, Hackman and Oldham (1974) propose that "positive personal and work outcomes (high internal motivation, high work satisfaction, high quality performance, low absenteeism and turnover) are obtained when three 'critical psychological states' are present (experienced meaningfulness of work, experienced responsibility for the outcomes of the work, and knowledge of the results of the work activities). All three of the Critical Psychological States must be present for the positive outcomes to be realized."

These Critical Psychological States are created by the following five job characteristics:

Skill Variety: the degree to which a job requires a variety of different activities in carrying out the work, which involves the use of a number of different skills and talents of the employee.

Task Identity: the degree to which the job requires completion of a "whole" and identifiable piece of work (i.e., doing a job from beginning to end with a visible outcome).

Task Significance: the degree to which the job has a substantial impact on the lives or work of other people whether in the immediate organization or the external environment.

Autonomy: the degree to which the job provides substantial freedom, independence, and discretion of the employee in scheduling the work and in determining the procedures to be used in carrying it out.

Feedback from the Job Itself: the degree to which carrying out the work activities required by the job results in the employee obtaining direct and clear information about the effectiveness of his or her performance.

Jobs that are organized and managed using the values and policies of the Commitment Paradigm tend to show these characteristics. Effectively designed jobs support the success of redesigned work processes.

Organizational culture

Organizational culture is "a pattern of beliefs and expectations shared by the organization's members. These beliefs and expectations produce norms that powerfully shape the behavior of individuals and groups in the organizations." (Schwartz and Davis, 1981) An organization's culture, therefore, shapes the way people behave as encouraged by the organization's values and beliefs. Culture can be analyzed by observing communication, teamwork, and management practices.

Culture can have a significant impact on a company's ability to implement new technology successfully. Sanker (1988) points out, "Advanced technologies change the very foundation of the firm that uses them. Hence, a change in culture is an organizational imperative for adoption of new technologies."

In conclusion, all four of the Elements of Success require attention to achieve the desired results from new technology. It is not enough to focus on each one in isolation. Rather a holistic view of the organization treats the people, the process and the technology in an integrated fashion.

Technological change management: putting theory into practice

Putting these concepts into practice requires a change management plan. This plan is designed to enable the organization to move from its current reality to a desired future state.

Just as technology projects demand detailed plans for implementation management, the same requirements exist to plan transformations of culture, workflows and work structure. The first step in designing these plans is the articulation of the Strategic Triangle.

The strategic triangle: integration of business strategy, technology strategy and organization change strategy

The most important contribution senior executives can make early in the project lifecycle is to participate in a strategic planning session very early in the project lifecycle. The purpose of such a session is to develop the "Strategic Triangle" (Walton, 1989). See Figure 6. This consists of a clearly articulated and tightly linked technology strategy, business strategy and organization change strategy.

Figure 6. The Strategic Triangle. © 1989 Walton

The Strategic Triangle provides direction for developing a change management plan and guidance for all major decisions throughout the project.

Most often, technology strategy drives organizational change. While the business strategy may be clear, it is often not reflected in a linked organizational change strategy. Failure to define and link together all three strategies can have serious consequences.

For example, in moving toward the Commitment Paradigm, one organization had a well-publicized organization strategy to empower employees to take more ownership and responsibility for their work. At the same time, the project team for a new information system decided to take maximum advantage of the workflow management software's capability for work measurement and management reporting. They designed a system that monitored the time spent by each claims processor on each transaction. They even designed the system so that when the prescribed time was exceeded, a beeper went off at the workstation of the employee's supervisor.

Their technology strategy, which reflected the values of the Control Paradigm, was clearly at odds with their organization change strategy. This resulted in employees who were so angry and confused about the mixed message that, eventually, the information system had to be redesigned, at great expense, to reflect the company's new management approach.

User acceptance

Many organizations try to create change management programs without fully understanding the organizational and individual issues that will affect acceptance by users and, ultimately, system utilization. Before designing any change management program, organizations must develop a broad-based understanding of non-technical issues. An assessment of readiness, operations and culture highlight strengths and vulnerabilities in the organization's ability to assimilate change. This knowledge is critical for the development of a systematic and comprehensive implementation plan.

> workflow technology is not an end in itself

As a result of such an assessment, a manufacturing company implementing technology and redesigning work process, was able to improve its implementation in four key areas. First, the company designed a communication program that included electronic mail, a biweekly newsletter and a suggestion box. Second, it undertook a work redesign process that enabled it to combine three separate functions into one department. Third, it developed new performance and career management systems so employees would understand the opportunities for advancement in the new environment. Finally, it conducted workshops to enhance the teamwork and group problem-solving skills of the newly combined department.

Employee involvement was evident throughout this project. Employees at all levels of the organization actively participated in all aspects of the change management strategy. This approach results in readiness and a culture that is able to effectively assimilate and support the changes in job design and technological tools.

Principles of redesigning work

Typical technical approaches to workflow analysis have focused on identifying the existing flow and then determining where to put various pieces of technology. A more thorough approach is recommended utilizing measurement techniques from total quality management (such as Pareto Diagrams and Cause and Effect Diagrams). The following principles are offered as guidelines:

Objectives:
- Design work around whole processes, products, customers or projects.
- Focus on the customer and on quality, and profits will increase.
- Design to jointly optimize human and technical systems.
- Maximize the performance of the entire organization, not just a portion.

Structure:
- Design for error prevention, not error correction; eliminate inspection and appraisal tasks; eliminate hand-offs.

- Develop source defect control. Errors, if they cannot be eliminated, are best controlled as close to the point of origin as possible.
- Reduce cycle times; eliminate delays; eliminate hand-offs through integration of tasks; eliminate setup times; eliminate transports; eliminate/minimize exception processing.
- Do as many tasks as possible concurrently, rather than sequentially.
- Increase source information flow, where information goes to the person where direct action can be taken.
- Design for minimum critical specification, (i.e., only the most critical aspects of jobs and methods are specified).
- Carefully locate team boundaries; be aware of "us vs. them" issues.
- Build business systems (e.g., reward and compensation) that support team behaviors.
- Design team structures where employees are involved in self-management tasks.
- Build mechanisms for continuous improvement through the redesign of work, experimentation, risk taking and the continual acquisition and application of information.
- Capture information once, at the source, and in its native form.
- Treat geographically dispersed resources as if they were centralized.
-

   People:
- Enhance the quality of work life; increase responsibility, empowerment and motivation.
- Create jobs in which employees are cross-trained, multi-skilled and highly flexible.

Culture: the transformational process

Initiating change from the Control Paradigm to the Commitment Paradigm has strategic benefit to new technology implementation. Organizations that are fully benefiting from workflow technology are recognizing the workflow must be embedded within a culture characterized by initiative, creativity, accountability and customer service. For this to occur, management must shift its thinking, provide skills training to managers and employees to ensure a highly committed workforce, and modify business support systems, such as compensation.

Workflow technology is not an end in itself. It is a catalyst for organizational change and ultimately organizational success. The realization of this dream is dependent upon the willingness of an organization to enter the realm of the Commitment Paradigm. Difficult as these changes may be, they are the keys to leveraging existing assets with new technological capabilities.

In the words of Will and Ariel Durant, "The Future never just happened. It was created." Only by managing the human and organizational issues can the promise of workflow and reengineering initiatives be transformed into reality.

BIBLIOGRAPHY

Belgard, William; Fisher, K. Kim; and Rayner, Steven R. *The Leadership Role in a High Involvement Organization.* Belgard, Fisher, Rayner, Inc., Development Systems Inc., Beaverton, OR 1989.

Hackman, J. Richard; and Oldham, Greg R., "The Job Diagnostic Survey: An Instrument for the Diagnosis of Jobs and the Evaluation of Job Redesign Projects," Technical Report No. 4, Department of Administrative Science, Yale University, May 1974. Available through the U.S. Department of Commerce, National Technical Information Service.

Sankar, Y., "Organizational Cultures and New Technologies," *Journal of Systems Management*, April 1988.

Schwartz, Howard; and Davis, Stanley M., "Matching Corporate Culture and Business Strategy," *Organization Dynamics,* AMACOM, Summer 1981.

Stewart, Thomas A., "The Search for the Organization of Tomorrow," Fortune, May 18, 1992; pp. 9298.

Walton, Richard E., *Up and Running: Integrating Information Technology and the Organization,* Boston: Harvard Business School Press, 1989.

Case Study: American President Lines

Jordan Libit, Vice-President, Marketing

FileNet Corporation

The experience of American President Lines (APL), a $3 billion shipping line, is an excellent example of the benefits of efficiency that a workflow system can bring to an enterprise both in serving customers and controlling costs. APL, based in Oakland, California, is one of the largest international transportation companies, moving some 150,000 containers at any one time. They operate a fleet of 22 container cargo ships and use the services of various trucking and railroad companies as transportation partners.

With its far-flung operations, shipping diverse cargo over long distances, APL's cargo damage claims processing is a busy operation, vital to customer service. A manual filing system hindered productivity and service, and cost the company millions in lost claims.

The firm was losing $500,000 a year due to a lack of documentation for claims damages. It was recovering only 50 cents on each dollar from its transportation partners because their paperwork could not prove APL was not at fault. The APL Cargo Claims Department was paying $10 million a year for damages on some estimated 6,500 claims.

> from the first day staff processed claims faster and faster

APL's solution, adopted in 1992, was a document imaging and workflow system.

Past Problems

As a national and international enterprise, APL receives paperwork on its shipments from all over the world. Approximately a million pieces of paper a year are received, including small cards and rice paper from Asia. Documents show the movement of cargo over sea and land, from port to port, from terminal to terminal. These include bills of lading, invoices, packing lists, correspondence and faxes between APL and its customers.

The company also receives color photographs with approximately 35 percent of all claims. Whether it is spoiled fish or moldy oranges, photographs are used to show damage. Claims files of 100 to 150 documents of all types are common. An additional headache for APL officials was customer criticism of tardy claims processing. It could take three weeks for the company to acknowledge the receipt of a claim. It could take three months to settle routine claims. When a customer called to check on the progress of a claim, APL staff scrambled to find the paper-stuffed file among their claims adjusters. APL's challenges are easy to appreciate.

Finding a Solution

APL set out to reform this system and believed imaging was an important step. They soon discovered that inclusion of a workflow system would be a critical component for the success of improving cargo claims and would be an ideal starting point for a corporate-wide strategy to reengineer APL information systems with workflow.

> the company made the employees part of the decision-making process

APL spent a year evaluating vendors, made its selection and began installing the system. It took only three months for the system to begin operating because by APL's project manager had already identified participants and set goals. A detailed project plan was created specifying start dates for each activity or task. Every document was identified by type, including claims, surveys, pictures, terminal control bulletins, phone logs, correspondence and pay requests. The next step was to design flow charts, develop workflow queues and create a matrix.

APL's research was thorough. The company clearly defined its workflow goals. It also knew the other technologies it wanted to add in the future, such as OCR, bar coding, voice capture and video. From the first day APL started to phase in the document-imaging and workflow system, staff processed claims faster and faster. Customers, in return, received prompt responses to their claims.

Managing the Flow of Work

Here is how APL's workflow system works:

When a claim is received, it is separated by type-dry or refrigerated-and by dollar amount, since certain adjusters have specific limits. Claims and their supporting documentation such as bills of lading and packing lists are scanned into the system.. The department's phone log is included in the electronic claims jacket. After scanning, claims are indexed. A preparation program, run at night automatically registers the claim data on the APL mainframe. WorkFlo software, a Windows-based product, is used to draft a letter to the customer acknowledging receipt of the claim. The letter is then automatically faxed or mailed. This used to take as long as three weeks. It now takes a day or two.

After the letter is sent, WorkFlo routes the claim to an adjuster. The adjuster brings up the new claim and reviews the documentation. If additional correspondence is required, standard letters can be generated automatically based on the information retrieved from the computer. That letter is then faxed or mailed to the customer.

APL took its system a step further by creating an automatic diary system so that claims will not be lost. Every transaction has to have either a permanent closing or diary date. Each transaction also has an open or closed tag. WorkFlo can review pending claims and activate it on a given date. Adjusters see the claim on their pending queues.

The APL system also provides quality and assurance testing. Supervisors can monitor claim processing, especially by new employees, to ensure proper handling. If an employee is sick or on vacation, claims can be routed to others. Supervisors can determine which adjusters are assigned to each customer.

APL also has a subsystem called Loss Prevention. Simply put, it allows adjusters to view a customer folder and compare with previous claims to see if they can identify trends or patterns, hopefully minimizing losses.

Another subsystem is a bulletin board service from an independent weather forecasting company that informs adjusters whether bad weather or a possible disaster, such as a hurricane, is imminent. This allows APL to document weather conditions occurring in some part of the world if a claim results. The benefits of the system were immediate.

Cost Savings

The system paid for itself in three months. Claims are easier to document. If a claim is not APL's liability, it is easier to collect paperwork to prove it. If it is APL's responsibility, it is easier for the company to discover that, too. APL now settles 85 percent of all claims in 45 days, up from 44 percent. Many claims are settled in only 10 days.

Improved Customer Service

Immediate acknowledgment of customer claims, and quicker investigation and resolution create greater customer satisfaction. When a customer calls regarding the status of a claim, any department member can immediately call up the folder instead of physically searching desks or file cabinets for it. Adjusters can do electronically what they used to do manually. With the folder management software product, FolderView, they can highlight important information, make margin notes and Post-It notes, use paper clips and organize their folders using icons to represent the bill of lading and other important documents.

Increased Productivity

Productivity has increased 25 percent. WorkFlo software makes it possible to track queues to ensure the workload is distributed evenly so the claim adjusters do not become overloaded. More significantly is the elimination of clerical work for the adjusters. They do not have to spend countless hours on tedious paperwork. They get to do what they do best; expedite claims and solve problems.

A Competitive Edge

In the transportation industry, APL can move cargo only at a certain speed. It is the quality of customer service that can make a difference. By addressing its customers' needs, the workflow system has become a marketing tool for APL's sales representatives. With the system APL was able to reorganize its claims staff. Those handling refrigerated claims stayed in Oakland. The Denver office, equipped with an RS/6000 server, handles dry goods claims. A fractional T-1 line connects Oakland and Denver, giving both operations simultaneous access to customer claims of both types.

APL took exceptional care in interviewing vendors and identifying company needs for handling large document files and tracking claims to payment. The company developed the following criteria that any company might find helpful when considering an imaging and workflow system:

1) Identify the Scope and Goals of the Project

Determine what you want to accomplish within a specific timeframe. Understand the degree that you really want to computerize. Be careful of 'scope creep,' do not get overly enthusiastic and run in too many directions at one time. APL had to use a good measure of self-discipline.

2) Don't Automate a Bad Process

Understand the nature of your business. Establish the areas of opportunity for making improvement. Actually walk each piece of paper through every step. Ask staff what they really do with it.

3) Develop a Detailed Project Plan

Identify all the steps that need to be taken by interviewing all participants. Create a matrix based on what the business unit wants to achieve. Do not consider any detail too small.

4) Do Your Documentation First; Then Select a System with the Right Software.

APL reviewed 25 vendors considering all aspects of their needs, from current demands to future considerations. Now that cargo is running, APL plans to implement workflow and reengineer other administrative functions as varied as employee expense accounts, vendor accounts payable, and Human Resources Department, making employee records immediately available.

5) Understand Your Audience

It's very important to have the people who are actually going to use the system buy-in to the project. In the beginning, the company found areas it did not want to automate because there was some resistance on the part of the staff, which ranged in age from 28 to 66. Some had been with the company three years, some 28. To use an executive's words, "The closest some had come to a mouse was at Disneyland." Other employees were using dumb terminals. At the outset, the company proposed—rather than told employees—what APL would like to do and why. The company made the employees part of the decision-making process.

> image storage and retrieval without workflow really only solve half the problem

6) Don't Overwhelm the Users

The company did not want to bring the claims adjusters into the world of personal computers with Windows workflow and imaging at the same time. First, APL let them get comfortable with the PCs and mouse devices, and reassured them the company was not going to rip out their dumb terminals immediately. They did have a time limit on the transition period, but long before the deadline, everyone had switched to the new system. The group learned imaging over a four-week period, starting out with a day spent with each individual, tapering off to an as-needed basis.

7) Offer On-going Support

After the imaging system was implemented, an APL project manager held weekly meetings. The company installed a suggestion box—paper and non-threatening, located where bosses would not see an employee drop in a suggestion or comment on the system. If a suggestion affected all the users, and they did not like a certain process, a vote was taken. The company let staff develop their own icons. By giving them decision-making power, the implementation process went very smoothly.

8) Prepare for disaster

Proper planning eliminates unpleasant surprises. Since the Cargo Claims Department is located at the terminal where the ships dock, brown-outs can occur when electric cranes unload cargo. If the system were operated on the same electrical network, it could crash from power shortages or blow out from power spikes. An uninterrupted power source was installed to ensure that does not happen, monitoring the electrical system at all times. It pays to have a disaster recovery plan in place.

In Conclusion

When judging the benefits of imaging and workflow software, the real value to the user is not in merely storing and displaying digitized images of paper documents, but in automating the delivery of all types of information to make better business decisions and gain a competitive edge. Image storage and retrieval products have their advantages, not the least of which are eliminating filing cabinets and solving some inefficiencies of handling paper. But image storage and retrieval without workflow really only solve half the problem. As the APL example shows, workflow allowed the shipping company to achieve its remarkable efficiencies.

A storage and retrieval solution give users only passive access to information. They put information (paper) in and they pull information (images) out. Workflow software allows people to manage images by putting "information at your fingertips," in the words of one industry observer. Workflow does not simply control the routing of work. Workflow software allows users to manipulate information to their advantage, to act on it and direct it to others in the organization. It allows them to understand how information is used and processed within the organization. For example, with workflow a claims adjuster now gets a complete folder of information from many different sources in one electronic jacket. With such detailed information, the adjuster is in a much better position than before to begin negotiation with the customer much earlier. If the problem must be referred to a supervisor, it can be done so immediately and completely, electronically.

As a result, the information allows them to change business processes for the better-to innovate and reengineer.

The results: higher productivity, better customer service, lower operating costs, enhanced worker satisfaction and more informed decision making.

Work Reengineering and Workflows: Comparative Methods

Dr. Stanley Soles

Professor Information Systems and Sciences, College of Business Administration, Fairleigh Dickinson University

Abstract

This chapter examines and compares techniques used in work reengineering and workflow products. Part One presents definitions, rationale, and general areas of agreement among major advocates of reengineering. The chapter compares the methods emphasized for a series of issues espoused by various advocates of reengineering and process innovation projects including radical and/or incremental change, quality or continuous improvement programs with reengineering, the roles of employee participation, and comparison of the information engineering model with reengineering.

Part Two examines types of emerging workflow products, compares workflow with work reengineering, and identifies purported workflow solutions to business problems. Many workflow products originally were found to solve specific short term problems. They were developed without theory. Other products were based more in theory and from research centers. Contributions from a series of research centers, and coordination research centers are noted. This part describes ActionWorkflow theory and work as a closed loop process. The need for standards among workflow products has led to the formation of an industry-wide coalition.

Part Three discusses and analyzes broader issues of work reengineering of which workflow is a part. It identifies elements of the basic change model. The reasons for success and failure in reengineering are explored. Other topics include: change management, importance of business and Information Technology (IT) as enablers of changes, authority and power, culture change and organizational issues. Finally, unemployment is identified as a major unintended consequence of reengineering and other restructuring programs that deserves national attention.

Introduction

The term reengineering has become one of many buzzwords and a shibboleth. General presentations about reengineering are filled with excerpts and samples of success from reengineered companies.

Many writers on reengineering present bold, glossy, and glowing accounts with too little attention to the nuances and difficult contingencies involved. Reengineering as a movement has many faces. To some, it is another form of downsizing, cost cutting restructuring, outsourcing, right-sizing, and a move toward client/server architecture. It is time to move the discussion beyond the hype. The purpose of this chapter is to present an expository statement on the emphasis and methods of various advocates of reengineering and workflow. This chapter compares techniques used in work reengineering, workflow products, and processes. It is based upon a review of textual records, case studies, and interviews. This paper is part of current research on reengineering. (Soles 1991, 1992).

> reengineering as a movement has many faces

Methods, Techniques, and Emphasis

Work reengineering and workflow are recent developments. Some of the distinctions cited here refer to tendencies, emphasis, and some differences in how the selected issues are handled. It is premature to regard these variations in techniques among reengineering and workflow programs as fully developed methodologies.

Definitions and Key Concepts

First, what is reengineering, and its key concepts? Under what circumstances do top managers decide that a company must engage in reengineering? "Reengineering is the fundamental rethinking and radical redesign of business processes to achieve dramatic improvement in critical contemporary measures of performance such as cost, quality, services and speed." (Hammer and James Champy 1993, p.32.) The core claims of reengineering may be stated as follows: In line with a business vision, the process teams or cross-functional teams focus on analysis of business processes. In reengineering, the business process analyses are combined with selected advanced information systems technology (IT). Information technologies, in turn, 'act as enablers to devise new products with customer satisfaction in view. Dramatic productivity gains are claimed to result in terms of lower costs, savings in time, and more customer satisfaction.

Business process reengineering seeks to overcome fragmentation due to the division of labor into so many narrowly specialized roles requiring so much coordination. The focus shifts from task management to business process management.

One key concept is the term *process*. Process means a structured measured set of activities. The process-set is designed to produce a specific output of value for a particular customer or market. (Davenport 1993a, p.5.) Processes may be interpersonal, interdepartmental, or interorganizational. A process involves input and output that adds value to customers across more than one task, and usually across more than one functional area. Thus, we have a key phrase: cross-functional business process (Davenport 1993a, See Appendix B pp. 311-326).

Generic Agreement of Overall Stages

There is general agreement overall about reengineering as a framework. Management consultant firms use variations of themes and steps used in reengineering. Some place greater emphasis on strategy formulation and overall system architecture. For example, Arthur Anderson Inc., emphasizes the importance of integration of process management for the organization to carry out. Another framework called core process redesign is advocated by Kaplan and Murdock (1991). Its framework includes four steps: identify the core competencies among the processes; define the performance criteria; pinpoint the problem areas; and redesign the process.

> those who use the
> output of the process
> perform it

The overall process of reengineering includes a series of phases or stages (Johannson et al. 1993). Reengineering starts with a recognition of the need to change and to reformulate of the company's vision. The reformulation, creation, and generation of their vision results from a fundamental examination of first assumptions. It identifies the firm's core competence, basic commitments, the nature of their competition, the central values, and its mission. The challenge is to evaluate the existing processes and create possible modifications using the world's best practices.

Business Process Focus and Cross-Functional Process Teams

Reengineering advocates agree to shift work analysis from a task focus to a business process focus. Structural reorganization is accomplished by using cross-functional teams and installing new information and measurement systems in line with a customer-oriented corporate value system. Process management guides cross-functional or process teams with an emphasis on quality and customer satisfaction.

There is general agreement on many steps as well as stages of reengineering. A top-down approach is followed. Leaders appoint key personnel. The head of reengineering (Czar) secures the resources and coordinates the entire reengineering project. The leader is usually top management such as a chief operations officer (COO). The process owners, governance steering committees, and other top key personnel are all appointed by the leaders and the Czar (Hammer and Champy 1993).

Process owners determine priorities and list targets. Process owners select the business process team members from cross-functional areas of the firm. The Czar has the responsibility to remove process owners or other managers if they cannot or do not carry out their new coaching and facilitator roles. The process owners' tasks are to shift from directing action to distributing responsibility for the flow of process quality.

Governance policies for the transition are generated by the top management team. Using the top-down approach, process teams or cross-functional business process teams undertake careful analysis of business processes. Eventually business processes are winnowed down to select a business process targeted for reengineering.

> to get to process innovation means to overcome inertia

Task and design teams are assigned for a limited amount of time. Teams identify a baseline, and use process based cost-value analysis methods. Benchmarking and search for world class best practices are carried out. Hammer suggests key guiding principles to combine and to streamline the old processes: "Organize around outcomes not tasks. Those who use the output of the process perform it. Subsume information into real work that adds value, not overhead. Treat geographically dispersed resources as though they were in one place. Put decision points where the work is performed." (Hammer 1990, pp. 108-109).

It is difficult to sustain the focus on business process rather than to shift back to a departmental task focus. Hammer and Champy offer some tips to help process thinking. They suggest renaming the beginning and end states to cut across functional areas: for example, product development becomes called "concept to prototype"; sales becomes "prospects to orders"; manufacturing becomes "procurement to shipping"; and service becomes "inquiry to resolution." (Hammer and Champy 1993, p 118.)

The design teams carry out the redesigns and implementation of reengineering processes. Consultants are often placed on redesign teams called insider-outsider teams. They are encouraged to use lateral, non-linear, and inductive thinking. The techniques are used to devise creative and innovative uses of information system technology (IST) to solve business problems as identified from business process analysis. Small teams are expected to perform the entire process from beginning to end with broad information access (Davenport 1993a.).

Lab teams may engage in actually using systems by the redesign teams. The pilot study may take place in a distant site to ensure a clean slate, or to be free from the conventional current operations of the company.

The shifts toward a new organizational structure are a temporary overlay upon the existing functional organization. The process approach connects the former vertical organization and new forms of organization on all levels. Some proponents claim that process management moves toward a horizontal organization. Other supporters state that a fundamental task is for the top management to identify the company's core competence from the business processes. The new systems exist in parallel to the old (Morris and Brandon 1993). These new emerging organizational forms are similar to matrix type organizations with business process much broader in scope than project teams. In effect, the reengineering design teams interlace the firm. Ideally, the technology architecture of the firm migrates toward client/server architecture with IT acting as an enabler.

> the challenge is to go with the current process improvement programs

Davenport (1993) gives a framework for viewing the transaction costs and time-based competition concepts. Davenport describes an explicit framework for action and ways to create new uses and solutions to business process problems.

When Do Companies Start to Reengineer?

Hammer and Champy have said, in a few cases companies start reengineering when business is doing rather well. Their visionary CEO recognizes that in five years the company will really have some problems. Hammer and Champy (1993, pp. 159-170) cite the example of the reengineering at Hallmark Cards. The company began reengineering in 1989. At that time, Hallmark was still the market leader. Many other companies wait until they are in deep trouble (Hammer and Champy 1993, pp. 39-44). In the case of Ford Auto Company, accounts payable was a problem. By reengineering, Ford replaced it with a system that does not use invoices and allows three-quarter staff reduction. Most of the companies that consider reengineering already have some crisis within a product line. The company sales may have declined in market share of product lines. If feasible, then the specific business process could be a target for reengineering, and would be likely to yield sizable gains.

Method Issue 1: Radical and/or Incremental Change through Process Innovation

Hammer and Champy (1993, p. 49) and others have said teams should try to think as though the companies are starting anew.

Ardent calls are made for reengineering to think radically, to make fundamental changes. In what has come to be called classical reengineering, Michael Hammer has said that in reengineering, radical change yields radical results. He is very serious about the importance to sweep clean from prior practices. The tone of the language that Hammer uses is bold. "Don't automate the past, obliterate!" "Create a future rather than pave over the old cow paths." (Hammer 1990; Hammer and Champy, 1993).

Tom Davenport disagrees with Michael Hammer. He contends that very few companies can sweep away all the current business operations and start with a clean slate. Davenport accepts the idea that many businesses have some type of continuous improvement (quality) programs in place.

Tom Davenport (1993; 1993b; 1993c) calls for "process innovation" that is a revisionist or pragmatic approach. He uses the terms, process innovation and process improvement, to include various continuous improvement programs. He acknowledges that corporations have many current business processes that are required to stay in business.

The challenge is to go with the current process improvement programs, and then to select one business process for the process innovation (reengineer). Firms are able to continue other business process improvements.

Evaluative Comments

There are merits to both the radical call for reengineering and the process improvement to process innovation positions. The bold radical call is to sweep the ship's deck clean. It is to sustain the focus on change in line with vision as maintained and updated. Some advocates challenge top management to be bold enough to engage in reengineering. Failure often is attributed to timidity, lack of resolve, or strong commitment. Hammer and Champy claim that unless there is conflict within teams, then nothing is happening. In their other writings, Hammer and Champy say a clean slate is not really necessary to start reengineering, especially if independent sites are used for pilot testing. The essence is that reengineering projects should develop, unobstructed by current practice.

The clean slate option implies a denial of the tough issues of culture change. Even a new independent site for a pilot test is not really a clean slate. People cannot escape from history, language, and experiences. The main point is that Hammer and Champy encourage a fundamental rethinking. Act as though the corporation is brand new and just beginning. The design teams are then free from current operational constraints. A favorite example is the Saturn Automobile company.

The incremental approach or process improvement, according to Davenport, is accepted as one part. It should have continual employee team support. To get to process innovation means to overcome inertia; it needs to shift from a narrow to broad scope business process. Reengineering can bog down and flounder. It may be unable to breakthrough the existing fragmentation and specialization. The incremental change may be the ticket for day-to-day survival, The risk is that "to get that long range survival, requires a new vision for a company, the organization and its direction" (Walton 1989, p.53).

Method Issue 2: Quality, and Customer Satisfaction in Reengineering Compared with Continuous Improvement Programs

Many companies currently have developed and used various types of quality and continuous improvement programs in their companies. In these quality programs, attention is given to small, incremental, systematic and gradual improvements. By contrast, in reengineering the focus is on holistic, broader scope business process. They are likely to produce major change in outcomes, but they may take longer to implement. Peter Keen (1990) said, "Any methodology for analyzing business processes must begin and end with customers, because it is the customer power that has reshaped the competition."

> the process owners are to serve as coaches and as facilitators

Both programs emphasize process, and focus on customers, operations, and team approach. One crucial difference is that reengineering relies upon information technology as enabler for new product development. Quality and continuous improvement programs encourage company-wide participation by all. They rely upon closely watched metrics and statistical quality control rather than IT as enablers. (Davenport 1993a; Hammer and Champy 1993).

Evaluative Comments

Reengineering champions offer critical comments about TQM. Kaplan and Murdock (1991) state that TQM programs have reached the point of diminishing returns. Others often use a chart to depict a continuous gradual slope of improvement in products, quality and cycle time, showing gradual linear improvement in production of ten percent per year. By contrast, purported reengineering interventions boost the production ten times to a plateau of best practice followed by gradual continuous improvements until another reengineering intervention boosts production again.

The widespread and varied practices of continuous improvement quality programs provide mixed results. The *kaizen* method focuses on ongoing improvement involving everyone in the steady improvement of production process and innovation in products. Kaizen is able to incorporate quickly the latest technological improvements (Masaaki Imai 1986).

Articles offer some critical evaluations of TQM and other quality and continuous programs. Gilbert (1992) wrote, "TQM Flops, Learning From The Experience of Others." The article illustrates how TQM programs have now matured and have developed a body of critical research to guide practice. Davenport claims that when continuous improvement programs are combined with reengineering business process, then dramatic upturns in production may occur. Others question whether TQM programs are becoming an end rather than a means to an end. One challenging question is how shifting from some continuous improvement programs to selecting some broad business processes for reengineering and boosting productivity.

Method Issues 3: What is the Role for Participation in Redesign?

In many corporations, all employees participate to improve quality and service to customers. In fact, many of the companies with continuous programs also use forms of business process analysis with their participative work teams. Davenport acknowledges that in continuous improvement, the company-wide participation does bring together activity and provides input into decisions. Yet, Davenport does not believe that participation is feasible on redesign or

workflow refers both to process and products

reengineering design teams. (Davenport 1993b). Hammer brushes aside the question with a quip that nobody loves being reengineered. He believes that attempts to reengineer from the bottom up are bound to fail. Business processes cut across functional boundaries, and so many career interests are embedded in the existing conditions. Ideas that bubble up would be strongly resisted. The authors say that authority to change the organizational structure and decision-making must come from the top (Hammer and Champy 1993, pp. 207-208).

Evaluative Comments

There is a sense of irony in the position taken on participation. Fundamental changes that reengineering calls for include dismantling current functional departmental areas and the way work is structured in organizations. Process owners and other managers are expected to shift from directing action to become facilitators and organize self-directed teams. The process owners are to serve as coaches and as facilitators. Participation in decision-making within process teams is encouraged in reengineering and process innovation. Process teams are claimed to be empowered. Is crucial decision-making still made by the steering committees at the top? Is participation in decision-making still confined to making recommendations on issues within teams? Do teams select their own team leaders? Participation is certainly not company-wide. Do employees have assurances that effectiveness and Quality of Working Life (QWL) criteria are criteria for redesign and not just cost-cutting, efficiency and growth criteria? Do privileges and authority structure remain intact? Are key metrics used such as time-based competition of business process cycles and transaction costs?

> business process analysis starts with customers

Davenport more recently (1993c) has qualified his views. He says that participation by employees in company-wide programs can help to sustain their morale. Teams provide decision input into the process improvement programs, which, in turn, may contribute to process innovation (reengineering).

If team participation in reengineering is only allowed so that employees *feel as though* they decide and then their recommendations are given no credence, it does not take long for participants to wise up.

A question remains as to how the basic authority structure for decision-making from top-down has changed? A considerable amount of research on self-management teams has shown that workers are able to carry out self-directed tasks. They have many ideas for improvement of productions and new operations and products. For over three decades, the movements from Quality of Working Life, Statistical Quality Circle, the current TQM, and continuous improvement programs clearly demonstrated employees in teams are able to generate ideas. They responsibly monitor their team work.

Methods Issue 4: Compare Information Engineering with Both Reengineering and Process Innovation

Information engineering (IE) is a major systems development approach with a rigorous methodology. Information engineering is a top-down approach to systems planning as an overall global architectural model (Martin 1991; Finkelstein 1992). The strategy forms a framework, then business oriented studies depict how the enterprise functions. The management-oriented studies point to how technology might help the firm to function better (Martin 1991, p. 351).

In business reengineering, the business processes and cross functional teams used to breakthrough to design and to pilot new processes are important. "To really benefit takes time to architect, build, test, and migrate into full operation.... Reengineering seeks radically new processes, but these must be integrated into a company's existing corporate culture. One can either design new processes and incorporate them or tailor the processes to fit as they are designed." (JM and Co. 1993).

Information engineering is part of strategic systems development plan for an overall systems architecture. "The information engineering model identifies objects (entities) in an enterprise about which information is stored. It decomposes the functions of the enterprise into processes, and builds data models and process models for each business area." (James Martin 1991, p. 341).

IE relies on both data models and process models. The priority of emphasis is on the data model rather than process activity models. The techniques of Information Engineering and state-of-the-art Computer Aided Systems Engineering (CASE) tools are used to prototype the design and to facilitate the analysis and process streamlining (JM and Co. 1993). The models are stored in the enterprise repository with rule-based processing. Martin uses "skilled with advanced tools" (SWAT) teams in what he terms rapid application development.

Evaluative Comments

These major approaches of information engineering and reengineering (process innovation) are models with methods for reorganizing business organizations. Both are methods for organizational development and restructure. The terms, process and workflow, have been used by other major models such as systems development, database development, and information engineering. While the terms are similar, the methods are different.

In information engineering, business process reengineering is viewed as program sub-sets that fit within the more global framework of strategic information. The information engineering approach emphasizes data modeling, and uses process modeling at the operational level (Martin 1991).

In reengineering and process innovation by contrast, the use of business process is the central focus. Business process analysis starts with customers, and then considers the highest and most abstract level for the enterprise. The process focus is on activity.

The information engineering approach has many reports of success, such as Consolidated Edison in New York. It also has a record of difficulties with its own complexity and integration. Companies such as Xerox Corporation abandoned or changed from information engineering to other approaches for its restructuring and organizational architecture.

Summary—Part One

In Part One, three issues discussed showed differences in technique, emphasis, and distinctions, if not method, among major advocates of reengineering. A fourth issue identified an alternative model of information engineering, compared with reengineering models for designing and changing organizations. All of the reengineering models use a top-down approach. All use cross-functional teams or SWAT teams. All presume advanced technology, seek cost savings, and new roles that require fewer jobs. They all imply layoffs among current employees.

Part Two: Workflow Process and Products

Part Two of this chapter identifies workflow. Since other chapters in this book describe various types of workflow, this part assumes that some details on workflow are covered elsewhere. This part emphasizes and compares workflow with work reengineering. It identifies varying types of workflow products. It compares the methodology basis of various product types. Many workflow products were developed without theory; other products were based more in theory and came from research centers. Contributions from a series of research centers; and the coordination research center are noted. This part describes ActionWorkflow theory and work as a closed-loop process. The emerging field needs and demands for standards among workflow products have led to the formation of an industry-wide workflow coalition.

> **workflow products go beyond routine work tasks**

Workflow refers both to process and products. Workflow refers to a new set of software tools for automating and improving business processes. (Dyson 1992). Types of workflow software include document based, image system based, message systems, and databases. Workflow systems go beyond the storage and retrieval of documents and images.

Work Reengineering Compared with Workflow

Workflow and work reengineering both focus on business processes and customers. Workflow products are part of the battle against the excessive use of paper. The uses for workflow products far exceed the uses with reengineering. Workflow software holds the promise to combine, to reorganize, and to compress a series of business processes. Workflow software can be used to automate the new process path, and track the steps of the new business process. Both reengineering and workflow are used in many major projects. (J. Verity, 1993 p.156.) Redesign teams on reengineering projects may use workflow software as a tool for complex tracking, metrics, transactional costs, activity based costing, and matrix type analysis. The process teams must rely upon considerable good judgment as well.

Key research centers have pioneered a way to combine flow tasks with the use of advanced technology. This is an example of how workflow software may add value by devising alternatives and allowing testing of alternative workflows before installation. Reengineering uses a logic that focuses on business processes, which, in turn, combines it with a focus on service to customers. Only after these analytic steps does information technology enter into the picture. Then information technology is aligned with the business processes.

Workflow may be congruent with work reengineering in many projects. Forrester Research (1993) has reported that the real gains from reengineering require attention to workflow. Workflow may include processing of metrics for cycle time of a case or record. Workflow may provide alternative routes to streamline routing and scenarios. Workflow products go beyond routine work tasks. If workflows are linked with customer support and flexibility, then more gains are likely (Dyson 1992). Workflow products are used more widely than just with reengineering. For short term gains, some workflow products may be added, but to devise customized applications requires systemic change. In the long term, to get the greater gains may require some form of redesign and reengineering.

> to get the major productivity gains with workflow products usually requires advanced staff training

Workflows as Solutions to Business Problems

There are many types of workflow vendors and products. The types of workflow products continue to increase. Workflow products include those that carry out specific functions or tasks. An increasing number of workflow products is combined as add-on products or in a suite of products. Many start-up companies have pioneered the workflow product lines.

Workflow products include groupware products such as e-mail, calendaring systems, meeting schedulers, and conference systems. A major series of workflow products is designed to monitor and track. They manage the automated routines of business processes. Another leading group of workflow products augments database management systems. Some of the workflow products have their own database as special features.

Imaging systems technology are increasingly used in information intensive industries such as banking, finance and insurance. Some of these installations are a result of reengineering projects. Major companies using document management systems are increasingly shifting to types of imaging technology and use a variety of workflow products.

Coordination issues are addressed by a series of products on arranging meetings, running meetings, and consensus building. Other products aid in devising policy, and some may be combined with teleconference capabilities. Some allow concurrent team work on common projects regardless of geographical locations. Action Technologies has been a pioneer in these areas.

In 1993, a comprehensive review of workflow products and their markets was completed by International Data Corporation/Avante (IDC/A). (McCready 1993). The findings were reported in four volumes. IDC/A used a three-way classification of business problems or tasks. Workflow market segmentation was divided into: production, ad hoc, and administrative issues and tasks.

Many companies now use workflow products. Some use workflow with reengineering projects, but most use workflow for other current business processes. The short term gains for installations may not actually lead to longer term benefits.

studies on decision-making rules, such as voting and nominal group methods have been carried out

Some staff ought to be able to refine and further customize applications of case entries and the workflow at their desktop workstation or as Computer Aided Systems Engineering (CASE) managers. To get the major productivity gains with workflow products, the addition of advanced software and advanced technology systems usually requires advanced staff training. Action Technologies has established a special training institute for their product users. Motorola University has its quality training program. Wang Inc. has been training CEOs. Novell requires certificated service personnel. WARIA, the Workflow and Reengineering International Association offers a school of business process engineering, and workshops at open sessions and in-house at customer sites.

Major companies recently entered the workflow area. They have added workflow type features and formed alliances with other companies. WordPerfect Office 4.0 integrates e-mail, personal calendaring, and group scheduling. WordPerfect Inc. has just acquired SoftSolutions technology. Lotus Notes had a joint arrangement with Action Technologies; however it has since opened up to other companies with many specific function workflow products.

Microsoft has Windows with Workgroups 3.11, including features of workgroup functioning. Workflow products are expected from Microsoft in the future. AT&T's NCR already has a suite of products including NCR's Cooperation that is an object-oriented set of tools running on UNIX servers with Windows clients One of the NCR's other products is called ProcessIT and is targeted for business process use.

Methods

Workflow Products without Theory

Most of the workflow products were developed as applications to solve particular business problems. The specific solutions were converted into some form of software; then commercial workflow products were born. Many of the workflow products are not used jointly with reengineering projects. (PC Week, March 1, 1993, p. 67). A few other workflow products have been development as a result of explicit theory.

Can Academic Research Centers Help Reinvent the Corporation?

In the past decade, a series of academic research laboratories called Group Support Systems (GSS) have been established. They do research and conduct field applications with businesses. Much of their research is directly relevant to reengineering and workflow issues. Several government agencies are engaged in reengineering projects and use workflow products. Effective team functioning is a core research topic of the GSS centers. The research topics include: collaboration, cooperative work systems, group decision-making, and meeting facilitation. In addition, they devise GSS software, and generate policies.

These research centers, along with others, have demonstrated that research may serve as a catalyst for change. The changes must be followed through within the corporations themselves. A second generation of research centers has emerged, including 36 university sites. IBM, BellSouth, Texaco, Greyhound Financial, and other corporations have sponsored projects and used their facilities.

> coordination focuses on goals that a single actor, if alone, would not perform

The various GSS research laboratories could be a valuable resource for projects in both workflow and reengineering. Some GSS centers have done research and conducted sessions with cross-functional teams that are directly relevant to workflow and reengineering. GSS labs do sessions that combine many levels of organizations to generate new enterprise. Research includes other topics such as effects of group size and anonymity. Still other topics include the importance of (active) facilitators and (passive) chauffeurs to aid in group process. Another series of studies is on features of effective group decision-making. Studies on decision-making rules, such as voting and nominal group methods have been carried out. The GSS Centers have devoted research to the study of varied conditions to generate ideas, to negotiate, to participate, and to build consensus. Other studies have considered how to avoid groupthink and mindguards. (Jessup and Valacich 1993)

Coordination Theory

The GSS research centers use a range of theories and methods. They have been sites for reengineering efforts from corporations and the government agencies (Vogel 1993). One academic GSS research center that pertains directly to reengineering and workflow is the Center for Coordination Sciences at MIT.

Coordination theory states that work groups (two or more actors) pursue goals. Coordination focuses on goals that a single actor, if alone, would not perform. (Malone 1988). CCS uses multi-disciplinary teams of scientists to undertake projects with business partners. "The Center not only studies how people work together now, but how they might do so differently with new kinds of information technology. Other projects focus on developing new collaborative tools." (Malone 1992).

ActionWorkflow Theory

Another approach to coordination, communication, and methodology is found in the work of Winograd and Flores (1987). Flores and his associates drew upon the philosophy in the Heidegger tradition in the study of language and linguistics. J.L. Austin's writing on theory of speech acts was used. John Searle's taxonomy of speech acts is used with special emphasis on the concept of commitment.

Several ideas are combined in ActionWorkflow theory. The combined philosophic outlook is applied to work settings in the offices and in businesses. Flores and associates analyzed communication: electronic systems, computer technology and the roles of designers, and human systems. A view of the systems as a collection of interacting components was generated. Organizations are networks of conversations. The design does not just link people and places, but coordinates conversations for action. Every organization contains three kinds of processes: material, information, and human. It is in the human processes and communication in which requests and commitments are made. Some commitments are broken, and others are fulfilled. Conversations through requests and commitments become implied contracts. Even in the systems world, only people make commitments. (Denning 1992)

Loop Interpretation as Technique and Method

In the light of these assumptions about communication and commitments, Flores and Associates reconsidered views about coordination. Action Technologies view the organization as a network of recurrent conversations. In work settings, we communicate through commitments. Flores and Associates have devised and patented the loop interpretation as a new way to think about systems. It puts thinking about human beings' mutual commitments back into the communication inputs and responses. A loop is a way to identify the actions two or more human beings take as a result of a communication. Requests are made of performers who mutually commit to carry them out. Upon the delivery of the product, a customer approves (or disapproves). In language, our requests and mutual commitments occur as we communicate with human beings. The "loops" connect the communication exchanges.

Loops Connect Customer Satisfaction and Work

Flores and associates have applied the loop idea to business processes and customer satisfaction. The four-step process for structuring and managing human communications in database and communications systems has been patented. In nearly any business transaction, the communication by human beings implies an atomic loop. The atomic loop graphically depicts the action in which a performer completes an action to the satisfaction of customers. The customer accepts or rejects. In this way, the customer gives approval or satisfaction, which closes the loop. The concept of customer satisfaction is thereby embedded within the workflow loop. The closed loop is implied in work transactions. Flores states, "Work implies a closed loop process."(Keen 1991; Denning 1992; Medina-Mora, et al. 1992).

> viewing work as a closed loop process is a fundamental refinement in workflow and business processes reengineering

The speech-act theory as interpreted and modified by Flores and associates provides one basis for development of a variety of software products that apply to communication and decision-making in the workplace. (For further details, see Raúl Medina-Mora et al. 1992).

Evaluative Comments

Workflow software is used at various levels to provide tools for tracking. Other workflow products are used to automate a given workflow path. Many workflow uses are quite independent from the current movement toward business process reengineering. Prior efforts have been made to design computer tools to help people work together on common projects. The traditional workflow analysts tend to view tasks, not the coordination of tasks, as requests and commitments. The loop interpretation is a powerful technique for observation, analysis and use. This method has a customer satisfaction end-user focus and an action focus. It does not ask, "What is the work (task) here?" It asks, "Who are the customers and performers?" Their requests and commitments are depicted in the action loops (Medina-Mora et al., 1992, p.4).

In other traditional workflow products, actions are seen as tasks or flow of information, but not as coordination structures with a customer focus. The commitments put the human being back into the communication equations depicted by the loop. Viewing work as a closed loop process is a fundamental refinement in workflow and business processes reengineering. ActionWorkflow loops provide a way of depicting work that someone is doing for someone else. "The structure is defined by language acts through which people coordinate, not by the action done by individuals to meet the conditions." (Medina-Mora et al. 1992).

The current products of Action Technologies are illustrative of what can be developed such as business process maps that may be created to show the connections and dependencies of the workflow structure. Numerous combinations are possible with other workflow products. These developments are part of the rapidly growing market of workflow products.

Let the Buyers Beware

The variety of workflow products on the market and predictions for future market growth are indicators to consider. Davenport urges some caution in the use of workflow products. He believes workflow may help to structure work and to track on the lower levels. Workflow software cannot replace the complex judgment called for from the redesign teams. He advises discretion be used by self-managing teams until the products have matured (Davenport 1993, pp. 104-105).

Currently, there is an increasing demand for consumer product review, specifications, and standards. The lack of common industry wide specifications is a problem. Consumers or customers want guidance and evaluation of the many new workflow products.

They want advice on products, not just for today, but for growth tomorrow. They also want guidance on today's purchase and on the hidden costs for connectivity and interoperability in the longer term (*Computerworld*, Feb. 28, 1994).

In recent years, special industry-wide association coalitions have been formed to address similar issues to provide independent review and common specifications. The Open Systems Foundation, Frame Relay Forum, and ATM Forums were established to review current diverse practices and seek common industry-wide specifications. Fortunately, workflow industry representatives took such a step on August 9, 1993. Workflow managers and vendors formed the Workflow Coalition to try to overcome obstacles such as devising Application Programming Interfaces (APIs), technical specifications for the varied formats and protocols. One critic raised doubts about the obstacles confronting the Coalition. (Hoard 1993, p. 1). The Coalition met again in December 1993 and in February 1994 to address issues for common specifications and other matters. (Workflow Management Coalition WFM, 1993).

Part Three: Evaluation of Reengineering Model

Part Three reviews business process management in perspective, and briefly analyzes four models. It then comments on the change model, and notes paradigm shift issues. A tentative diagnosis of the failures of reengineering suggests a review of ways in which research may clarify issues and serve as a catalyst for companies. What do analysis and review of research reveal? A dozen facets are listed. The chapter ends with an admonition about the third order effects of layoffs and unemployment associated with reengineering.

Perspective on Reengineering and Process Management

Reengineering and workflow projects have been underway for less than five years. The prospects of a new dawn have been heralded. There is very little in the way of systematic research and few in-depth longitudinal case studies at this date. Without such data, one is forced to review related research, case studies, and studies of innovation involving advanced technology.

In any study of reengineering, many faces appear. One must distinguish between the face of a presentation made by consultants for their firms and, the faces of the complex reality of actual reengineering projects. Presentations are pitches made to get contracts for their consultant services.

Amid the current hype about reengineering and process management, Tom Davenport provides a perspective. He points out there are no companies that are completely process-managed. Few companies have carried out the overall macro or mega level of process planning. They have reengineered only a few business process modules with remarkable gains in productivity for some product lines (1993b). These companies continue the work on their other business processes. There are hundreds of companies that have some type of continuous improvement or quality programs underway at the micro level.

> the critical point is to add value rather than increase overhead

Four Models Within Reengineering

Much attention is given to four models used within reengineering:

(1) **Business process redesign and workflow approach.** Here the rationale is improve business processes and streamline the workflow by cost cutting and simplifying workflows. This includes reducing space and reducing inventory. It creates few new roles and thereby eliminates other jobs.

(2) **Technology as enabler.** Start with business processes first, then later bring in information system technology fused to business processes. Here the rationale is that technology is necessary to save time, but must be subordinate to the business process focus.

(3) **Cross-functional teams become empowered.** Natural work teams know how to enhance operations. Teams are expected to bring out their energies and capabilities. The rationale is to save money by improving service and satisfying customers.

(4) **Strategic business processes are more complex.** It's carried out at high level of abstraction at first. It forms the overall information technology and organizational framework. Core business process redesign is generated with iterative prototype modeling. Market tests are simulated. The rationale is to provide integrated development and show real cost estimates.

These four approaches or models together constitute a more comprehensive model of reengineering. Even these four together tend to focus on internal changes for cost reductions, shorter cycle time, and savings with fewer employees.

Few proponents of reengineering have actually claimed increased market share, or major shifts in ROI. The performance criteria of cost, service, quality, and speed are commonly used. The emphasis is primarily on internal changes. The negative effects that occur during reengineering projects do pose problems of cost estimates and sources for resistance. The hidden costs occur when upgrading with advanced technology, with delays in cycle or delivery time, and in training and staff changes.

The critical point is to add value rather than increase overhead. (Straussman 1985). This may include giving attention to strategic new opportunities externally as well as the internal cost savings. Breakthrough thinking may include extending business process thinking externally to major suppliers. New intercompany alliances may streamline business processes for both. Hammer and Champy (1993, pp. 60-61) use the example of Wal-Mart, who worked out an agreement with Procter and

> you may lead from the top down, but you implement from the bottom up

Gamble. P&G agreed to provide just-in-time delivery and provide a single bill for Wal-Mart's entire order of Pampers. The interorganizational alliance benefited both P&G as major supplier (locking in the customer) and Wal-Mart as major retail customer. Wal-Mart not only reduced costs of internal order processing, they eliminated storage space and inventory of Pampers. They reduced fixed costs and variable costs at the same time. The firms seek to move toward long-term competition and profit, while concentrating on customer service.

Change Models Used in Reengineering

What are assumptions about change models that are used in reengineering projects? The many models of reengineering are combined like Chinese boxes, each within another. Reengineering is mainly a managerial change model. Reengineering seeks to reach across the entire enterprise. It is not a strategic change model. It does get into the strategic plans as the vision of the company is developed and the core competencies are identified. Reengineering constitutes a shift to a customer satisfaction-based management system. It is complex and long term. It requires sufficient finances and commitment.

Reengineering uses an amalgam from other types of organizational change models. Reengineering in both theory and analysis addresses organizational units, not individual units or personalities. Yet the appeal is made that individuals on teams feel empowered. The analysis of business process sets focuses on organizational units, the norms, and the roles. It seeks to change corporate culture. This includes changing rewards and incentive systems. The overall approach combines a top-down one with cross-functional teams implanted across the organization. Insider-outsider teams as change agents are commonly used by organizational developers in temporary roles on large innovative projects.

> more case studies of actual reengineering projects are needed

What are the actual changes made in the authority structure and top decision-making structures? Interventions take place at the top, but changes occur on sites and on all levels. On one level, reengineering seeks to change the organizational policies and procedures. What is espoused may not be what is actually practiced. On another level, reengineering seeks to change some of the behavior and skills used by employees of the company. In effect, the emerging structure shift is toward some new form of a virtual matrix organization or virtual corporations (Davidow and Malone 1992). The new evolving structure and cross-functional teams are captured in the phrase, "You may lead from the top down, but you implement from the bottom up." (Morris and Brandon 1993, p. 215).

Reengineering is a bundle of beliefs and practices about how to change the way work is done. It changes the way new products and services are provided. Reengineering is not an end in itself. It is a bundling of the means to identify, to design, to set-up, and to install. It is to implement new products and the emerging new work structures of business process. Davenport's *Process Innovation* (1993) is one of the few books that devotes considerable attention to issues and draws upon research. He is explicit about many aspects of process, and structuring enablers in the process change. He discusses measuring cycle time, transaction costs, and exiting costs.

In the reengineering models, customer satisfaction is the end in view. Business processes are to be fused with advanced technology as enablers. Enablers interact with the embedded culture and bring some shifts in the normative beliefs, the patterns of practice and values. Some of the recipes provided for reengineering appear to underestimate the fusion. The flux of change becomes the norm. One day, it is a new vision and business plan. The planning, learning, and adjusting necessary for the conversion are worked through. Next week or month, the changes call for installation and implementation of advanced foundation technologies. All these developments entail culture changes. Have the breadth and depth of culture change of these emergent structures and experiences been taken into account?

Analysis of Failures in Reengineering

The lack of complete systematic evaluative research information about reengineering projects from the companies that have tried reengineering is a major limitation. Consultants' case examples and glowing success stories do not tell the whole story. They are bound by client confidentiality not to reveal negative results. Reengineering projects report that between 50 to 70 percent of the companies failed or did not meet to meet their goals (Hammer and Champy 1993, p. 200; Stewart 1993). CSC Index Corporation reported to Computerworld that the failure rate was about 25 percent (Schwartz 1993). Morris and Brandon (1993 p. 92) defend the early reengineering projects. They said that the projects were discontinued, or abandoned, but they did not fail. They imply that the model was sufficient, but the commitment and the resources were lacking.

Review of Research

The analysis of breakdowns in reengineering leads to reviews of research in a dozen areas. It starts with case studies. Then, to learn from mistakes, clarify theory, guide and practice. Then, suggestions are drawn from empirical research on cross-functional teams. Interpretive in-depth longitudinal studies reveal more on technology and structures. Still untried is to combine "work as closed-loop process" with major reengineering projects. More use of research clearinghouses would save time and costs, and avoid costly mistakes and repetition. Limitations are cited with migration plans and calls for research beyond the technical aspects. Research could include cultural, social psychological aspects, and human resources matters.

Case Study Research

Without direct research, we turn to case studies and draw from research on closely related subjects. More case studies of actual reengineering projects are needed, and not just another survey of clients. For example, Benefit Life Insurance Company was reengineered. It made the news with its new case manager role. Later, MBL went bankrupt mainly due to its unwise real estate investment (Berkley and Eccles, 1991). Another case study sought to learn from a "perfect failure." It revealed that high expectations and the effort needed were underestimated as the main reasons for the disaster (Hess et al. 1985 p. 20). A recent report, "TQM Flops: A Chance to Learn from the Mistakes of Others," (Gilbert

1992) echoes the point that we can learn from negative findings and may be of value in clarifying theory to guide reengineering efforts to bring about changes. One survey, based upon 100 companies with 20 reengineered projects, found that the newly redesigned businesses are likely to achieved long term successes if they thoroughly consider two factors: breadth and depth. Reengineering is complex. Business processes must be broad in scope. This means that processes must be defined in cost and customer values across the entire business unit. Restructuring all levels includes getting into the company's core organizational elements to change. It includes roles and responsibilities. This means both measurement of and changes in incentives. It means attending to organizational structure, information technology, and the shared values and skills (Hall, et al. 1993, pp. 119-128).

Research and Development of Cross-Functional Teams

Cross-functional teams are a linking pin for reengineering projects. Some related empirical research on cross-functional teams, team building, and decision-making has been done by Anaconda and Caldwell (1990). Three points they reported are worth restating:
(1) Some conflict of interests arose if a design team member's evaluator was still based in the unit being redesigned.
(2) Issues of internal review and external relations with customers for business process teams are very important. Teams must manage not only to get along internally, but must coordinate relationships with external stakeholders.
(3) The cross-functioning teams showed some synergy. Their diverse technical skills with differences in knowledge did express some creative expertise. Concurrently, the cross-functional teams were found to lack cohesion (Anaconda and Caldwell 1992).

Redesign teams include insiders and outsiders (consultants). They are encouraged to engage in inductive, non-linear thinking in attempting to create new solutions. Redesign team may require training from consultants.

Many reports of reengineering imply teams become empowered. In fact, considerable prior research (Zuboff, 1988) found that teams did not automatically know how to work toward common goals. Many times team members continued in the computerized setting to pursue their own individual goals. Team structuring does not automatically mean success in collaboration. As Michael Schrage (1992) pointed out, team members may unwittingly engage in self-deception. They may use the words, "sharing" and "collaboration," but they are not reflected in their actions. Here again is the distinction between espoused theory and actual action.

Team building and development are not automatic. Training in team building and team skill development may be required. Process owners may not be skilled facilitators. They may not be able to bring out the trust, confidence, and belief in the decision-making judgment of team members. As Walton (1989) commented, cross-functional teams alone are not sufficient as a strategy to improve organizational performance. These studies illustrate how research may help to refine the vague guidelines of reengineering. Findings may be useful in the skill development needed by redesign teams.

In-Depth Studies on Power and Resistance to Change

Three in-depth longitudinal studies provide additional interpretations. Kling and Iacone (1987) studied what happens when advanced technology systems are installed. They found that the shifts that occur in power and rewards in organizations have impact throughout the organizations. Research showed that when MRP was installed, perception of shifts in power was pervasive in the organization. The teams experienced fear of loss of bargaining power. These research reports are similar to the vivid reactions among employees in companies engaging in reengineering projects.

> little overt attention is given to the power impacts in reengineering reports

Kling and Iacone (1987) reported that control goes beyond the vertical management control. Influence is exercised by many employees in a complex social fabric of the organization. When key end-users of computers participate in the larger institutionalized world of computers, their status and prestige among other employees went up. This was true, regardless of the user's relative position in the formal hierarchy (Kling and Iacone 1987, p. 77).

In a second study, Markus (1983) used an interpretive interaction theory over time, and found resistance to implementation of financial information systems. She showed how the shifts of power had impact throughout the organization on divisional and centralized accounting functions. It was a source of major conflict between these units.

A third study was on accounting and control systems. Markus and Pfeffer (1983) found the resistance was minimized and accounting and control system installations were more likely to be a success if the "system can be designed consonant with (existing) organizational power distributions and cultures." Markus and Pfeffer found, "It is quite another matter if the goals includes significant organizational change. The issues of resistance to organizational implementation, then, need to be addressed explicitly." (Markus and Pfeffer 1983).

In the light of the research, once employees realize the power shifts that occur and how they effect them or their interests, then they are likely to resist. Does the basic reengineering model underestimate the importance of shifts in power and authority of multiple stakeholders? Does it emphasize only formal management prerogatives and stockholders as stakeholders? Reengineering expects significant organizational change, but it is explicitly silent about power transfers. Little overt attention is given to the power impacts in reengineering reports.

Changes in Technology and Structures Unintended Outcomes

In much of the reengineering literature, the writing style is similar to pronouncements. Reengineering champions presume only intended managerial outcomes. Other research has shown that dual outcomes, some of which are unintended. Zuboff (1988) used the term "infomate" to point out that, beyond automation of procedures, new views emerge. The results produce new information with dual managerial options and outcomes. Computer-aided smart technology, once installed, may produce more surveillance or more autonomy. Structures and technology are both constrained by and constraining.

> the medication may have been good, but the side effects were detrimental

Weick has similarly views of the dual role of technology and structuring. Dual outcomes occur because structuring is an ongoing process. Structuring shapes the meaning of artifacts (technology), and the technology, in turn, is shaped by structuring (Weick 1992, p. 22).

Why does installing a similar advanced technology produce such different results? If research views technology as social process, then research shows the results vary depending on how the technology is introduced. One research approach, Adaptive Structuration Theory (AST) actually views technology as a social process. AST could be used to understand and to improve effectiveness of cross-functional teams and team meetings. AST suggests that meeting outcomes are less a result of the use of the type of structures and technology used. They are more a result of how groups appropriate and modify these structures and technology. This again points out how teams function may be critical for teams to be effective (Poole and Jackson 1993, p. 281)

Reengineering Models and Work as a Close-Loop Process

The current models of information engineering, business process reengineering, and process innovation are all basically information models of work. The focus of business process teams is within both information input and output models. The same is true of the time and motion models of work.

Many describe meetings that imply parent-to-child communications rather than adult-to-adult. The reengineering models do not make assumptions about human communication in terms of requests and mutual commitments models as espoused and patented by ActionWorkflow Theory (Medina-Mora et al. 1992) as described in Part Two.

Reengineering relies on information models with an input-process-output scheme. Reengineering projects could make use of the concept of work as a closed-loop process. Cross-functional teams could trace commitments, and graphically depict loops in their analysis of business processes, benchmarking, locating breakdowns and other tasks. There are many ways to use loop interpretations, observation, and analysis in work settings. Requests and mutual commitments and customer satisfaction are embedded into the Action software tools systems. The speech-act theory and applications development provide a strong basis to address communication and decision-making in the workplace.

Michael Schrage cautions, "Language must be viewed as a medium to create meaning and shared understanding rather than simply to exchange information. Communication is more than a medium to exchange contracts. There are many levels to conversations, but the best conversation are acts of collaborative creation which did not exist before." (Schrage 1993, p. 83)

> ...if teams are not in contention, then nothing is happening

Research Clearinghouse for Projects and Research

Given the variety and number of reengineering projects, some form for gathering information about the many projects in reengineering is necessary. This cannot be left to the major consulting firms, nor to the companies themselves. Some independence may be necessary to acknowledge success, recognize errors systematically, and learn from mistakes.

Another source is the series of academic GSS laboratories. Their central mission is to use computer based information systems (CBIS) to support intellectual collaborative work (Jessup and Valacich 1993). The GSS could constitute sites for collecting, analyzing and conducting research.

The Center for Coordination Sciences (CCS) at MIT has one research project that has collected many examples of how different organizations perform similar processes. These amount to a database inventory of IT enablers. These have been placed on-line with information regarding relative advantages of alternatives. The process handbook has three purposes that help: (1) Redesign existing organizational processes. (2) Reinvent new organizational processes that take advantage of information technology. (3) Automatically generate software to support organizational processes." (Malone et al. 1993., pp. 2-3).

Other academic institutions have clearinghouse centers including: PlexCenter at University of Arizona and Xerox PARC in Palo Alto. The University of Minnesota has worked with the state government of Minnesota on phases of reengineering. At the University of Arizona, Tucson, sessions have combined personnel from Army, Navy and other agencies. Sessions held in COLAB use the Federal IDEF model to carry out business process reengineering.

In 1993, many government agencies have used the collaboration facilities, and Ventana Inc. Software using GroupSystem, VisionQuest and other software (Vogel 1993).

Reengineering Migration Plans: Technology and Culture

Reengineering may be viewed as a wonder drug that holds promise. Initially, it has miraculous effects. It seems to work, but then side-effects begin to appear. Eventually other difficulties develop. A decision is made to stop the wonder drug treatment. The medication may have been good, but the side effects were detrimental.

One may hypothesize about the stages in which the breakdowns occur on reengineering and business process redesign projects. There needs to be more research on where and when the breakdowns happen in reengineering projects. Then there would be answers to the questions: Are the stages and steps of implementation adequate? Is the complexity of fusing new technology with business more complex than anticipated? Are some current employees overwhelmed by the pace and complexity of change? Are others threatened by shifts in power or anxiety over possible layoffs? Are many inspired to engage in work teams with the hope to be on redesign teams? Are the changes in roles challenging to the mindsets of some current managers and other employees?

Without research findings, one cannot say for sure what causes reengineering projects to breakdown eventually. Elaborate theoretical speculation may be presented. Champions for reengineering certainly have disseminated their pronouncement through access to the media. One could conjecture that in middle or later stages, the leaders and teams miscalculate. They may underestimate the complexity and difficulty of changing the information technology architecture. The shift entails the complex choices among varied types of IT enablers or delivering technology. The change to CASE tools and Object Oriented Development (OOD) are not simple transitions. The users of the new technology require higher level of skills than may be present among current employees. Education and retraining take time. The shift from legacy mainframes to new image-based technology and client/server architecture is complex. In addition, these new technologies need servicing. Beyond the complexities and difficulties of technologies are the new roles and shifts in the distribution of power and distributive leadership.

Research on Cultural and Social Psychological Changes

The conversions and transitions are not just in advanced technology, but involve cultural changes to new behaviors and beliefs. Davenport (1993a) devoted major sections of his book to discussions of organizational changes in the context of process and work redesign. Reengineering advocates generally talk about culture change, but usually their references are more to change management. One purpose is to calibrate the effort required to bring about the changes as planned. Management of change is often treated only as mechanical and organizational variables. The larger context and subtle nuances are ignored.

Too little attention has been given in the reengineering guidelines to social psychological aspects of team meetings, and team deliberations. The reactions by team members to each other and to nuances of those management memos and directives may be critical. As noted by Walton (1989, pp. 14-15), subtle differences in such statements as: "securing compliance" versus "eliciting commitment" from process owners produce quite discordant outcomes from team members.

The importance of change management and changing culture is repeated by Hammer and Champy (1993). They acknowledge the importance of conflict. They say that if teams are not in contention, then nothing is happening. The resistance to change is ubiquitous. Difficulties that teams experience in decision-making are not fully understood. Weick and Meader (1993) probe the importance of how people come to frame events as problems prior to decision-making. They call this sensemaking. GSS research centers could study the interaction of cross-functional teams. They could study the patterns of sensemaking and team deliberation. Research could find out how teams learn, ways they construct meaning, and how teams decide. GSS research centers are, in fact, engaged in studying such problems.

how much can human beings change?

Research on Organizational and Human Resource Issues

The broad transformation of corporations as we know them today is underway (Morton 1991; Kochan and Useem 1992). The process teams are constituted cross-functionally throughout the company. As these teams interlace the company, a shift toward process management starts to take place. Reengineering calls for fundamental re-examination of many assumptions about what and how work is being conducted. New models of corporate governance are being used (Kochan and Useem 1992; Maynard and Mehrtens 1993).

How much can human beings change? How much life span learning is possible? Some express doubt and impatience with the prospects for lifetime learning. Some assume that reengineering requires rapid changes, and that some human beings cannot withstand the pace and complexity of change. Others realize that reengineering requires a range of special needs for more services, including training, retraining, and job shifts. Many of the tasks call for collaboration across areas. As Davenport (1993) put it, "If process innovation is to succeed, the human side of change cannot be left to manage itself. Organizational and human resources issues are more central than technology issues to the behavioral changes that must occur with a process."

Unemployment and Reengineering

Most articles on reengineering and companies are silent about the unemployment issue. Every project has anticipated and unanticipated effects and outcomes. Reengineering actually works, but what are some of the unanticipated effects both negative and positive?

We know the rationale for the corporate strategy. As firms reengineer, they revise and streamline the business processes. In the past, many middle management jobs served as information channels between top management and operations. Restructuring organizations around information invariably results in fewer middle-management and other jobs. Reengineering creates fewer new roles with higher skill sets required. In the new corporate order, many prior jobs and roles are no longer necessary, and are eliminated (Bell 1993, p. 26).

> change involves mutually and continually adjusting directions and goals

A detailed presentation this topic is beyond the space allowed for this chapter. The discussion and rhetorical questions raised are designed to provoke a commitment to the issues.

To call simply for jobs, jobs, jobs, may have worked in a political campaign. It implies a continuation of the old industrial model. After reengineering, the virtual corporation becomes a network organization. The former department is now merely a drop-down menu at the case manager's workstation on the network (Davidow and Malone 1992).

Many accounts and editorials on reengineering, downsizing, rightsizing, conversions, and other forms of restructuring acknowledge layoffs as tough decisions, but say they must be made. In reengineering literature, very little rigorous attention has been given to the human resources issues nor the organizational impact of reengineering, and to downsizing and restructuring into new work systems.

Any plan for restructuring has some costs and benefits. Calculations are made of alternatives on what various changes may cost. Shifts in fixed and variable capital costs are compared. Questions that occur are: How often is labor regarded as a variable cost, while new advanced technology treated as a fixed cost? How often is labor is treated as a cost on profit? In the new workplace model, employees are viewed as assets (Applebaum and Blatt 1993).

High performance work practices show both productivity and long-term financial performance (U.S. Department of Commerce and Labor 1993). As Charles Handy (1989) points out, human beings are regarded as assets, not just part of balance sheets and profit and loss statements. Questions that occur are: In how many reengineering cases and projects are employees been treated as assets rather than as costs? Are expenses for training and education regarded as investments in assets? What are employment policies? How can one make sure that alternatives are considered before layoffs?

It is Structural, Not Frictional Unemployment

When the question about unemployment is raised, a frequent response is that massive unemployment is not the responsibility of the corporation. The figures for overall layoffs, displaced, and unemployed, should not be viewed only in terms of a single firm. Many of those displaced employees, or unemployed are not frictional unemployment of shifts from one job to another. Changes take place not just in one firm or one industry sector, but across nearly all sectors. These are structural changes in industries where jobs have been lost.

> reengineering is viewed as part of major larger paradigm shifts

Response to Structural Unemployment in Civil Society

Companies in the past have not completely ignored their civic and social responsibility for their current employees. The layoffs are phased over time to minimize the impact of unemployment and plant closing on the communities. Citizens, representatives, and governments do not passively accept the fate of unemployment. In July 1993, a joint conference by U.S. Departments of Commerce and Labor in Chicago gave attention to The Future of the American Workplace. Research reviewed during the conference showed that skilled and dedicated or high performance work practices were associated with both productivity and long-term financial performance. Evidence showed that specific practices such as ongoing training, alternative pay systems, and employee involvement were often associated with higher productivity (U.S. Department of Commerce and Labor 1993; Applebaum and Blatt 1993).

Employees and those unemployed are citizens and voters. They are also consumers of products of other companies. The cumulative effect of layoffs and unemployment from one company to another are bound to reduce purchases of those products that have been redesigned to satisfy customers. People who are not working have lower effective demand and are most likely to buy fewer products.

Questions to provoke commitment on the issues are: Can corporations afford not to seek alternatives and to address the issues? (Kochan and Useem 1992). The cumulative numbers and the immense size, variegated aspects of dislocation make the country ripe for unrest, distrust, disgust, and anger. Do businesses along with professionals, labor unions, civic groups, government have joint responsibilities?

Paradigm Shift Issues

Reengineering is viewed as part of major larger paradigm shifts (Tapscott and Caston 1993; Morris and Brandon 1993). In a similar vein, Maynard and Mehrtens (1993), use the metaphor of waves to depict major transitions of how institutions are organized, and how wealth is defined. The authors show how the corporation relates to the surrounding community. The Second Wave was a shift from agriculture to industrialization, where the challenge was to create products. The Third Wave is more post-industrial and information-oriented. The focus was to create value and to beat the competition. The Fourth Wave corporate models are emerging in the world today. The authors outline main points of the Fourth Wave: Corporations will relate to community. They will accept responsibility to internalize social and environmental costs; they will be committed to use resource accounting, and to create safe environments that are being demanded in the Fourth Wave. The emerging shifts are from local, to national, to regional to global service;

- Shift from adversarial relations to mutual trust between labor and management
- Shift from stockholders only, as owners to widespread ownership (pension systems)
- Shifts in governance from stockholders as the only stakeholders to multiple stakeholders guided by a sense of stewardship toward the environment of the planet.

(See also: Kochan and Useem, 1992.) The authors of the Fourth Wave provide possible resolutions of the many dilemmas among paradigms today.

As the paradigm shift issue continues, here are some of the questions: Do varied sectors of society have joint responsibility to consider alternative models? How real is the shift in corporate governance to multiple stakeholders not just stockholders? (Kochan and Useem (1992), (Maynard and Mehrten (1993). Do global corporations expect to view employment in local, in national, in regional, and in global terms? Does the unemployment call out for national, regional, and global policies and strategies?

Beyond Rhetoric to Reality With Unanticipated Effects

The patterns emerging from restructuring, reengineering and redesign are new modes of operation with side effects both positive and negative. The new patterns of work contradict the deterministic industrial models of the past. What do the Virtual Communities (Rheingold, 1993) and Virtual Corporations (Davidow and Malone, 1992), and reengineering imply in the near-term prospects? The bold rhetoric and promises of reengineering and workflow often imply a quick fix or master plan for change. These claims have contributed to very high expectations. Can change can be planned? Yes, but not by simply following a Grand Master Plan. That is the fallacy of programmatic change. Change involves mutually and continually adjusting directions and goals. (Michael Beer et al., 1990.) Change is always accompanied by unanticipated effects that are both negative and positive.

With reengineering, there are many signs of mutual adjustment as well as the grand master schemes. We have both paradigm changes in business and new paradigms of technology combined. As one writer put it, a new paradigm may not be required to start reengineering. You will need it by the time you finish.

REFERENCES

Anaconda, D.G. and D.E. Caldwell, "Cross functional teams: blessing or curse in new product development" in T. A. Kochan and M. Useem eds. *Transforming organizations*. New York: Oxford. 1992 154-166.

Applebaum and Blatt, *New American Workplace: Transforming The Work System in the United States.* Ithica, NY: Cornell University Press.

Beer, M. Eisenstat, and B. Spector, "Why Change Programs Don't Produce Change" *Harvard Business Review*, Nov.-Dec. 1990.

Bell, Trudy, "Jobs at Risk," IEEE Spectrum Aug. 1973, pp. 18-35.

Berkley, J. D. and Eccles, "Rethinking the corporate workplace," Case Management at Mutual Benefits Life. N9 492-015 Boston: Harvard Business School, 1991.

Computer World, Special Issues: Guide to Workflow Software: Feb. 28, 1994.

Computer World, Special Supplement Workflow Software Applications, BIS White Paper. June 28 1993.

Davenport, T. *Process Innovation*. Cambridge, MA: Harvard Business Press, 1993.

Davenport, T. Seminar at New York University Corporate Affiliates Session. Sloan School of Business. MIS Dept. 1993b

Davenport T. Book Review of Hammer and Champy "Reengineering the Corporation" *Sloan Management Review* Fall 1993c.

Davidow, William H. and M. S. Malone *The Virtual Corporation*, New York: Harper Collins Book. 1992.

Denning, Peter, "Work as Closed Loop Process" *American Scientist* June, 1992.

Dyson, Esther, "Workflow: software that automates routine tasks," *Forbes*, Nov. 1992. P192

Finkelstein, Clive, *Information Engineering Strategic Development Systems,* Reading Mass: Addison Wesley. 1992.

Gilbert, James D. "TQM Flops—A Chance to Learn from the Mistakes of Others." *National Productivity Review.* Autumn, 1992. Pp. 491-453.

Hall, Gene, J. Rosenthal, and J. Wade, "How to make reengineering really work," *Harvard Business Review.* Nov. Dec. 1993. Pp. 119 132.

Hammer, M. "Work Reengineering: don't automate, obliterate!" *Harvard Business Review* 1990

Hammer, M. and Champy, J. *Reengineering The Corporation.* New York: Harper Business, 1993.

Handy, Charles. *Understanding Organizations.* New York: Oxford, 1993.

Hess, Peter, et al. *"Learning from an Unsuccessful Transformation: A Perfect Failure."* in *Corporate Transformation* edited by Ralph Kilmann. San Francisco, Jossey Bass 1988. P 202).

Hoard, Bruce. "New Workflow Consortium Faces Up hill Battle" *Imaging World* September 1993 p.1

Imai, Masaaki, *Kaizen.* Cambridge, Mass.: McGraw Hill 1986.

Information Week. How do you fit into reengineering and how you don't. May 6, 1992.

Jessup, Leonard M. and Joseph S. Valacich. *Group Support Systems: New Perspectives.* New York, Macmillan, 1993.

Johannson, Henry U., P. McHugh, J. Pendelruin, and W. Kelley. *Business Process Reengineering.* New York: Wiley and Sons, 1993.

Kaplan R. and Murdock, L. "Corporation Core Competence" *McKinsey Quarterly,* Dec. 1991. P 51-90.

Keen, Peter G.W. *Shaping The Future.* Harvard Business School Press Cambridge MA. Harvard Business School Press. 1991.

Kling, Rob and Suzanne Iacono. "The Case of PRINTCO" in Casebook for Management Information Systems Readings: by Henry C. Lucas, Jr. New York: McGraw Hill 1987. P. 94-98.

Kochan, Thomas H. and Michael Useem. *Transforming Organizations,* New York: Oxford 1992.

Malone, T. W., K. Crowston, J. Lee, B. and B. Pentaland. "Tools for inventing organizations: Toward a handbook of organizational processes." *Center for Coordination Science* WP # 141 SS. WP # 3562-93. Massachusetts Institute of Technology, Cambridge, MA. May 1993.

Markus, M. L. Power, politics and MIS implementation. *Communications of ACM,* 1983, 26, 6, pp. 430—445.

Markus, M. L. and J. Pfeffer. "Power and the design and implementation of accounting and control systems" *Accounting, Organization and Society* 8, No. 2/3 1983b, pp. 205-218.

Marshak, Ronni T. "Action Technologies Workflow Products" *Patricia Seybold's Workgroup Computing Report.* Vol. 16, No. 5, May 1993.

Martin, James. *Rapid Applications Development*. Prentice Hall, Englewood Cliffs, NJ. 1992.

Maynard, H. B. and Susan E. Mehrtens. *The Fourth Wave*, San Francisco: Berret-Klohler Publishers, 1993.

Medina-Mora, Raul, Terry Winograd, Rodrigo Flores, and Fernando Flores. "The ActionWorkflow Approach to Workflow Management Technology" *Communications of the ACM* CSCW 1992 Proceedings November 1992.

Moad, Jeff. "Does Reengineering Really Work?" *Datamation* August 1, 1993. p 22

Morris, D. and J. Brandon. *Reengineering Your Business*. New York: McGraw Hill, 1992.

Poole, Scott and Michael J. H. Jackson *Communication Theory and Group Support Systems* in Jessup and Valacich. 1993, p. 281.

Rheingold, Howard. *The Virtual Community: Homesteading On The Electronic Frontier*. Reading Mass: Addison Wesley, 1993.

Scott-Morton, Michael. *The Corporations Of The 1990s: Information Technology And Transformation Of Organizations*. New York: Oxford Press, 1991.

Schrage, Michael. *Shared Minds: New Technologies Of Collaboration*, New York: Random House, 1993.

Schwartz, J. "Here Today, Here Tomorrow" *Information Week* (1993) May 10, 1993. p 35.

Shipper, E.C., E.G. Eccles, and T.L. Soske. "Consulting: has the solution become part of the problem?" *Sloan Management Review*, Summer, 1993.

Soles, Stanley. Reengineering Work: Prospects for Transformation and/or Unemployment." *Proceedings of Association of Management Conference*. Aug. Atlantic City, NJ, 1991.

Soles, Stanley. Reengineering Work and Business Process Redesign: What Role for MIS? *Proceedings of International Academy for Information Management*. December 12th, Dallas TX, 1992.

Stewart, Robert. "Reengineering the company: How it works and Doesn't." *Fortune*, Aug. 23, 1993. Pp. 41-60.

Straussman, Paul. *Information Payoff*, New York: Free Press, 1985.

Tapscott, Don and Art Caston. *Paradigm Shift: The New Promise Of Information Technology*. New York: McGraw Hill, 1993.

United States Departments of Commerce and Labor. "High Performance Work Practices and Firm Performance" at Conference on Future of The American Workplace. Chicago, Ill., July 25-25, 1993.

Verity, John. "Getting Work to go with the Flow." *Business Week*, June 21, 1993, p. 156.

Vogel, Douglas. Personal interview regarding the work at GSS COLAB at University of Arizona, Tucson. 1993.

Walton Richard. *Up And Running*, Harvard Business School Press. Cambridge, MA, 1989.

Weick, Karl. "Technology as Equivoque" in P. S. Goodman and L. Sproull, *Technology and Organizations.* Jossey Bass, 1990, pp.1-44.

Weick, Karl and David K. Meader. "Sensemaking and Group Support" in *Group Support Systems: New Perspectives by Jessup and Valacich* (1993). Chapter 12, pp. 230-252.

Winograd, Terry and Fernando Flores, *Understanding Computers and Cognition.* Reading, Mass: Addison Wesley, 1987.

Zuboff, S. *The Age Of The Smart Machine.* New York: Basic Books, 1989.

Case Study: Logicon Software Engineering

Louis C. Rose, System Architect

Logicon, Inc.

Abstract

In today's competitive environment, there is an increasing demand to produce more sophisticated and complicated software systems with greater productivity and increased quality. New tools, including groupware tools, associated methodologies, programming language enhancements, and shared data repositories help to address this demand by incorporating technology advances into the software development process. However, these factors alone do not provide what is needed to progress the software industry beyond where it is today. Software engineering and management disciplines (for example, software process, policies, procedures, standards, and conventions) are needed to provide the structure that is required to take advantage of technology advances.

Organizations adopt a software process model, or develop their own, to describe their software process at a high level. A mature software process can accomplish the goal of producing a quality product on schedule and within budget. However, these gains can be magnified by the addition of disciplined software management and the use of process control tools that automate much of the software process creating a process-driven software engineering environment (SEE).

Logicon is a systems integrator and software development company providing high technology services to the government and civilian agencies and helping them solve their large scale systems and software requirements. Several years ago, the management in Logicon reviewed the processes that drove several projects, looking for areas of improvement as part of the instituting of a Continuous Process Improvement (CPI) program. During this investigation, they discovered that most projects were not working with an explicitly defined process and furthermore, there were few metrics that were available about the process used. There were a reasonable amount of metrics relating to the application being built (for example, size of the documentation, size of the code, and amount of test procedures) but very few metrics on the tasks used within the process. Logicon set out to determine how it could better address these deficiencies in future projects by starting an investigation into the availability of automated process/workflow tools.

Applying the workflow paradigm

In the past, workflow was enacted solely by individuals. The processes that controlled the workflow were informal at best, and only experienced managers were capable of orchestrating efficient and productive coordination of a complex set of tasks. However, as the processes have become more formally defined, the burden has shifted from individuals controlling the workflow to automated control systems.

Logicon has automated the software development workflow process as part of a software engineering environment (SEE) called LOGICORE. LOGICORE's implementation began three years ago by initiating an internal effort to design and develop a SEE to address the problems related to the control of a large team's collaborative effort. Past experiences revealed several specific areas that impacted workflow. As a team increases in size, the efforts needed for the team to communicate technical ideas and share data increases at a greater rate.

This causes significant inefficiencies and opportunities for misinterpretation of instructions and assignments. Additionally, a set of related problems exist for management to control and monitor the process being exercised by the development team. The larger the project, the more devastating the loss of control is on the project's success, and the later in the process a serious problem surfaces, the more costly the solution of that problem is to implement. The managerial problems are further complicated by the size and complexity of the information requirements of developing large software systems. The larger the information requirements of an application, the more difficult it is to ensure consistency and completeness in the requirements, traceability, design, and implementation of the system.

> the larger the project, the more devastating the loss of control is on the project's success

To address the first two sets of problems, Logicon defined a set requirements that the SEE must include an automated control system with the ability to define, control, and monitor a software development process for a large development team. At the time of the initial investigation, about two and a half years ago, Logicon found no system that met these requirements. As luck had it, Logicon attended a presentation of a prototype document control and development system, then called the XEROX Document Object Manager (XDOM). The framework for XDOM was an automated process/workflow control system that appeared to directly address the majority of our requirements. Logicon made arrangements to visit the facility developing XDOM for an in-depth technical demonstration and discussion. They came away from that meeting quite impressed with the technical foundation of the product and Xerox's plans to develop it commercially. Logicon started by evaluating the prototype software and eventually became a Beta test site. LOGICORE now incorporates the current releases of the product, InConcert. While working with XSoft, the XEROX division that markets InConcert, Logicon provided insights that influenced product releases benefiting both parties.

The working relationship with XSoft during the early phases of the product development was both interesting and exciting. Logicon found it extremely satisfying to observe some of their suggested modifications implemented in the new releases of the product. In some cases, XSoft extended the implementation of some suggestions beyond the concentration of our concerns and produced a more flexible capability. For Logicon it is also satisfying to have its opinions solicited on occasion before modifications are implemented to determine the company's feelings on the effectiveness of these future changes. Not all suggestions were implemented, however, as the application of InConcert as a framework of a SEE has some requirements that diverge from the main marketing thrust of InConcert as a document production control system. But the generally elegant and flexible capabilities of InConcert has allowed Logicon to continue to adapt it to meet the significant majority of our requirements.

> process-controlled information baselining is a key benefit of this level of process integration

Before discussing how LOGICORE adapted the InConcert process control system to be the framework of the software engineering environment, a brief overview of the process definition and enactment capabilities of InConcert is in order.

InConcert process definition

InConcert is an object-based, dynamic process management system that facilitates the interactions of people, software, hardware, and information. InConcert includes a collection of utilities to define, instantiate, and enact a process by using an object management system that controls access to a shared data repository. InConcert is built for operation in a distributed, open-system environment. The architecture consists of a set of graphical user-interface clients supported by one or more InConcert servers. These servers control access to the process and object management systems implemented, using a relational database management system (RDBMS).

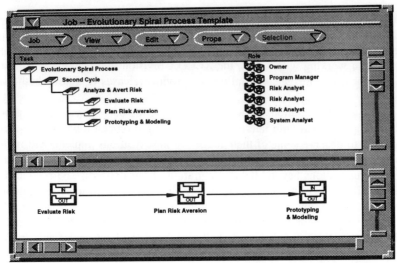

Figure 1: InConcert Workflow Editor

A process (or Job, in InConcert terms) is a hierarchical network that is the collection of process activities (or tasks) identifying the work to be done and the order in which the activities are to be enacted. Each activity has a Role associated with it that is used to represent the required skill of the task performer. Activities also contain Document Objects that perform the activity. The Document Objects are generic objects that encapsulate the data and the associated method or tool. Process definition with InConcert is accomplished using the Workflow Editor. The Workflow Editor provides the ability to define process templates graphically. *Figure 1* shows the decomposition of the risk management activities of an Evolutionary Spiral Process cycle.

The number of levels of decomposition can be tailored to organizational needs.

InConcert process instantiation and enactment

InConcert provides all the capabilities needed to instantiate a process model and prepare the process for enactment. The process model template is instantiated into to an active process by generating a copy of the process model. The active process is modified to address the process drivers that identify project specific characteristics.

The process activities must be customized, Pools assigned to Roles, and project specific Document Objects registered to the process activities. All of this work is accomplished with the InConcert Workflow Editor. All of the Document Objects that are registered to the opened activity are presented in the lower window. Access to the tools and information is provided by selecting the Document Objects. Selecting a Document Object causes the tools associated with it to be launched referencing the appropriate information. Tool launching methods are provided by mapping user-defined information types to particular tools on the network. With this capability, all of the information and tools are available to perform the process activities.

When the User has finished the activity, the User marks the activity as complete. When an activity is completed, the InConcert server scans its database to determine what successor activities in the process network can act after the activity completion. The server then notifies the applicable Users that new activities can now be opened. This process continues until all activities in the process network complete.

LOGICORE Life Cycle Information Repository

To address the final set of problems that deal with control and interrogation of the information requirements of the development of a large application, Logicon defined a set of requirements that the SEE must contain in a central information repository. This repository must contain the data from all of the tools used in the software system development as well as project management information. InConcert's implementation of process control, although comprehensive, does not address all of the requirements of a software engineering environment. For instance, while the InConcert Object Management System does control access to information within the process context, it does not provide semantic data integration of information about the system under development. Semantic data integration is necessary for a team of developers to gain the maximum benefit of a shared-data repository that contains complete life-cycle information integrated into a comprehensive data model.

After an industry investigation, Logicon discovered that there is no commercially available repository that provides semantic data integration, so it set out to developed its own repository. The structure of their repository data model is based on analyzing available industry and military standards used for software development (For example, DOD-STD-2167A, MIL-STD-7935A). The top level architecture of the repository contains a staging area and a baseline area. The staging area is a temporary storage space used to receive information from design tools, and the baseline area is a persistent storage area used to store validated information. The major focus of this repository structure provides the ability to query the repository for consistency and completeness validation of the objects. This identifies errors early in the process when they are more cost-effective to correct.

Integration of process control and data integration

A semantically integrated shared repository is not sufficient on its own. Large numbers of people arbitrarily accessing large amounts of data can lead to significant inefficiencies. To accommodate this, the controlled access to the repository must also be properly coordinated within the context of the process.

Logicon views this as integration of process control with data integration. This is easily accomplished with LOGICORE, using the task decomposition to control the access to our data bridges and consistency queries. Access to the repository is focused and executed within the context of the process defined in the workflow implementation.

Process-controlled information baselining is a key benefit of this level of process integration. An easy way to lose control of a large software development project is a lack of good configuration management. With automated process-controlled configuration management, the baselining processes are executed when required and the configuration management status is readily attainable.

Management control features

InConcert provides a large set of automated capabilities that address many of the management monitoring and control requirements that Logicon placed on LOGICORE. InConcert has an Audit Log that maintains a history of key events occurring within the InConcert environment. The Audit Log is stored in the control RDBMS. For example, during process enactment, the times and causes of process activity status changes are recorded. Also, the user modifying the process and the time of modification is recorded as are Role/Pool assignment changes, indicating an activity reassignment. This Audit Log provides the foundation for many of the metrics needed to address most of the CPI issues discussed previously.

> as a software development project grows in size, the task of monitoring its progress grows more difficult

As a software development project grows in size, the task of monitoring its progress grows more difficult. Management needs the ability to monitor the progress and make needed dynamic adjustments to improve the process or adapt it to new situations. This is accomplished using the Workflow Editor that displays the process enactment status.

Other management monitoring problems occur on a large software development project by relying on human interaction to determine task or milestone status, whether it be verbal, e-mail, or memorandum notification. Furthermore, often notification is after the fact, causing further problems or delays not yet reported. InConcert has a built-in event-triggering mechanism with which the environment can automatically notify management or take automatic action for over 60 critical events in the automated process.

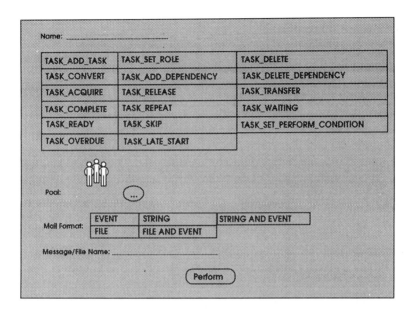

Figure 2. Trigger Registration Window

This facility is provided by the registration of an event trigger to any collection of the InConcert events can initial an e-mail notification to a pool of users or execute a program.

In *Figure 2*, the trigger registration window for process tasks shows the available event types for which a trigger can be created. Some straightforward uses of this facility are global triggers registered to send e-mail for all tasks that start late (TASK_LATE_START) or tasks that have not completed in the allotted time period (TASK_OVERDUE). Later, there is a discussion of how these triggers are used for the integration with a program management tool.

Extended attributes

The InConcert control database can easily be tailored to meet the data needs of differing organizations. All InConcert object classes can have user-defined extended attributes added to them, and each object class can have a subclass hierarchy defined with the sub-classes containing unique user-defined attributes. In addition, the sub-classes inherit the attributes of their parent's classes. For example, with this capability, InConcert user and pool objects can be structured to match the labor category structure of an organization. These user- defined extended attributes can be a string, numeric or date and they can have default values assigned optionally. Later, there are discussions how this facility was used to provide the integration with the program management tool.

145

Tool launch integration

The integration of tools into the InConcert environment is flexible and straightforward. The InConcert document objects provide the facility to launch tools and have specific data passed to the tools. This is accomplished by first defining a data type for the document object. This data type is user defined in a data type definition file as shown in *Figure 3*. Note that each data type in the first column can cause the tool to be launched with a VIEW (read only) or EDIT (read/write) access mode. The tool to be launched with each specific data type is the system command, or script file, in the fourth column.

Following the commands are optional arguments that can include the data file associated to the document object and any number of document object attributes. When a document object is opened, the InConcert server determines the data type of the document object and the mode of access (VIEW or EDIT), the server then scans the data type definition file for a match on the data type and access mode.

When a match is found, the command is executed, passing to it the specified arguments. This capability allows access to any tools that are available in the development environment.

```
ascii, EDIT, Application, textedit %FILE
ascii, VIEW, Application, textedit -read_only %FILE
audio, EDIT, Application, audio_in.sh %FILE
audio, VIEW, Application, audio_out.sh -read_only %FILE
audit, EDIT, Application, audit_log.sh %ATTRIBUTE(PROJECT_NAME)
audit, VIEW, Application, audit_log.sh %ATTRIBUTE(PROJECT_NAME)
image, EDIT, Application, image.sh %FILE %ATTRIBUTE(PROJECT_NAME)
image, VIEW, Application, image.sh %FILE %ATTRIBUTE(PROJECT_NAME)
query, VIEW, Application, query.sh %FILE
query, EDIT, Application, query.sh %FILE
```

Figure 3. Example data type definition file.

In the case of LOGICORE, data types were defined to access project management, CASE, implementation, test and other software development tools. InConcert does have a current constraint related to the data associated with a document object, however, that caused Logicon to adapt the use of this associated data. The constraint is that the data associated with a document object can only be a single file. This association is sufficiently adequate for tools such as word processors, spreadsheets, image tools, and voice. But the tools involved with software development, such as program management, CASE (for example, Teamwork or Software through Pictures) and requirement traceability tools (for example, RTM and RTRACE), have multiple control data files sometimes contained in a hierarchical directory structure.

Therefore, these tools with multiple file databases could not be placed under the control of the InConcert object management system. The solution to this constraint was to use the InConcert document object data file for control information for the launch of tools with multiple control files. When the document is opened and the tool is launched, it is passed information that identifies the tool database location for a specific project and the form in which the tool is to be launched. Using this facility, Logicon has integrated over 50 tools from over 20 vendors, in addition to Logicon's developed tools, to form the foundation of its SEE.

This situation has been discussed with the InConcert developers and they have agreed to work to incorporate the ability to handle tools with multiple control files in a future release.

Program management tool integration

InConcert does not contain the capabilities of a program management tool such as costing, scheduling, Gantt charting or critical path analysis. Therefore, Logicon had to include a comprehensive program management tool in LOGICORE. But this resulted in creating different tools to handle the project task network. InConcert provided defining of the project process task network (process management), and the program management tool provided the ability to define a PERT chart of the project tasks (project management). Clearly, if the program management tool used a different network than the one used by InConcert, the program management reports would not be indicative of the true status of the process as enacted under InConcert control. To alleviate this problem, a coupling of the two capabilities was needed. Since InConcert is implementing a development organization's process model in a set of existing process templates, it was decided that the process, as implemented in InConcert, should be the controlling factor.

> an organization should tailor the active process from a template before the project begins

An organization should tailor the active process from a template before the project begins. With the initial structure of the active process, Logicon developed an InConcert client program that reads the process task hierarchy and creates the files necessary to import this structure into the program management tool. To accomplish this in comprehensive fashion, it was necessary to add extended attributes to both the task and role objects of InConcert. These added attributes are editable in the attribute-scrolled region in the property sheet of the task and role objects. The program manager enters the attribute information as the active process is being initially tailored for the project, and then executes the client program to create the import files for the program management tool.

This capability provided only an initialization of the program management tool at the start of the project. More dynamic integration was needed to keep the program management tool in synch with the status of the active process as it was enacted. This capability was created using the event trigger mechanism mentioned earlier. In this case, client procedures were developed to react to each task start and completion and these actual event times were then automatically updated in the program management tool. Also, any process structure changes, such as task additions and deletions as well as task dependency changes, were also automatically updated in the program management tool. With this facility, the program management tool automatically updated at the time the actions were occurring, so the program manager did not have to rely on the verbal or written progress reports of the staff and had an up-to-date accounting of the project status.

Summary

While many of Logicon's managerial goals are being achieved with LOGICORE, there is an issue that is particularly acute in the software development industry. That is the historically strong independent attitude of the software development personnel. The incorporation of process workflow needs to be presented to the software developer as an environment that makes everyone's job more efficient to execute. Also, the process workflow definition should be high level at first to allow management and staff to determine how to adapt the automated workflow to fit their way of Operating projects. A process workflow that is excessively detailed at the start is most likely to be a burden on the project, start lightly and add the detail as experience grows and the conditions dictate.

Although InConcert was not envisioned by the XSoft developers as a framework for a software engineering environment, their dedication to providing a general and flexible process/workflow control system made adapting InConcert to support a SEE straightforward. Even though Logicon began working with XSoft over two years ago, the production version of InConcert has been available for less than one year. Logicon efforts continue to expand the adaptation of InConcert to provide a more robust environment. In-house use of LOGICORE has just begun within Logicon and there are ongoing discussions with some strategic vendors to assist in the commercialization of LOGICORE.

Managing Technological Change

Susanna Opper, President
Susanna Opper Associates

"Information is the new raw material. And as the material is applied to products, companies, and entire businesses, everything changes."
Alan M. Webber, *"What's So New About the New Economy?"*
Harvard Business Review. January-February 1993

Work has gone though only a few fundamental changes in the whole history of humanity. The first radical change came when our forebears began raising crops and husbanding animals rather than gathering and hunting. Work changed again when we moved to the industrial age. And it is changing once more—in ways equally as profound as these previous revolutions.

It is easy to underestimate the enormity of this change. Worse still, it is easy to consider the changes as mechanical ones—installing networks, selecting software, writing programs, and automating processes. Yet the early evidence from workgroup computing pioneers is that the shift from paper-based to computer-based workflow is

> I believe it's far better to learn a little bit and play and then learn more

much more complex and much more challenging than expected. As the other technological changes that came before—the telephone and the automobile—this shift will make its impact known in waves, over a considerable period of time.

This chapter is about managing technological change. It is important to say at the outset that we are early in the process. Business guru Tom Peters believes that this transition may take 40 years. Since we have, at best, only two or three years of real business experience with desktop-oriented, large networked computer systems, it is far too early for definitive prescriptions.

Still, there is evidence that paying attention to three interrelated critical factors will foster a smooth transition to workflow and support individuals and organizations through the potentially chaotic process of moving to computer-based work. See Figure 1.

Having an educational perspective is critical to the process. By setting learning as a key objective for both the individual and the group, the transition to workflow has more to offer than just improved cycle times and more efficient processing. Taking this view, workflow becomes a keystone of the learning organization.

When education is the context for a workflow effort, experimentation becomes a major ingredient of the learning process. Just as students learn chemistry in the lab, workers will learn elements of the new work environment by exploring various possibilities.

The end product of both the education and the experimentation will be enhanced teamwork. The complexity of most of our contemporary work environments, and the interrelatedness of most business tasks, require nearly everyone to work in teams. Yet we know relatively little about how the team process functions in a networked computer environment, so workflow projects will therefore promote the necessary learning.

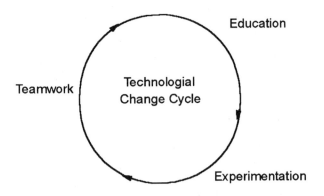

Education

Teamwork

Technologial
Change Cycle

Experimentation

Figure 1.

To explore these assertions, we will use examples from an actual workgroup computerization project at a major multinational East Coast bank. The activity was well into its second year when a series of one-on-one interviews and electronic focus groups were conducted to determine the results of the workgroup computing effort. The quotations included in this chapter come from that material as does much of the other specific information.

Project expectations

These are the expectations set for the project at its outset:

- Efficiency improvements in the administrative process by eliminating paper flow within the division (planning, scheduling, budgeting, reporting)

- More effective meetings through networked prework (presentation of background material, initial statements of position, documentation of proposals)
- Record keeping and communication to be combined in most routine management processes
- An increase in the direct personal contribution of managers at all levels

The benefits research showed clearly that the electronic environment improved administration in the department. People at all levels were able to process routine information much more efficiently and move forward in their work without bottlenecks. In many instances, the nature of work changed. Managers at all levels, for example, were doing more of their work directly without assistance from secretaries and clerks. Workers, on the other hand, encountered fewer delays waiting for decisions from management.

The nature of meetings changed as well. There were fewer meetings and those that were held changed focus from the routine to the controversial. Traditional memos all but disappeared. In their stead was immediate, on-line communication.

Managers were able to be more involved in their staff's work because the workgroup computing system gave them better access to tasks in process. Like many other elements of work automation, this can be a double-edged sword. Effective workflow systems must allow managers to get the information they need without inviting them to be involved in the process prematurely.

The project at the bank was based on the premise that workgroup technology is an educational process that requires an open mind and an experimental attitude. With these it can foster teamwork. Let's consider each of these elements in more detail.

An educational process, not a technology change

Education—that is the key to improved use of the new platform. I think it will also help to increase the audience. People are afraid of change, but with education it does become easier to embrace.

I continue to be impressed with the fact that at the bank, education was stressed with the rollout of this new work environment.

All too often when people plan to computerize workflow, they consider education and training "last but not least." More effective for a successful workflow effort is to see education and training as first among equals. Automating the work process is changing the very tools with which people work. And this, in turn, changes everything about the work process. To overlook or undervalue the magnitude of this change is to hobble the process at the outset.

Education and training are separate, but related, endeavors. Training refers to the learning of the actual workflow tool or tools. Without abundant training, people are being asked to do their work differently, but are not sufficiently skilled to do what is expected of them. Needless to say, such a situation engenders anger, resentment, resistance and even rebellion and sabotage. All have been known to occur in office-automation projects over the decades since machines first entered the white-collar work arena. Most, if not all, of these negative results are unnecessary.

Education is learning about the changed process and understanding how it will alter the way people work together. The learning is mastering new ways to interact with others in the organization, with customers, clients, suppliers, and anyone else with whom the organization routinely does business. Even though much of the educational process is evolutionary, it is equally as important as tool training to making an effective transition to computer-based work.

In the next section we will consider training. We will return to the subject of education later.

Training should be incremental, well-planned and varied

I believe it's far better to learn a little bit and play and then learn more, than to start from scratch and be taught more than you can comprehend at that time. We should have tutorials when we want to know how to do something specific.

We need to build in the time for people to be trained. We have strong feelings that training is important, but most companies are lousy at it. In fact, training never stops. We are constantly honing skills. Companies don't provide enough training and should make more time for training.

Almost everyone understands that before a workflow project is implemented, users must be trained. Most also realize that the timing of this training is critical. Users must be schooled and then return to their work environment to begin using the new tools. All too often, hardware delivery or scheduling difficulties separates the actual classroom learning from the inaugural use of the tool. This is to be avoided at all costs. In addition to the fear of the unknown and natural human resistance to change, people moving into an electronic work environment have enormous performance anxieties. This is severely exacerbated by any separation between learning and doing.

But having said this, there is a temptation to train everyone in everything they need to know all at once. Sadly, human beings cannot absorb most of such intense instruction. Thus it is better to provide limited sessions for the basics and add to these as needed. Lest this sound too difficult to manage and schedule, additional instruction need not take place in a classroom, need not be scheduled way in advance and may be highly informal. But it does need to happen.

These incremental training elements can be provided through computer-based training or video tape, for example. People can manage their own learning from libraries of appropriate material, if they know what is available and if it's easily accessible.

We will see in the next section that involving workers in the workflow process is another key to success. Skilled users can share tricks of the trade with other workers at regularly scheduled brown-bag lunches. This strategy shares the learning of one individual with the rest of the group while giving one person the opportunity to shine with his or her peers. Such sessions require planning and management, but once they become a habit in a group, employees will want their time in the limelight.

A third approach for on-going, incremental training is one-on-one or small-group tutorials. Using this approach, power users spend part or all of their time coaching others in the use of the tool.

Countless studies of how people learn stress the differences in style between how individuals absorb information. Using varied strategies honors those differences. For the visual and auditory, a video tape may be the best learning device. For the kinesthetic, a hands-on, computer-based program may help some individuals learn most comfortably.

Furthermore, offering varied training elements meets one of the greatest challenges in a workflow environment—dealing with individual differences in competency. One worker may take to the new tools like the proverbial duck to water. Another may be slow, awkward, unsure, and error prone. Admittedly, there are some people who simply cannot learn new technology. These, I believe, are fewer than imagined. Most people learn what they need to know and can use computers productively. But each person needs to be treated as an individual with the ultimate responsibility for his or her own learning. This can be done when training is deeply honored, fully funded and management understands that constant training will, in the long run, ensure a good return on investment.

> resistance is the normal human reaction to such changes

In this section, we have mostly been talking about training. To understand and respect the subtle distinction between training and education, we need to consider the next caveat of workflow adoption.

Experimentation—go with the flow

Educate that the evolution of the platform is a process, not a goal which we will reach.

As the network grows, many more rules and standards must be put in place to avoid chaos.

There is a certain inherent, natural chaos that results from fundamental change. Resistance is the normal human reaction to such changes. And some resistance is inevitable. But workflow can actually strengthen the organization, improve the product and, yes, make work more fun but only if individual needs are honored and workers get to control the process, not follow someone else's rules.

Let's try to unravel the relationships between automated workflow, increased teamwork and empowerment. Taken at its highest and simplest level, when you link the work processes of individuals though a computer network connection you restructure relationships. The individual pieces of work that each person used to do and the effort of the whole team, department, or workgroup are recast. Certain human and organizational results will flow naturally from this process.

Decision-making ability changes with information availability

The platform has delayered—flattened—the organization. Information is whizzing by; flows are no longer hierarchical. We can't stop the information:

Sometimes it's disconcerting as a manager because others know things before I do. Net effect: More information is available about what we do and why we do it.

There is an inevitable relationship between the use of networked computers to do work and the moving of authority and decision-making to lower levels in organizations. It is not clear which is cause and which is effect, nor does it matter. In fact, the two are inexorably linked.

While it's possible to predict that there will be change, it's not so easy to know in advance precisely what that change will be or who will rise to new levels of leadership. In a sense, workgroup computing creates a whole new game. In this new game, the rules are not yet determined and the star players have yet to make themselves known.

Even the simplest workflow implementation makes information available to members of the workgroup whose access was previously limited. And it allows work to be restructured away from the traditional assembly-line processes and more toward all individuals in a workgroup being able to respond to a customer query or assemble a report.

Especially in the early stages of an automated work project, it's critical to stay open to specifics of leadership, roles, and responsibilities. And it's hugely important to keep listening to the people who are using the system and keep responding to their requests. One way to do this is to use the networked technology itself. If electronic discussions are not part of your workflow system, then find another way to use the network to collect and disseminate electronic group conversations. Best of all, design the feedback loop right into the development of your workflow process so that user suggestions are funneled directly to the development team.

Use electronic workgroups to redesign work process.

The biggest temptation is to take the existing work process and automate it. Roads built by paving cowpaths lack responsiveness to new environments and changed patterns. By now that's a cliché, but it's one worth remembering. Effective reengineering is about radical, fundamental, dramatic changes first to business processes and then to organizations. While this approach looks initially at jobs and structures, it ultimately affects values and beliefs.

The most effective way to keep the workflow project from becoming another paved cowpath is to involve everyone who will be affected by the process in the design of the workflow. Understandably, this is not a happy prospect. We have all heard that the camel is a horse designed by committee. But workflow can be designed by workers incrementally. One of the greatest advantages of bringing design tools to the desktop is ease of modification.

If an outcome of the workflow automation process is to empower the worker, then that goal needs to be embodied at the outset. That means teams or groups of potential system users will help design their new work environment. The selection of the members of that team is a key issue, one that has trapped many system designers.

For example, if you design the system to meet the needs and capabilities of the most skilled worker in the group, what happens to the less competent worker? On the other hand, where is your quality program if the system meets the needs of the average, or still worse, the least skilled worker in the group? This is where the directive "create and adjust" becomes useful.

Expect the unexpected

Requests for technology will grow in unpredictable ways. The well-used phrase, "What have you done for me lately?" epitomizes the evolution of technology in a typical organization. After a year-and-a-half of computerized work at the bank in our case study, people noticed that some days they worked exclusively on their computers. This raised the issue of telecommuting, created demands for machines at home and calls for notebook computers.

Your new workflow system will also create unpredictable heroes. The insignificant claims processor who used to sit unnoticed at the last desk may become the technology guru. She may be the person everyone in the section seeks out to answer questions about how the system works and how certain tasks can be processed. Though it's difficult, if not impossible, to predict who will be the departmental technology wizard, you can be sure there will be one or several. Capitalize on these unexpected champions. Support their efforts to coach their co-workers; give them expanded roles, perhaps using them as coaches and tutors for the adjunct training sessions we described above.

By its very nature the specifics of the unpredictable are unknown, but we do know that you will have surprises. Users will find new ways to work with and work around the technology. Whole new sets of behaviors will be needed, and the people who are doing the work are the ones to make the necessary rules and standards.

Develop teamwork and foster diversity

We are orienting more toward teams and sharing. I was a member of one team. Initially people were drafted; no one wanted it. But it turned out to be an enjoyable project. It was very informal. There was collaboration and sharing; everyone owned the problem and the solution and contributed equally, even though people were at different levels.

Staff meetings are transformed; day-to-day project stuff has gone to on-line meetings. My own leadership is different. The new technology provides a common ground; a language. Our department head has changed the model of leadership. I am trying to emulate this change. Collaboration and teamwork are greatly enhanced. People are more accessible; whether or not they are in their offices. Now we keep the ball moving; things used to come to a standstill.

Workgroup computing is not a magic pill. And teamwork is not automatic. Groups of people who were not working well together before the introduction of technology will not automatically become collaborative. An efficient, clearly directed team certain of its objective and supportive of group efforts takes commitment and skilled leadership.

At the bank, the technology's sponsor, the department head, was also a master user. He believed in the technology, invested the time to learn it well, and set an example for his staff about how they could communicate with their own staffs. He was also committed to the technology as a teamwork tool. He experimented with ways to share information on-line so that face-to-face meetings were richer and more productive. With routine day-to-day information handled electronically, there was time at regular meetings for discussion of long-term vision and overall direction.

> as teams begin to collaborate electronically, they will build a body of knowledge

One of the most challenging elements of effective team-building is to support diversity to provide an environment in which different points of view can be expressed, welcomed, and allowed to thrive. That's why it's critical in any process-oriented workflow environment to provide a discussion-oriented electronic workspace as well. This provides an opportunity for team members to express themselves and creates a place where everyone involved in the project can work well together. This is especially beneficial when team members are geographically dispersed.

There is a caveat to this recommendation. Do not ask for peoples' opinions unless you are committed to honoring what they have to say.

Every workflow project has a built-in opportunity to practice the art of teamwork. By their very nature, workflow projects are marriages between business process and technology. And traditionally business people and technologists come from diverse points of view. By establishing a workflow team at the inauguration of the project, the scene is set for learning about teamwork. Once the project is launched, a team continues to be beneficial to support the growth of the effort and to fine-tune the system. The specifics of your work environment will determine whether the team members remain the same or shift once the project is under way.

We all have much to learn about how to work effectively in groups. In some ways, computer networks—serving as electronic umbilical cords—help the process. But there are other ways in which they add to the challenge. The commitment to teamwork is primary. And the openness to experimentation is also critical. As teams begin to collaborate electronically, they will build a body of knowledge.

This knowledge, in turn, becomes part of the educational process we mentioned earlier in this chapter. Thus each team has something to contribute to the whole and to the continuing process of education. The cycle supports itself in growing a body of knowledge and experience that enables new generations of workers to thrive with workflow

Implementation Requirements
James H. Bair, Research Director
Gartner Group

Introduction

This chapter offers a view of workflow that goes beyond current implementation practices. Based on examples, it will list and describe some prevailing perspectives and biases. The basic necessity for improved workflow system implementation is increased awareness. It is essential to transcend the limits of narrowly defined perceptions, roles, and disciplines. Although the examples will illustrate the potential of expanded awareness of the work situation, these recommendations are grounded in over 15 years of experience and research into the improvement of organizational productivity.

The "aware-workflow" paradigm creates new requirements for system implementors. It requires that management, end-users, and customers be brought together into a process that ensures the effective use of the new technology, not just the design and implementation. This approach is more user-centered than previous methods of understanding requirements. The process has three components compared to the traditional focus on technology alone:

Workflow Systems: Computer-based technologies used by people working together in virtual offices on common work objects such as forms, documents, and folders.

Methods: Proven techniques for involving end-users and management in the design of the work system based on total quality management and communication science. The work system includes how the technology is used, the activities and processes that have to be changed, and the ongoing support requirements. It integrates end-users into the design and ongoing success of the system, and provides increased support of management's objectives.

Communications: The interpersonal communications between individuals including meetings, phone, e-mail, teleconferencing, and paper-based interaction that can be quantified through the application of user-centered methods.

Implementation methods

User-centered implementation methods

Special implementation requirements result because workflow technology fundamentally changes the way users work together. Changing work processes and activities requires understanding the current work system and then consciously redesigning it to take advantage of the technology. Implementors need to go beyond traditional systems analysis by gathering collective insight into all of the work related behavior. Implementation requires assessment of the key communication behaviors including team membership, communication patterns, and customer relations. Workflows, document/form life cycles, and information sources also must be identified.

Implementors need participatory methods such as workshops, interviews, and questionnaires prepared to ensure that workflow technology is willingly used. Involving end-users, managers, and customers in the design of a new system will result in improved acceptance by users and by the organization. User acceptance can be overlooked when systems are installed through management edict. This can greatly increase the probability of system breakdowns that could have been avoided by motivated and involved users.

The methods take a team through the following steps:

1. Clarifying work objectives for teams
2. Identifying the inhibitors to achieving objectives
3. Determining how workflow systems can remove the inhibitors
4. Reviewing communication requirements to include all persons in the related communication network
5. Developing a team action plan.

The Need for User-Centered Methods

User-centered methods are needed when computers are used for collaborative work such as co-authoring a document, circulating a memo, preparing a briefing, sending mail, filing and retrieving documents, managing engineering drawings; or for applications based on forms such as expense claims, personnel action requests, budget planning documents, travel requests. These methods can also can be used for more data-based work, such as insurance claims processing, loan applications, airline reservations, and purchase order processing.

> office work cannot be designed without the participation of office workers

Research into why there has been such a "puny payoff" from office computers has brought attention to the necessity of designing office work, not just installing workflow systems. Office work cannot be designed without the participation of office workers because it is less structured, requiring worker discretion in the treatment of each work object. Decisions are often made on the spot regarding the actions to be taken and when. This is the nature of white-collar work: It requires decision-making capability on the part of each worker. For example, consider the array of alternatives and tradeoffs in making business travel arrangements, developing a marketing plan, or processing a loan application.

The user-centered methodology provides an approach to successfully involving end-users by:

- Systematically obtaining end-user input to the analysis and design of the work system
- Involving management to ensure the execution of their delegated responsibilities
- Involving all the success "influencers" including senior management, customers, related members of the management team, and other stakeholders
- Identifying and supporting their communication needs.

The benefits of user-centered methods

User-centered methods ensure that workflow applications reflect the work actually being done in organizations rather than reflecting an abstract representation. It will enable organizations to obtain payoff from the widespread use of networked PCs and client/server architectures. New workflow applications will achieve ROI (return on investment) because of:

- Increased workflow acceptance and usage by the organization
- Technology that better leverages the organization's mission-critical processes
- Enhanced competitive position
- Planned access to information as a corporate resource
- Increased opportunities for organizational effectiveness as:
  - Labor is reinvested in revenue activities, not in communication overhead
  - Alternative activities and processes are selected for increased efficiency
  - Workflow inefficiencies are reengineered

- Meeting user needs better:
  - The use of the technology will be planned, not left to chance
  - User needs will be fed back to workflow designers
  - Methods for the continued improvement of work processes will be part of the system
  - Interpersonal communication is treated as a fundamental component of the work system.

The foundation of user-centered methods is communication

Implementation requirements focus on human communication when the user is emphasized in the implementation process. Human communication includes the everyday interactions among individuals. In the context of workflow, the interactions include the transfer of work objects among workers and the use of other media such as telephones and meetings. This is a broad definition of communication that treats the use of any media in a similar way. By looking at the user as an individual in a communication network that uses many different media to accomplish work, we avoid missing critical components of the work process. We also can apply rigorous methodologies from the research world with very practical consequences.

Communication science is an interdisciplinary field with academic departments and industrial applications. The focus is on understanding and improving human communication media such as meetings, telephoning, e-mail, and documents. Communication is viewed as the critical process in the functioning of organizations, if for no other reason than 75 percent of all white-collar time is spent in communication with an average of 35 percent in meetings alone.

> a system must show the overall context of workflow and allow for the imprecise nature of work

There is a strong relationship between human communication and organizational performance. Over the past 15 years, an organizational model has been developed based on pioneering work at Stanford Research Institute. This model shows how to improve the performance of teams and organizations based on experiments with communication including workflow, and its validity has withstood the test of time. Most recently, workflow has been recognized as a communication process in which the behavior of participants must be a major consideration in the design of the technology implementation.

The "communication-aware" approach has been developed and tested in several major corporations, including an international engineering company and a major satellite communications company. Various forms of this methodology have been used extensively in the implementation of workflow systems. Focusing on the broader issues of human communication has overcome the limitations of traditional workflow implementation methods.

Problems with current workflow implementation

Engineering Orientation

Improving the approach to a complex process requires identification of the problem areas; unfortunately, the basic orientation of current implementation practice appears at fault. But the fault is only apparent if we align ourselves with the user's values and perspective. The traditional design is driven by the highly technical, precise, and demanding computer and engineering sciences. To produce good programmers our educational system begins infusing them with the utmost of empirical rationality at an early age. A new way of thinking and problem solving is inculcated, derived from the abstract tools of mathematics and engineering. At the end of 4-6 years, this educational process has forever engendered a new thought process that is brought to bear on design. Collectively, a culture with its own language is created, the rigorous, logical domain of pro-gramming languages, rule specification, and input-output devices.

In this culture, the questions posed do not arise from user needs for the most part, but rather from technology potential: "What neat thing can I get my software to do?" The result of competent effort is a system that functions well for the programmer-designer. Of course, accommodating the user is merely a matter of adding some user support documentation, training, and an introduction to computers for good measure. The end result typifies message systems and other office systems today: *a working non-solution.*

The resultant system typically can be demonstrated and shown to perform in some way; for example, routing and managing pur-chase orders. However, the user is confronted with op-erational opacity, indecipherable error conditions and error messages, and a plethora of control characters, function keys, and rigid steps that must be followed unconditionally. Rarely does workflow software permit the end-user to view the overall flow, resulting in lost time when questions beyond the immediate processing task arise. This unpredictable time loss has negative bottom line impact. To meet the needs of users, a sys-tem must show the overall context of workflow, reflect communication needs, and allow for the imprecise na-ture of work.

> workflow implementation requires that we become aware of how we work together

Divergent Perceptions of User Needs

Once the engineering orientation is overcome through a user-centered ap-proach, we are faced with another set of alternative perspectives. Implementation problems would be solved if the solution were merely to meet user needs. The question confronting implementors is, "Who is the user?" There are four very different perceptions of user needs that confound even the most user-oriented design approach: (1) what the system-chooser will buy, (2) what the user says he or she needs, (3) what industry can develop, and (4) what analysts say will ac-tually increase user effectiveness.

(1) The system chooser is the buyer or decision maker in an institution ac-quiring a service. His or her criteria are primarily economic, including a limited investment per person, a predetermined rate of return, and a defined amortization period. Very often, up-front economic constraints prohibit investment in imple-mentation and support that are fundamental to long range viability.

(2) A classic misconception is that the user can tell designers what he or she needs. No different from life in general, the process of self-diagnosis is woe-fully inadequate as the sole determinant of needs. Certainly, users must be polled and seriously regarded in selecting opportunities for system application, but su-per-human powers of prediction should be left to others. A user cannot anticipate

the form of a technology unknown to him; energy is much better spent determining the user's objectives and criteria for success in the context of his current work environment.

(3) Even if the user could anticipate the optimum workflow design, the industry currently would have difficulty delivering such a workflow product. In numerous studies, it has been found that currently available systems could not meet the chooser's or the user's criteria. Perhaps we are seeing industry's reaction to user demands that results in a situation where neither user requirements nor industry capability is met. Industry, dominated by the working non-solution approach, perceives users' needs in light of the current capabilities of marketed technology. For example, if users want an integrated credit purchasing and purchase authorization management system, they most likely will get an image management system that simply maintains digitized purchase records. The larger issue of the company's interface to the purchaser will probably be overlooked (c.f. Peter Senge's book on systems thinking). The limitation is not the potential of industry, but industry's perception of system design.

> workflow systems are different because they fundamentally change ongoing, human working relationships

(4) The convergence of the foregoing three perspectives still does not address the most important question: What will increase organizational effectiveness? Plagued with two sub-problems, how to measure effectiveness changes and how to determine the causal relationship to design variables, this perspective remains a frontier for the new workflow paradigm. A surprising conclusion from research is that users cannot judge what will improve their effectiveness. Measurement of productivity factors must be done indirectly, regardless of whether the factors are the efficiency of screen layout or the robustness of rules in workflow activities.

Thus, user's perceptions must be taken as only one of four perspectives of system implementation, and do not reflect complete requirements. However, the user's perspective as stated above is a very important component in implementation success. User's perceptions can provide an understanding of expectations of system characteristics, and provide the basis of user participation in implementation, both critical for successful system implementation and acceptance.

Limited Awareness of Work

The reason users' perceptions should not be the basis of workflow implementation is straightforward, resulting from limits in awareness. Once the awareness issue is understood, the work system design can be a powerful and permanent improvement over the existing system. In offices or any work situation, we know what we need to be aware of to execute the immediate tasks. Work is actually so complex that if we were aware of every detail, it would be overwhelming. If we had to think through every motion in the process of walking, we would never get anywhere.

Awareness is more limited when we use tools, ranging from a hammer to a computer. When we are using the hammer to pound in a nail, awareness focuses on the act of hitting the nail, not on the hammer itself. But if the hammer handle breaks, then our awareness dramatically shifts from the nail pounding process to the hammer and the different process of fixing it. Designers call tool unawareness "transparency," a major goal of current graphic user interfaces.

Philosophers have studied the issues of awareness for ages and written volumes of complex treatises on awareness, consciousness, and existence (existentialism). From all this, there are two phrases that describe the shift in consciousness from one part of experience to another. "Ready-to-hand" describes the behavior (use of the toolhammer) when we are not aware of it. "Present-to-hand" describes the awareness of the behavior when something happens such as an unexpected breakdown.

In the implementation of workflow systems, much of the work behavior is not addressed in the workflow design. Consequently, working non-solutions are implemented as if the work would never vary from the first analysis. But work is unpredictable, non-deterministic, and fraught with breakdowns. Breakdowns are usually resolved through communication that is not defined in the initial workflow. Workflow implementation requires that we become aware of how we work together in order to implement computer technology that builds toward to improvement.

The behaviors of interpersonal communication are largely ready-to-hand. Not only are we generally oblivious to the ways we communicate, but we spend most of our work time communicating. Meetings seem to be comparable to the "nail hammering process" where we invest enormous amounts of time with little awareness of results and even less of the process. Previous writings have questioned the use of meetings in organizations and millions of dollars of research and improvement programs have been conducted to little avail. Meetings may be "broken" as an effective tool for investing business labor resources, but the breakdown has not yet resulted in widespread "present-to-hand" for meetings. Similarly, the use of communications tools has not become "present-to-hand." Certainly, phone, fax, e-mail, and paper have become "ready-to-hand" tools, but there is no thoughtful set of behaviors for optimal use. In fact, e-mail may actually be approaching a present-to-hand level of awareness as users become overloaded with e-mail items.

The most important problem facing workflow design is the lack of awareness of the actual behaviors of work. When workflow is ready-to-hand, designers will miss the breakdowns that are causing inefficiency and loss of effectiveness. Designers may model the flow of a document through a series of workstations only to bypass necessary information acquired by phone or meetings. Or they may overlook the flow of information through the use of "Post-Its" or yelling over the office dividers. Research into offices has documented the importance of serendipity conversations at the water-cooler or copier. Note that the contribution of research is to identify behaviors that are ready-to-hand before a breakdown makes them present-to-hand. The challenge has been to convince users that working differently will improve effectiveness. We have not had much success in the area of meetings that are run the same as they have been for fifty years, and fewer than a thousand electronic meeting support systems are installed. However, workflow systems are different because they fundamentally change ongoing, human working relationships.

Awareness of the human communication network

The organization is a communication system

Viewing the organization as a communication system overcomes the limitations of more narrow perspectives. It can enable users to make their work processes present-to-hand so that designers can model all of the relevant behaviors. Instead of tracking a form as it moves from one workstation to the next, the conversations that comprise all the work can be supported.

For example, tracking special health insurance claims when there is an exception illustrates the importance of the larger communication system. The straightforward description of the form with data fields such as insured's name, ID number, Plan ID, MD's name, illness name, treatment, is done first. Subprocesses are built to transfer data from handwritten forms to electronic and to update the data base. Steps are coded into the system for connecting the incoming forms to the corresponding work steps, usually associated with a work station. Thus, when a claim form arrives from a client, a data entry clerk calls up the client's record on the screen and requests a new electronic form. The data is entered from the paper form and compared to the database that shows current eligibility.

The breakdown in this example occurred when the clerk saw that eligibility was expired because the client terminated employment. Of course, insurability should continue under the new laws (COBRA). But the employer had not forwarded the application for continued coverage under COBRA to the insurance management company responsible for administration of the plan. In this case, the breakdown was compounded by the use of different companies for administration and insurance. The clerk had no choice in this data processing system but to deny the claim or pass it on to a supervisor (who also denied it). This actual case illustrates how exceptions lead to uncoordinated processes (the employer not delivering the authorized application for COBRA to the insurance manager) that cannot be resolved because communication beyond the basic workflow is not supported.

Work flows and people communicate

The previous example illustrates the traditional approach to business processes that focuses on a narrowly defined task (insurance claim processing) and does not enable communication with related functions. In this case, the clerk should have been able to reach the employer in some way to check eligibility, either through access to a common data base or through personal contact. Since this is such a rare exception (most COBRA applications reach the manager before the first claim is submitted), providing special access to the employer is relatively expensive. However, an e-mail connection with the employer's representative would have cleared up the exception in a few minutes of effort. The lack of coordination resulted in much more effort as the client called, wrote letters, resubmitted the claim, creating additional processing overhead.

An example of a user-centered solution

In some cases, workflow is not the solution even though a workflow system is planned. One case involved the operation of geosynchronous satellites for telecommunications services. The major satellite operations company was responsible for maintaining the digital communications network worldwide as a commercial service. Revenues from services had to offset the enormous cost of launching and maintaining satellites. The charges based on data transfer for units of time were (and are) a profitable business. But

> if people do not communicate, then work does not flow

satellites require maintenance and constant monitoring to ensure they remain in service. Since data transfer rates for each satellite are in the terabits, any downtime for a satellite is extremely costly.

The satellites are monitored by a round-the-clock engineering team in Southern California. Engineers work for eight-hour shifts, sitting at workstations with Star-Trekian equipment including displays of real-time data. Each engineer is responsible for relaying any observed conditions to the succeeding team that might forewarn of impending difficulty. Different ways of ensuring this transfer had been implemented, such as a 15 minute overlap of the engineers' shifts. Despite attention to the transfer of critical information, conditions observed in one shift were not being communicated to the succeeding shift resulting in excessive satellite downtime. Various techniques were explored, but none seemed to ensure the transfer of information, leaving engineers to their own devices, such as Post-It notes, scrapes of paper, and spoken conversation. Indeed, one failure was traced to a Post-It note falling off the workstation surface.

The solution was clear once the need for alternative communication media was recognized. It became a simple matter of providing e-mail, electronic bulletin boards, computer conferences, and voice-mail for the engineers. In numerous other situations, the hi-tech environment belies the unsophisticated approach to supporting the flow and coordination of work. Once the engineers could leave messages in a computer, the transfer of information became managed rather than random. The arriving shift would immediately be presented with in-baskets, blinking alerts, and other signals that information was being transferred from the previous shift. When information was not read, alerts would be sent to a supervisor who would then follow-up in the case of unscheduled absence or oversight.

Additional advantages included the sharing of knowledge that was previously lost, a result intended by the system implementors, but a welcome surprise to management. Engineers could read all appropriate items and learn of conditions in other satellite systems that would help them with their own. As communications were stored, a shared database of experience grew that further enhanced engineers' abilities. In addition, the extended reach of e-mail informed other concerned people, such as managers and R&D people. At the risk of hyperbole, the advantages represented a transformation of the working organization to a much more highly coordinated and error-free, responsive system. The specific problem of transferring information across shifts resulted in the opportunity for improvement in the overall communication system—both the human and the data communication system.

This example illustrates the extreme case when the solution was to support communication rather than apply traditional workflow technology. It is a contrast to the insurance claim processing example. However, the point that all work is composed of workflow in the context of all other communication is precisely the point. The satellite engineer's work could have been defined as a precise work package that would be routed to the next engineer for specific actions. The workflow could have included rules such as, "If satellite failure is eminent, route to supervisor." Such a limited assessment of user requirements would have led to the increase of bureaucracy, the decrease of individual capability and the loss of organizational learning. By increasing communication options, no bureaucracy was added while the process was made much more effective. The bottom line is, *if people do not communicate, then work does not flow.*

Implementation that supports the organization

Workflow analysis vs. Communication analysis

In the previous example, the communication process was ready-to-hand until the breakdown became so costly that it required attention. The solution was based on the straight-forward notion of adding communication options for the users involved. This contrasts sharply with the traditional approach to workflow. Workflow vendors and consultants today analyze a workflow setting by starting with work objects and tasks to be performed on them. The work object is described by fields in a form that become a database structure. Tasks are usually associated with workstations, a place where individuals work. Completing an action or a task on a work object then moves the object onto the next station. Presumably, all the information to complete the task is available to the operator at the station. Training must enable the operator to understand the necessary tasks at his/her workstation.

This workflow paradigm is quite limited by a number of assumptions. First, the information environment must be unambiguous, like the database structures that support it. Secondly, all the information must be ready-to-hand, not requiring any awareness of the overall process on the part of the user. Thirdly, it must be structured so that it can be described with little textual explanation. By contrast, when the entire communication context is examined as part of implementation, the workflow system will be far more effective and long-lived.

Communication subsumes workflow

We have emphasized the importance of human communication in the implementation of workflow systems. Communication subsumes workflow, which is actually another form of communication. When individuals work, they interact with each other through a variety of media, beyond the flow of work objects. A communications perspective views each person as a node in a communication network with linkages to others through meetings, phone calls, e-mail, documents. These links can be drawn (graphed) showing the proportions of media used during a typical period. These proportions can reflect the amount of time, the quantity of text, or the number of pages. The links also can represent the frequency of communications showing the relationship to time; for example, showing periods of frequent communication versus slack times.

> when individuals work, they interact with each other through a variety of media, beyond the flow of work objects

There are several techniques for gathering quantitative information about communication. The user-centered methods collect communication data through interviews and other self-reports by the individuals in the implementation setting. Each person's subjective recollection of who is communicated with, when, and how much is accurate enough to provide the context for implementation. Other methods can be used for more objective quantification of communication such as specially designed questionnaires, diaries, and observations done by the implementors. A range of accuracy is available depending upon the precision required. Usually, users' report that they need interaction with other workers, a certain number of times a day, within a certain time period, to facilitate the processing of a work object, is sufficient for implementation planning.

A typical workflow implementation would begin by identifying the work objects and their related tasks, such as a loan application form and the decisions to be made as it moves through an organization. Tasks are accomplished at each station based on the communication of information beyond that available in the data bases. A far more effective implementation results if the sources of information, the persons communicated with, are identified. Then those communication channels can be supported through e-mail (address lists can be provided for easy identification of the related persons), phone mail, computer conferences (collaboration bases), PC-fax, shared-screen conferencing.

Conclusion

The new requirements for workflow system implementors center on users' need for interpersonal communication. Uncovering user needs is best done by applying user-centered methods as part of the implementation process. User-centered methods involve users directly in the description of their work including the traditional concept of workflow. User-centered methods have far more longevity than traditional approaches that rely heavily on engineering perspectives. The methods bring together users to describe their work in terms of objectives and inhibitors to achieving objectives. The historical roots of workflow are in engineering systems analysis that overlooks fundamental work behavior, such as human communication. The concepts, *user-centered* and *communications perspective,* have a lot of overlap. A user-centered approach will ultimately arrive at communication requirements.

> the concepts, *user-centered* and *communications perspective*, have a lot of overlap

The benefits of combining user-centered and communication approaches are listed in this chapter. There are two key benefits. First, users will be involved in the implementation process in a meaningful way and thus will be more committed to system success and more accepting of the new technology and the accompanying work changes. Second, the vital communications-based work that usually occurs outside the workflow system will be identified for support. The approaches outlined here create awareness of the often overlooked interpersonal communications that complement workflow.

Improved implementation has been confounded by four divergent perceptions, none of which will provide an accurate understanding of the implementation requirements. The views of the system chooser (buyer), the end-user, the vendors, and the analysts must be combined. Reliance on any one perception, even that of the end-user, will lead to a short-lived implementation with severely limited ROI.

Increasing awareness is the crux of successful implementation. Years of experience have reinforced this conclusion. Workflow systems are ostensibly implemented to improve work through increased efficiency and effectiveness. In actuality, there are "breakdowns" in the process that warrant the consideration of any improvement in the first place. The vapid notion of "cost reduction" is most often cited as the justification for workflow. Inevitably, analysis of the entire work environment, especially the interpersonal communications, reveals breakdowns that have been "ready-to-hand." Becoming aware of and repairing the breakdowns leads to sustainable implementations, extending the payback period for the overall investment. This extends ROI beyond the short sighted "downsizing" that obliterates jobs showing savings in the current quarter or at best the current year.

The brief examples of workflow projects that addressed the broader issues of communications are the tip of the iceberg. Several million dollars worth of projects have supported similar findings. Workflow as typically defined by the workflow and image processing vendors is much too limited a perspective. Workflow implementations are often "working non-solutions" because they address a narrowly defined process, but overlook the communication system in which the workflows are imbedded. They "work" by processing transactions and routing work objects, but they do not make the fundamental improvements to the human-computer system. Increasing awareness and treating the entire system with workflow as one important component, will yield the best implementation for today and the future.

Notes:

Bair, James H. "Contrasting Workflow Models: Getting to the Roots of Three Vendors," Proceedings of Groupware '93 (David Coleman, Editor) San Mateo, CA: Morgan Kaufman Publishers, 1993.

Bair, James H. and Laura Mancuso. The Office Systems Cycle, Palo Alto, CA: HP Press, 1986.

Bair, James. H. "A Layered Model of Organizations: Communication Process and Performance," *Journal of Organization Computing* (2)1, 1991, pp. 187-203.

Bair, James H., "Computer Support for Cooperative Work: Addressing Meeting Mania," *Proceedings of COMPCON '89* (Institute for Electrical and Electronics Engineers Computer Conference), Washington, D.C.: IEEE Press, 1989.

Bair, James H., "Communication Network Analysis Tutorial," Presented at Seybold Executive Forum (Long Island, NY.), Patricia Seybold Office Computing Group, Boston, MA, 1992.

Bowen, The Puny Payoff from Office Computers, *Fortune Magazine*, May 26, 1986.

Kolbus, David, Alexia Martin, James H. Bair, et al., Collaborative Technology Environments, Multi-client Study, SRI International, Menlo Park, CA, 1992 (5 Volumes).

Senge, Peter M. The Fifth Discipline: *The Art and Practice of the Learning Organization*, New York: Doubleday, 1990

Automating the Business Environment

Dr. Bruce Silver, Principal
Bruce Silver Associates

Why the explosion of interest in workflow technology?

Perhaps the most significant legacy to date of the document imaging vendors is a totally new software discipline, technically unrelated to the technology of imaging. It is the concept of business process automation, or workflow. Where it once was sold mainly as a feature that enables productivity gain in image-based transaction and case processing solutions, now workflow technology is asserting itself as a business in its own right, with or without document management or imaging. And the technology of workflow software is changing, expanding beyond the narrow requirements of the imaging market. Now, workflow is also becoming a key battleground in the war for supremacy in LAN-based e-mail and other mass market network applications.

Why the explosion of interest in workflow technology? Driving it are two principal factors, one based on economics, the other on technology. The first is a recognition among business and information systems executives that competitiveness in the '90s demands automating the entire *process* of a business activity, not just the individual discrete tasks. The second follows directly from the emergence of a new desktop computing environment—one capable of integrating multiple windowed applications, and networked to other equally powerful desktops throughout the enterprise.

Despite the huge investment in automation of white collar work over the past 25 years, many studies have shown that office productivity has not substantially increased. This stands in stark contrast to factory automation, where investment in computing technology has dramatically increased the manufacturing output for each worker. The rise of global competition for markets has now made productivity a basic survival issue for most companies, and we have seen in recent years tremendous changes in the way companies are organized to perform office work: leaner organizations, decentralization, flatter management structures. These organizational changes certainly could not have occurred without many of the recent innovations in computing, such as client/server network computing and the incredible power of the desktop PC.

But while companies continue to invest in computing power, it has become clear that there is something in the nature of office work itself that resists improvement merely from the sheer application of computing horsepower. A new kind of software is required that deals directly with the nature of the business process, the need to integrate information from multiple applications, and the contributions of multiple individuals within the organization. Fortunately, the office computing environment in the '90s is suddenly finding itself *capable of* running that kind of software, with desktop operating systems capable of running multiple applications at once in separate windows on the screen and exchanging information automatically between them, with electronic mail reaching across the enterprise and beyond, connecting workers in a way never before possible.

The combination of tremendous economic pressure—creating the demand for business process automation—with recent transformations in the office computing environment, the technology enabler has given rise to a wide variety of new software products that are grouped under the umbrella term, workflow automation.

What, then, do we call "workflow?" Simply defined, it is the process by which individual tasks come together to complete a "transaction"—a clearly defined business process—within an enterprise. Such a transaction may occur repetitively in the normal course of business and follow a standard set of processing procedures—handling an insurance claim, for example or it may be purely ad hoc, perhaps occurring once only, but nevertheless a process that involves the coordination of multiple applications or users, and that needs to be tracked and automated.

Some transactions fall in between. They are not part of the regular business process, but recur from time to time, and follow a more or less standard procedure: a check request, for example, or scheduling job candidate interviews, or a travel authorization.

The transaction or process may be relatively simple, consisting of only of a few steps: For example, take a customer's call; find the requested information or activity status; and pass the requested information back to the customer. Or it could be extremely complex, spanning many different departments, requiring the involvement of a dozen or more individuals, and consisting perhaps of hundreds of discrete tasks. Workflow automation in the broadest sense includes all of these.

Production versus ad hoc workflow

While the business need for workflow automation is broad—perhaps universal—defining the *market* for workflow automation software and services is not a simple task. The market is still in an early formative stage, and most users are still wrestling with the basic concepts of workflow software and the relative value of specific features and functions.

There are many basic ways for users to draw distinctions among the many workflow products currently being offered: Is the product intended to automate a line-of-business process or a general office procedure? Is it intended to be used by clerical workers, by professionals, or "knowledge workers"? Is the work driven by the processing of documents or folders, or is it better viewed as a set of task instructions and user decisions, that may or may not involve attached documents? All of these are valid distinctions, but probably the most basic differentiator of workflow software products is whether they automate Production Workflow or Ad Hoc Workflow.

Production Workflow involves repetitive processes, typically ones critical to the core business function. Examples include insurance claims, loan origination, accounts payable, or sales order entry. Most often—but not always—they are clerical, document-driven, and tightly integrated with line-of-business computer applications. They could, however, represent routine office activity: a travel authorization or expense report, for example. What distinguishes a Production Workflow environment is that the process obeys a set of codified rules and policies that are consistently applied to every work item.

Ad Hoc Workflow, on the other hand, automates unique or occasionally used processes. These processes may be mission-critical to the core business, but are more often associated with routine office procedures: correspondence management, interview scheduling, or document revision and approval. They are typically used by knowledge workers, are not usually document-driven, and not tightly integrated with line-of-business application software. What distinguishes Ad Hoc Workflow is the fact that the process required for a given work item is not predefined, but more a matter of individual judgment and decision. Where Production Workflow seeks control and transaction efficiency by integrating computer activity, Ad Hoc Workflow is more concerned with coordination and integrating human activity.

> defining the
> *market* for
> workflow
> automation
> software and
> services is not a
> simple task

Workflow and imaging

The segmentation between Production and Ad Hoc Workflow reflects a real division in the nascent workflow software market. The majority of the workflow software business today is concentrated on the Production side. Even more specifically, most of the workflow automation implemented to date has been associated with document imaging technology, using workflow software provided by the document image management vendors. However, the use of imaging technology with workflow is certainly not a requirement. The need for workflow automation goes far beyond the imaging market, but the link is historical, and in many ways natural.

FileNet Corporation in the mid-1980s was the first to perceive that the largest benefit of document imaging for businesses overrun with paper was not so much storage and retrieval as moving and coordinating the flow of paper-based information throughout a department or enterprise. FileNet put workflow automation tools at the heart of their document imaging software, and defined the core set of services, development tools, and administrative functions that virtually all document imaging vendors offer in some form today.

The association of imaging with workflow is a natural one because the businesses with the biggest transaction processing costs are typically ones with high volume paper-driven operations involving complex interactions between multiple users: claims, loans, credit operations, etc. Because the paper-processing costs are high, the value of improving transaction efficiency with workflow software is also high. For this reason Production Workflow software, particularly in conjunction with imaging, can command prices on the order of $2000 per user or higher, and still be regarded as generating a high return on investment.

While Production Workflow usually can be justified by cost-reducing a particular business process, Ad Hoc Workflow is geared to a less specific need. The buyer's motivation for Ad Hoc Workflow comes from a sense that routine office work needs new tools for coordinating and tracking activities that involve multiple users. Despite the proliferation of low cost productivity tools like project management, calendar software, and even electronic mail, these products by themselves do not allow the coordination of processes that involve multiple steps, or multiple users, or that tracks the activity status.

Unlike Production Workflow, this need is quite broadly based, touching essentially all office workers, and the ultimate Ad Hoc Workflow market, as measured by the number of users, will be far higher. The demand for Ad Hoc Workflow is a logical byproduct of the tremendous growth in PC networking and e-mail, which is truly the most significant computing phenomenon of the 1990s. Without workflow, users may be connected over the network but their work is not, and the productivity of the workgroup suffers accordingly. Workflow aims to create that connection and that group productivity gain.

Unfortunately, to most business line managers, the cost of inefficiency in routine office work is invisible. It is at least certainly hard to measure. That means that the value of Ad Hoc Workflow software is hard to justify on a return on investment basis. It certainly cannot command thousands of dollars per seat. Instead its price, or value, is being set by the norms applied to mass market PC applications, a few hundred dollars a seat at most.

Perhaps for this reason, the Ad Hoc market is likely to be driven by the mass market players in electronic mail and network applications.

Workflow market segmentation

While Production versus Ad Hoc Workflow represents the basic division of today's workflow market, there are other factors that help sort out the growing list of new workflow products. One interesting dimension considers whether the tasks in the process are Document-Centered or User-Centered. In other words, is the work defined by the processing required by the routed document or folder, or is it defined as a more general set of tasks to be performed by multiple users in a coordinated fashion?

Document-centered production workflow

The most mature portion of the workflow market today is the Document-Centered Production segment, the upper left quadrant of Figure 1. This segment is dominated by the image management vendors. In this segment, the work process is document-driven, mostly as paper. Because of the high cost of processing transactions using manual paper routing, the combination of workflow and imaging.

Technology provides a particularly high return on investment. The benefit of workflow automation today often represents the key to payback on the whole document imaging investment, still an expensive technology. Even at prices exceeding $1000 per seat, production imaging workflow can often be cost justified on a hard dollar basis. For this reason, this segment is also the "high end" workflow market.

More than simply work routing, workflow in this segment is increasingly concerned with automating complex processes involving information from multiple computer applications. The capability of integrating information from multiple sources is a workflow feature that the Production Workflow vendor typically stresses even more than automatic work routing. The integration usually involves automatic exchange of data between multiple applications simultaneously running in windows on a single user's desktop. Typically these might include a terminal emulation program running a mainframe application, a LAN-based document management database, and a desktop word processing program.

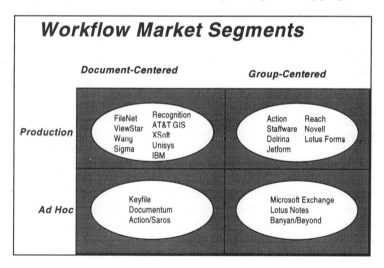

Figure 1. Workflow market segments.

When document processing is part of a production environment, often multiple users are performing similar tasks.

Workflow software allows work to be routed to shared processing queues, from which it is dynamically distributed to the next available user, in assembly-line fashion. Saying that the work process is "document-driven" means that the particular set of tasks that must be executed fits a standard pattern associated with a particular document type or set of documents. Examples include the processing of an application for credit, an invoice, or an insurance claim. Today, the "source documents" for these documents are often paper, but increasingly they will be electronically generated.

Standardization and proliferation of Electronic Data Interchange (EDI) will force Production Workflow products to embrace these new types of documents, while continuing the need to handle paper. So will the growth of a host of new technologies connecting mobile sales, service, and professional workers with a centralized administrative processing center: pen computing, wireless networks, even cross-enterprise e-mail. The nature of the document may change, but the process remains one of transaction automation.

Group-centered ad hoc workflow

The bottom right quadrant of Figure 1 represents a contrasting vision of workflow automation. Group-Centered Ad Hoc Workflow starts from the assumption that the work management problem is essentially coordination and tracking of the activity of multiple individuals. Workflow is essentially work routing from user to user.

> the nature of the document may change, but the process remains one of transaction automation

The work being routed is a request to the user to perform some task, or make a decision (for example, "approve or reject this proposal").

At its simplest level, this type of workflow exerts no control at all over computer applications. It just routes messages embodying these requests for action or decision. A common mechanism uses an electronic "form." Each user performing work indicates completion of the requested task or decision by a checkbox or action button on the electronic form. This automatically forwards the work package to the next user defined in the workflow, possibly dependent on the specific action or decision indicated. Each user receiving the work package in succession may see a different version of the form, reflecting the particular work request and decision options defined by the workflow originator.

Such a baseline capability—delivering instruction messages to users on a network—is already within the reach of most networked computer users today by the technology of e-mail. Adding workflow in this sense of sequential "intelligent forms routing" will be a major enhancement provided by most e-mail vendors in the next year, including Microsoft and Lotus. This form of workflow will become nearly universal within two or three years as simply a standard e-mail function, at little or no additional cost. This will represent the workflow "mass market," or the low end of the workflow spectrum.

Even the workflow automation built into e-mail will offer significant benefit. While the work processes it affects may not generally be "document-driven," documents—including images and annotations—can easily be included as e-mail attachments. In addition, software "agents," or background programs monitoring a user's mailbox for incoming messages, will be able to filter and detect arriving workflow packages, and initiate certain desktop functions automatically. Even deadlines for each workstep can be assigned, and alarm messages sent automatically if the work is late.

Such functionality can provide significant task coordination with little change to today's mail systems. By itself, however, this form of workflow automation provides little control over the work process. It cannot answer basic questions like, "Where is the work now? What has been done to it? What are the actions remaining?" These kinds of questions require a central tracking database that is updated by all the individual workflow processing events. Such a capability is something beyond what standard e-mail will provide. Such a workflow tracking database is a key component of specialized workflow engines that will allow the Group-Centered work model to deal with critical business problems.

Group-centered production workflow

The ability to organize and track complex processes performed by workgroups leads to a grander vision of workflow, one in which regulation and tracking of human activity is as important as integrating computer applications. The Group-Centered Production Workflow quadrant, in the top right of Figure 1, represents that vision. Here the processes to be controlled or coordinated obey a definite and stable, albeit sometimes fuzzy, set of rules and procedures; they are not Ad Hoc. Examples include processing purchase requisitions, field service problem resolution, or even new product development. The goal in each case is a faster and smoother process achieved by coordinating the activities of multiple individuals or groups.

In contrast to the Document-Centered Production segment, these processes are often measured in weeks rather than seconds or hours. They also do not require dynamic distribution of work from shared work queues. Consequently the Group-Centered production segment fits well with e-mail as a work transport, but will go far beyond the capabilities provided by the mail system itself.

For example, intelligent rules-based routing will be required, as well as interfaces to exchange information with external applications both on the LAN and on legacy hosts. Automatic retrieval and assembly of documents from various sources may be specified for different users in the workflow, even though the work is not simply document processing. Administrative utilities that override the workflow route and move work from one queue to another will also be typical in this type of workflow. But the most important differentiator will be work tracking and reporting.

Document-centered ad hoc workflow

Finally, the fourth quadrant, Document-Centered Ad Hoc Workflow, includes some special cases. Like the Group-Centered Ad Hoc segment, the workflows represent unique or unstructured processes, but ones revolving around the processing of documents, either electronically generated or scanned images. This category includes products oriented to document authoring and revision. Other examples include correspondence management, or document routing for comment or approval.

Products in this category provide tools for any user to initiate an Ad Hoc Workflow, but they are often closely integrated with a document management system. Such an arrangement is useful if workflow involves the sharing of significant document volumes, particularly images or other large object types. The link to a document management system allows documents to be moved "by reference"; that is, without moving the physical file over the network, since all users are assumed to be connected to the document server. In the near future, facilities for indexing and high volume storage of large objects will become a capability of network operating systems, such as Novell's Image Services for NetWare. This may spur the introduction of a number of new products that provide much of the functionality required for this segment.

> **the payback from workflow comes from handling the exception cases**

Workflow and reengineering

Because of the strong association of workflow software with the business process, the implementation of workflow software often occurs in conjunction with a broader initiative of reengineering that process. Business process reengineering involves analyzing how an organization does its work now, and how it could be changed to make the process more efficient, particularly with the application of technology. This is typically a significant effort, involving the use of third party services—often either by the software provider or an independent consultant.

Many of the details of current work processes are merely the legacy of age-old rules based on outmoded organizational structures and constraints of handling and communicating information, particularly the physical movement of paper. Workflow software allows new structures and new flexibility not available when these rules first were created, and tends to strongly encourage business process reengineering.

While business process reengineering helps greatly to maximize the economic benefit of workflow software, it is important to bear in mind that it is not required, and sometimes not even recommended before the initial application of workflow technology. A lesson learned by the first generation of workflow users is that often the "ultimate solution" cannot be predicted by analysis alone. It has to be evolved through experience. Today, users are increasingly getting their feet wet with workflow software on a pilot basis, and reengineering the business process incrementally as they go.

What users want

Even though the workflow market is still in its early stages of development, some aspects of what users want are already clear. Most users today are looking for workflow products that:

- **Allow them to get started quickly.**

If developing a workflow application requires months of study and massive program development as part of a monolithic reengineering effort, users are wary. They have a right to be. Experience has shown that an incremental approach, evolving from a quick pilot application to embrace a gradually increasing number of users and reengineered process functions, has a greater chance of success. This means users are looking for workflow software tools that encourage this quick-start incremental approach and rapid application development.

- **Allow them to modify and evolve the workflow themselves.**

Sophisticated users know intuitively that the "right" workflow design will require their own experience, plus a certain amount of trial and error. They certainly do not want workflow modification requests to add to the MIS application backlog. Quick response is mandatory. For this reason, users are demanding increasingly graphical tools that allow non-programmers such as themselves—to modify and maintain workflow applications, even develop new ones.

- **Handle Real World Expectations.**

Handling a fixed sequential process is easy. The payback from workflow comes from handling the exception cases. The old maxim that 80 percent of the time or cost is spent on 20 percent of the work is especially true here. That 20 percent represents the cases that do not obey the standard rules, but require special handling. Workflow products that allow complex branching based on identifying these exception cases are already the norm, at least in the Production Workflow segments. A new area of development is the ability of a user processing work in the middle of a workflow route to note an exception condition totally unanticipated by the workflow application developer, and add Ad Hoc processing steps to a workflow in progress. The use of object-oriented technology in workflow is a key part of this development.

Beyond the products for workflow automation, users are also looking for professional services to help them analyze their existing processes and reengineer them. Here, too, they are looking for a few basic essentials:

- **Services based on proven experience.**

Many computer vendors are rapidly expanding their service business as hardware margins shrink, but not all have the process redesign or analysis experience to back it up. Users want to see evidence of past success, preferably in a similar industry or application.

- **Reduced investment risk.**

Users are willing to spend money on workflow analysis and design services when they believe they reduce, rather than increase, the risk of a bad technology investment. Gone are the days when users readily accepted a $200,000 design study for a $350,000 investment. If there is risk, users want the service provider to share it, and perhaps provide the services incrementally to be a part of a gradual workflow implementation.

> users want to see evidence of past success, preferably in a similar industry or application

- **Use of a standard methodology.**

Process redesign and application development services that make use of a standard methodology give the workflow vendor much greater credibility with users. It usually means better trained consultants and a better means of leveraging previous experience. Methodologies that use software tools to model and analyze the workflow, simulate performance to identify bottlenecks, and tie into workflow application development are especially welcome by users.

Workflow market profile

BIS Strategic Decisions, in conjunction with *Computerworld*, conducted a survey of 600 users in the U.S. to determine the current profile of the workflow market and project future trends. The respondents represent purchasing decision-makers spread across a wide spectrum of industries and company sizes. Two thirds of the respondents come from the Information Systems side of the company, the rest from a line of business.

Judging by the survey respondents, acceptance of workflow software technology is already quite high (Figure 2). A healthy 11.9 percent of all respondents have already installed a workflow application, and another 2.6 percent say they have selected a product, but have not yet installed it. Acceptance is especially strong for the line-of-business users. Over 19 percent of them have installed or selected a workflow product, as compared to only 12 percent of the IS respondents.

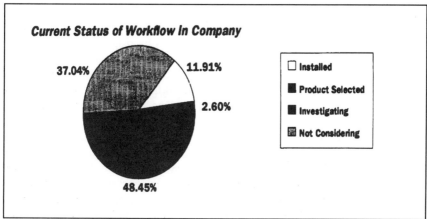

Figure 2. Profile of survey respondents

In addition, 48 percent of all respondents are investigating the need for workflow. Only 37 percent are not considering the adoption of workflow automation at this time, again with IS more inclined to say no to the technology.

Certain vertical industry groups (Figure 3) are particularly bullish on workflow: financial services, transportation, communications, utilities, and insurance. On the other hand, wholesale/retail, government/education, and professional services are slightly more conservative in their workflow adoption.

Overall, respondents rated today's need for workflow to facilitate general office processes equally to the need for workflow in line-of business applications (Figure 4). Today's workflow market, however, is predominantly concerned with production applications in line-of-business processing. Counting only those respondents with workflow installed, workflow automation of line-of-business applications is viewed as significantly more important than for office applications.

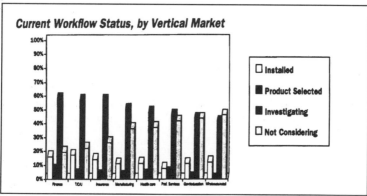

Figure 3. Workflow adoption patterns vary by industry.

In particular, the importance of workflow for line-of-business applications is rated higher than for office or ad hoc processes by respondents interested in document imaging, and by those favoring large system workflow platforms: mainframes, minis, or UNIX client/server. Line-of-business workflow is viewed as significantly more important than office workflow in certain vertical industries, as well: banking and finance; insurance; and transportation, communications, and utilities.

On the other hand, the converse view is held by wholesale/retail and education/government users. Line-of-business processing covers a mix of production and ad hoc functions, but tends toward the production side. Workflow procedures for line-of-business applications are viewed by most survey respondents as structured and relatively static, versus ad hoc and frequently changing. This view is especially strong in banking and finance, insurance, and government, as well as by imaging users reinforcing the strong connection between document imaging and "paper mill" industries with Production Workflow.

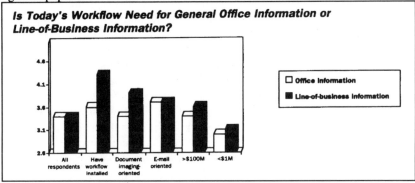

Figure 4. Line-of-business information will be workflow-enabled first.

Workflow in line-of-business applications rates higher in the largest companies (over $100 million in revenue) than in smaller ones. On the other hand, office automation workflow is rated equally important by respondents in all company sizes except for the smallest, under $1 million.

Surprisingly, over the next three years, respondents foresee a stronger rise in the importance of line-of-business workflow than for office workflow. This is surprising because workflow software for production line-of-business automation is already more mature and better established than the ad hoc office workflow technology.

Of course, the proof is in the actual adoption plans. Adoption rate as measured by plans for an initial pilot within one year favor line-of-business workflow over office workflow by a two-to-one margin (43 percent to 23 percent). Within a three-year time line, however, adoption of workflow office automation should occur in nearly as many companies as line-of-business workflow (69 percent versus 78 percent). Overall, the adoption rate of workflow for office automation appears to be about one year behind that for line-of-business applications.

Users are more optimistic than IS about initial adoption plans for both types of workflow in the near term, within a one year horizon.

However, looking ahead two years or more both users and IS predict the same rate of initial workflow adoption. Similarly, large companies are planning much more aggressive implementation schedules for workflow than small ones.

Who are the likely users of workflow technology; clerical workers, knowledge workers or management? Overall, respondents view the importance of workflow for clerical workers slightly higher than for professional workers or management. In three years, respondents rate the importance of workflow software higher for all three worker groups, but still tops for the clerical segment.

When asked to select a preferred workflow platform, survey respondents picked PC LAN Client/Server as the leading workflow platform today. That preference will only increase in the future. Overall, 55 percent picked PC LAN as their current workflow platform, compared to 44 percent for the next choice, the Desktop, followed by Minicomputer (24 percent), UNIX Client/Server (18 percent), and Mainframe (17 percent).

Looking ahead one year, PC LAN was the anticipated workflow platform of 69 percent of respondents, compared to only 33 percent for Desktop. In that time, UNIX Client/Server rises to 29 percent, while Minicomputer drops to 20 percent. MIS is more inclined than Line-of-Business to favor PC LAN and Minicomputer as workflow platforms, while the reverse is true for Desktop.

The survey clearly shows that users view workflow application development as a responsibility of the customer organization, not of a vendor (Figure 7). Overall, 64 percent of respondents look to their MIS organization as a primary source of workflow applications, and 24 percent view line-of-business end users as the primary workflow developer. System integrators follow in third place (20 percent), with the workflow software vendor (14 percent) and independent software vendors (12 percent) trailing.

Respondents also indicate a strong preference for the incremental reengineering approach. Asked to rate four approaches to reengineering on a five-point scale, respondents clearly favor gradual reengineering after implementing an initial workflow application. In second place was a complete reengineering before initial implementation. The alternatives of complete reengineering after workflow implementation, and no significant reengineering at all, have relatively little support.

Workflow in action: Aetna Health Plans

Aetna Health Plans processes approximately 80 million health insurance claims a year through 34 claims offices nationwide. Their use of workflow in conjunction with document image management is a shining example of the benefits of the technology in a Document-Centered Production environment. AHP's implementation was based on software from ViewStar, a California-based vendor of Production Workflow technology packaged as part of a document management system.

Processing health claims is one of the most paper-intensive transactions in business today, one that typically involves the movement of documents among many individuals in an office. Customer service representatives, who answer questions for policyholders, require constant and timely access to new and historical documents. Claims representatives must know that claims have been received, their current location, and their processing status virtually from the minute they arrive in the mail room. Before the implementation of workflow at Aetna, this information was unavailable until the claim processing was complete, up to nine days after it was received.

AHP's workflow thus starts in the mail room where the incoming claims are bar-coded and scanned. The workflow software automatically imports barcoded information into the ViewStar database, logging in the claim, assembling all the attached documents into a folder, and generating a unique ID number before forwarding to an indexer. The indexer retrieves work from a queue and key enters claim data from the scanned images. After indexing, each folder is forwarded to a Workflow Server, which makes complex processing decisions based on instructions programmed in ViewStar's 4GL script. Software on the Workflow Server does the following:

- Confirms that each folder represents only one family. If a folder is mis-- prepped with two claims in one, the Workflow Server will automatically split it into two.

- Checks the claim data against mainframe-based eligibility files, routing the folder to an Exception queue for research if necessary, or to a Fax queue if the claim must be forwarded to another Aetna office.

- Adds additional data to the folder from the policyholder file, such as group number, patient name, and codes, to assist in claim processing or automatic generation of form letters.

- Searches the system for other folders for the same family, merging them if found for processing.

- Identifies "special handling" claims, such as by high dollar amounts, for example, and routes them to priority queues for fast review.

- Distributes validated claims to the appropriate work queue for adjudication and payment. Claims processors drawing work from these queues are presented with a customized Windows screen including a 3270 host window, an image window, and a data form. They can key information into the host application from the images, place folders "on hold" pending additional documentation, or attach annotations and send the folder to a supervisor or analyst for further review.

In the first nine months after initial implementation, AHP was enjoying a 25 percent reduction in claims processing time, a 15 percent reduction in the processing of invalid or duplicate claims, and a tremendous improvement in customer service. At a scale of 80 million claims a year, these increase efficiencies add up to millions of dollars. In addition, now customer service representatives can access submitted claims within 24 hours of their arrival, instead of nine days. Improved customer service by the use of workflow provides increased revenue as increased market share to complement the reduced processing costs.

Workflow in action: Consolidated Edison

Document-driven Production Workflow does not require imaging, although the imaging vendors today have the most mature tools to handle high volume transactions. In this example, an imaging workflow vendor, Sigma Imaging Systems, has employed the workflow component with ASCII text files, not images, to solve a major customer service headache for Consolidated Edison, New York City's electric power utility.

> Con Edison anticipates it will save almost $2 million annually

Con Edison of New York has 20 sites and 1000 service representatives in its Customer Service Organization. Each day, meter readings are taken by field support staff throughout the New York metropolitan area. The readings are transferred to the central mainframe, which identifies inconsistencies and generates account investigation listings for problem resolution. Approximately one million such listings, or AILs, are generated each year.

Prior to the implementation of workflow, AILs were printed, manually sorted, and delivered to customer service representatives for follow-up, amounting to thousands of pages a day. The representatives were limited in their ability to respond promptly to customer inquiries because supporting documents were not at hand, and much time and energy were required to retrieve filed (and misfiled) documents. Using Sigma's OmniDesk software, Con Edison was able to load mainframe AIL data directly into OmniDesk forms. This data is automatically indexed and queued for workflow processing and distribution to customer service representatives.

Workflow routes are constructed to meet a wide variety of local needs, and can involve hundreds of routing rules. Because of the graphical nature of the OmniDesk workflow tools, however, these routes can be defined by nontechnical customer service managers; they do not require a programmer. Customer service representatives now retrieve the AILs from their workflow InBox, and by accessing multiple windows on the workstation can view the data, compare it with mainframe-based account history, and resolve the problem. Con Edison anticipates it will save almost $2 million annually with this system.

Workflow in action: Young and Rubicam

Group-Centered Production Workflow is still in its infancy. A pioneering example is the project traffic control system at Young and Rubicam, one of the nation's largest advertising agencies. The traffic system, an internal client project management process well established throughout the advertising business, is a complex process involving a mass of paper forms and the coordination of activities between many groups. It starts with a work-order form created by the Account Executive. The work-order is copied and distributed to creative services, that prepares concepts and layouts. Layouts must be approved, distributed, and filed; cost estimates must be prepared by the art director, production manager, and media planner; client signoff must be obtained; final art must be prepared and approved by the client; and purchase orders must be created. In the traditional traffic process, this is a paper nightmare.

Y & R's workflow implementation used Action Technologies' workflow companion product to Lotus Notes. Notes forms the document database environment for Action's somewhat unique workflow methodology.

Action views every major activity within a workflow as consisting of four steps: a request, an agreement, work completion, and acknowledgment of satisfaction. Their methodology consists of analyzing workflows and breaking them down into graphical "loops," each embodying this four-step cycle.

A difference between Y & R and the Aetna and Con Edison examples is that the workflow does not require integration of computer programs so much as the coordination of human work. Even so, assistance by Action's workflow consultants was necessary to analyze and map the workflow. This analysis forced Y & R to apply a logical structure on a sometimes chaotic process. At the same time, it identified bottlenecks and gray areas in the current process, and even created a higher sense of responsibility for Y & R's client in the work process.

While many users and managers were skeptical at first, the initial pilot involving a single advertising client has proved to be a very successful. No formal cost payback data is available, but a survey of users before and after three months of the pilot shows a dramatic improvement in users' qualitative perceptions of the efficiency of their daily work. For example, the number of users stating it took too long to prepare a brief dropped from 71 percent to none. Those saying it took too long to file and sort documents fell from 50 percent to none; frequent duplication of effort fell from 42 percent to none. Jobs finished on time with no rush rose from 32 percent to 52 percent; jobs completed on budget rose from 73 percent to 87 percent. Y & R naturally expects to roll out the Notes/ActionWorkflow to other clients in the near future.

Workflow technology concepts

What exactly does the workflow user see upon retrieving a work package from the InBox? The "work package" typically consists of a form, displaying coded data fields, and perhaps a text message of instructions or comments, plus document attachments. The user interface to the work also includes a constrained set of decision options for the user: "Done, Approve, Reject, Suspend." Beyond what the user sees, sometimes the work package may also pass instructions to the workflow application program on the user workstation. This causes the workflow application to perform specific functions on the desktop, perhaps retrieve remotely stored objects or initiate external applications, and arrange the sources of information on the screen in a particular way, and exchange certain data between them.

A typical screen for a Production Workflow user would show windows for document display, folder or document retrieval, browsing, and perhaps terminal emulation access to an external host application are presented. In a Production Workflow application, the work will often be handed to the user by the system in priority order, one package at a time. On the other hand, a typical screen for an Ad Hoc Workflow use will often feature an e-mail style InBox, from which the user can pick items to on which to work. Each selected work item will present a form with an instruction message from the sender, and action buttons representing the user's decision options.

Production Workflow and Ad Hoc Workflow differ in emphasis, but share many common technology elements designed to address basic workflow functions:

- Work routing
- Work distribution
- Work prioritizing
- Work tracking
- Management reporting

Work routing

The ability of the workflow designer to predefine the sequence of job steps is an essential concept. A user receives work by an electronic "InBox" and when the processing of that job step is complete, the work package is moved automatically and electronically to the next step in the sequence. The next step in the sequence usually depends on the result of the current job step processing, and, because of this, the routing logic is often tightly coupled to the business application.

Beyond simply a fixed sequential route, there are two basic types of work routing. The first, response-based routing, forwards work based on the user's selection: Approve, Reject, Revise, No Comment. These choices are specified by the workflow originator and usually appear to the user as graphic action buttons or menu picks. This is the primary routing mechanism for Ad Hoc Workflow, as exemplified by new electronic mail products from Microsoft and Lotus, as well as in some document management products such as Keyfile.

The second is rules-based routing. Here the routing destination depends upon a condition of the work package after processing. For example, if the claim amount is over $1000, route to A; otherwise, route to B. The rules can be extended to high degrees of complexity, and involve many of the workflow variables that are fields in the form component of the work package. The ability to link workflow variables to fields in external databases and applications is a new and evolving area of workflow development. This type of routing is not only the mainstay of document imaging workflow vendors like FileNet, IBM, ViewStar, and Recognition/Plexus, but is an important feature of the Group-Centered Production Workflow vendors such as Reach Software, Action Technologies, and Delrina.

Dynamic work distribution

The workflow routing logic often does not specify an individual user for activity processing, but a **job function** that may be performed by many users in the organization. This is a requirement for Production Workflow, and may gradually evolve into Ad Hoc Workflow as well. The ability to distribute work dynamically to achieve load balancing was seen to be a major contribution to improved efficiency even in the earliest workflow products of the mid 1980s. The traditional work distribution method has been to assign users to a specific job function when they logged on the document server (workflow and application processing were usually tightly coupled as well). For a given user to perform a different job step, the software often required logging off and using a different logon for the new function.

> the ability of the workflow designer to predefine the sequence of job steps is an essential concept

Because the activity logic processing was still tightly coupled to the workflow, this one-to-one mapping of user to job step function simplified the workflow software, but has come to be seen as not flexible enough for "real life" work. The new directions in work distribution involve the ability to construct more complex models of the user-to-job step processing assignments, such as assigning a set of functions that a given user has the skills to provide, or simply has access rights. In this case, the workflow software can distribute work efficiently, and relieves the "sender" of the need to know the name of the individual who performs a particular job function.

Work prioritizing

The ability to prioritize work is a benefit especially important in Production Workflow software. It was recognized early on in workflow systems that first-in-first-out (FIFO) is not always the best priority scheme, and that certain work processing steps or work item types should be assigned a higher priority. In the past, these priority assignments were fixed by the original workflow program or manually by the workflow originator, but today's workflow products allow much more flexibility. Leading edge workflow products such as Sigma Imaging Systems' RouteBuilder 2.0 allow dynamic priority assignment by the workflow software as a function of work aging, queue buildup, or as a function of virtually any workflow variable. Even in the Group-Centered products, an administrator or privileged user's ability to override the original priority assignment is now seen as a basic requirement.

Work tracking

The ability to track a work package and find out instantly its processing status, who has it, and how long it has been waiting for its current job step is another basic requirement for all but the simplest workflow products. One tracking function today getting more attention, particularly in the Ad Hoc Workflow products, is deadline/alarm reporting. This feature allows the workflow designer to define a date and time for completion of a given job step—either absolute or relative to the start of the workflow or particular job step—and have the software generate a warning message if the work item is approaching or past the deadline. This helps prevent work packages from being stuck forever in "suspense queues" (waiting for supporting documents) without attention. Some newer products even allow the expiration of a processing deadline to initiate new activities automatically, perhaps re-routing the work package to a special handling queue.

Management reporting

Logging workflow events for management reporting is necessary to track work. Production Workflow systems also use the information in the workflow tracking database for management reporting: How long on average does a particular activity take? How long does a package wait in a queue? How many transactions a day can be processed? Since the original acquisition of the workflow system was in many cases viewed as a part of a general program of "business process reengineering" in the customer organization, users often have a need to track and measure the new work process, if only to demonstrate cost justification. Some products provide reporting capability directly while others merely log events and update database tables for use by external report generators.

Workflow as an architectural element

A major area of innovation in workflow products—as they have evolved from their origins as a component of a document management system—is the attempt to *decouple*, as much as possible, the routing logic from the application or business logic. Architecturally, this allows the workflow component to be viewed as a generic "application service" rather than bound to a specific application or document database.

Each job step in the workflow can be divided in two basic parts. The **activity processing logic** is the combination of application software and decision-making that comprises the work of the job step; for example, the approval of an invoice, or insurance claim for payment. The software component of the activity processing logic often combines multiple application windows; for example, one tied to the business application or transaction database, perhaps on the mainframe, and another accessing folders containing images or electronic source documents driving the transaction—invoices, claim forms—generally on a document server.

The activity processing logic is what we usually think of as the workflow-enabled application. When the activity processing logic is complete, the second piece of the job step, the **routing logic,** takes over. It moves the work package to the next job step, usually based on the state of the work package following the activity processing. This processing state can either be calculated automatically by the software or manually selected by the user. Like the activity processing logic, the routing logic also interacts with a database, but keeps track of work packages and users, rather than documents or customer accounts. This is the workflow database--a key component of all workflow software except for the simplest forms of routing capabilities built into e-mail.

For many Document-Centered Production Workflow vendors, particularly document imaging companies such as FileNet, IBM, Sigma Imaging Systems, and ViewStar, tight connections between the core workflow component, the document management system, and the workflow-enabled business application are very important to achieve the necessary level of application integration and performance. A few vendors in this segment, notably Recognition/Plexus, NCR, and now Wang, have recently succeeded in opening up the connection between workflow and document management, and still maintain production-level performance.

On the other hand, for a new generation of independent workflow vendors, like Action Technologies, Reach Software, and Delrina, the broader potential market for Group-Centered Workflow requires loose, or totally open, interfaces between the workflow routing system, the document management system, and the business applications being workflow-enabled.

But the ability to workflow-enable external applications in a way that is open and accessible to non-programmers remains a challenge. Today there are no standards for passing data between applications and the workflow routing logic; that is, between application data and workflow variables. Simplifying the connections between user-defined routing logic and programmer-defined application code will be one of the "cutting edge" areas of workflow development, and there is at least some initial movement toward defining standards that will make this possible across multiple vendors.

The creation of software tools that allow complex workflows to be defined, tested, and modified by non-programmers, without tight coupling of the core workflow and business application components, is likewise at the forefront of workflow product development. A third critical feature of new workflow products is the ability to modify the routing logic without taking the system off line, or "flushing" all current work packages. This allows the introduction of Ad Hoc exception handling to deal with unanticipated cases.

> the workflow vendors are responding to user demands

Workflow software components

Virtually all workflow software products have three basic components: the workflow development toolkit; the workflow client and server functions; and the administrative utilities. The workflow server includes the internal database that tracks the status of each work package, maintains the queue tables, and keeps track of the forms or workflow variables. The administrative utilities include the functions of assigning users to processing functions, defining security and privilege levels, viewing the status of the various queues, and generating management reports. These are all important functions, but the most significant differentiator today between workflow products is in the application development tools.

The demand for tools that do not require an application programmer, but are capable of constructing, maintaining, and modifying complex and constantly changing workflows, make this area the most challenging one for the workflow vendors. The current trend, at the high end as well as the low, is to provide graphical point-and-click or "visual programming" tools that allow ever-increasing levels of application complexity. These are augmented by script languages or application program interface (API) calls for programmers or power users for the most complex application development, but the trend is to reduce the programmer dependence at all levels of workflow.

The latest idea in high-end workflow today is the encapsulation of script-based functions as "task objects" that non-programmers can rapidly "snap together" and reuse in a variety of workflows. FileNet, ViewStar, Wang, and Delrina are actively pursuing this object-oriented approach. New task objects beyond those supplied by the workflow vendor can be added by programmers capable of using the script language tools.

The concepts of a 4GL script for programmers and iconic maps and menus for non-programmers remain essential building blocks in the current vision of the "complete" workflow toolkit. That ideal can be roughly summarized to include the following:

End user tools

- Iconic route definition represents individual job steps by icons, and the programming of work package routing paths is achieved by the placement and interconnection of these icons.
- Table-driven rule definition allows non-programmers to describe routing/ prioritizing logic, data field validation rules, and other work processing conditions by filling in an "electronic form" from menus. The generation of programming logic in this way prevents programming syntax errors and promotes logical consistency.
- System simulation provides a way to discover bottlenecks, "black holes," and logical errors in the workflow design, with minimum effort. As a result of the simulation, staff allocations and routing logic can be changed, and the reconfigured workflow simulated again, without the pain of a trial-and-error approach.
- External application access allows individual work step processing to initiate external applications and extract data from them into the workflow, or to pass workflow data to them. In the past, this was difficult to implement within an end-user toolset, although today a graphical interface to Windows DDE, integrating word processing, spreadsheet, database, and host terminal emulation by simple point-and-click, is rapidly becoming a standard workflow tool component. Also, access to workflow services from external application builders like Visual Basic from DDE is an increasingly popular method of application integration.

Programmer tools

- A 4GL script language allows complex logical processing but insulates the programmer from the complexities of image manipulation code, queue and database definition, and C programming, using the Windows SDK or equivalent. The basic difference between "workflow script" and other image-oriented 4GL tools is that they include verbs that deal with predefined work queue data structures, including "rendezvous" queues, changing priorities, and event logging.
- Program exits to external code and mechanisms for passing data between the 4GL script and the external code give complete flexibility to the programmer. Ideally this would include the ability to insert C statements in the middle of a script program.

- Links to end user tools, particularly graphical form-fill screens, greatly simplify script programming. FileNet, for example, includes the call, "Do Form," in its WorkFlo script to process an entire form in one 4GL statement.
- APIs to external programs allow them to read data from or write to the work queues and other data structures defined within the workflow system. This allows external applications to generate work packages, make processing decisions (including the integration of expert system shells), and compile management reports, for example.
- Debugging tools are crucial to any programmer, and are needed as part of the workflow toolset as well. These should include syntax checking, instruction tracing, step execution, breakpoints (automatic stop at a designated point in the script), and watchpoints (tracking the value of script variables).

Workflow: business tool for the '90s

The workflow vendors are responding to user demands for this technology with an increasing number of product and service offerings in all segments of the market. Products that even bridge the Production/Ad Hoc divide are emerging, as established workflow vendors seek to broaden their markets. Interest among users is high, but they are asking for robust tools they can use themselves. Major PC software vendors are just now getting into the arena, and this will greatly advance the education of the mass market, creating additional opportunity for small workflow specialists. But an incredibly wide spectrum of price and functionality expectations still exists, so all vendors still face a prolonged period of buyer confusion and market education. This will be followed by a slow convergence toward accepted price/value relationships of specific workflow functions and capabilities.

One thing is certain, however. The economic pressures to increase the productivity of office work, in combination with the nearly universal networking of powerful multi-windowing desktops, make the future growth of workflow automation software a sure thing.

Case Study: Dow Corning

Dr. R. Kraft Bell, President
RKB Limited and
Executive Consultant, Prism Performance Systems

Abstract

This case study shows how Dow Corning demonstrated the foresight to preempt a future competitive situation by reengineering the level and type of process innovation and change required to ensure an ongoing competitive advantage, including a 74 percent reduction in commercialization cycle time.

Overview

Even though Dow Corning was eminently successful, an executive leadership team determined that they were in a "future challenged" competitive situation. They defined and communicated a captivating vision, empowering values, and clear direction, along with the appropriate route for change through renewal. Macro and core processes were analyzed and prioritized for appropriate reengineering. These executives personally led training-by-doing sessions and used computer-augmented tools to educate and involve over 300 middle managers and key professionals in managing this company wide change effort.

Cross-functional core process teams collaboratively redesigned workflows to both frame and integrate bottom-up efforts across the company. Targeted pilots and staged implementation were based upon a customer focus and process orientation that involved a balanced set of changes to shift mindsets, instill new principles, enhance team capabilities, and develop enabling infrastructure. Ongoing commercialization teams with product, market, and manufacturing members spearheaded the implementation of the time-driven, radically redesigned commercialization process.

Dow Corning's renewal achieved dramatic results. Commercialization cycle time was reduced 74 percent from an average cycle time of 48 months to 12.3 months for 1,000 new products. Quality increased and customer satisfaction significantly improved, while costs were reduced.

Competitive situation

Strategic/organizational issues

In today's turbulent competitive environment executives are increasingly confronted with critical strategic organizational issues. The questions reflecting these issues are:

Have restructuring, quality, cost, timeliness, and other change efforts lead to increased profitability and a competitive advantage?

Has the organization overcome gridlock, set and met priorities, linked and aligned work, handled conflict, and eliminated counter-productive efforts, while cost- and time-effectively serving customers?

Has the leadership learned to manage across functions, establish a customer focus, enhance teamwork, be process oriented, and develop core competencies?

Have we found an approach and tools that augment and expedite this work, including ways to build knowledge capital, and internalize capabilities?

Strategic issues: change dilemmas

In addressing these issues, companies must resolve three dilemmas:
Vision/upheaval
Immediate results/ongoing improvement
Caring/accountability
The first dilemma of vision/upheaval emerges because a worthy vision, like a competitive strategy, requires upheaval, that is, dramatic change and struggle. This destabilizes the status quo for which many have worked so hard, creates conflict many do not want or know how to resolve, and complicates managing, especially for existing mindsets and tools.

The second dilemma is immediate results/ongoing improvement. It involves working harder, smarter and relying on restructuring to achieve better immediate results. It also involves learning that ongoing improvement for significant long-term results requires the critical transformation of work processes, team relationships and capability development. Unfortunately, for most managers and employees such transformations are in their blind spot. If addressed, they are rarely approached in a systematic manner.

The third dilemma of caring/accountability is deeper and more difficult to discern. It reflects the unwillingness and inability to blend the soft and hard. The soft personal caring and the hard accountability are rarely balanced in the workplace that undermines the work ethic, empowerment and proper service to customers.

Dow Corning's Renewal

Dow Corning had a series of revenue and profit records with the highest market share in their industry, making it one of the most highly successful joint ventures in the world. Their matrix structure had been published in the *Harvard*

Business Review. The opportunity existed for an integrative large scale change renewal effort within a company that was not forced into changing. Dow Corning could be a model for other companies by saying, "Our competitive threat is not imminent, but it is real. We need to be honest with ourselves, discerning, and confront this potential competitive threat."

Guideline I—Top/Middle/Bottom Change

Dow Corning's application of integrative strategic change empowers people, focuses on meeting customer expectations, uses continuous improvement and develops world-class capabilities to create and sustain a competitive advantage for a profitable and growing company. The most unique aspects of this effort, reflective of the guidelines above, are its foresight—a profitable market leader recognizing future competitive challenges, while analyzing and acting now to renew;

- depth—delving beneath symptoms and problems to their root causes, while making changes accordingly
- breadth—prioritized reengineering through a core process strategy, while linking and aligning workflows at all levels across the entire company
- balance—developing balanced leadership, while internalizing critical capabilities.

Renewal at Dow Corning involved significant changes that were systematically integrated into a large scale change effort on a company-wide basis, encompassing the U.S., Inter-American, European, and Japan/Pacific operations. The executive committee and renewal leadership team (top 30 global executives) lead the top-down aspect of this effort. They completed a competitive analysis, established and monitored corporate milestones and a change road map, and solved problems on the underlying causes of the company's issues. Based on this analysis they framed and coordinated prioritized business process reengineering through ongoing team sessions.

These sessions used the computer-augmented WorkFrames product by RKB Ltd. to help educate, train and develop over 300 middle managers and key professionals.

Through these sessions, middle management was involved, both up front and on an ongoing basis. Many of these managers lead or were involved in the process reengineering teams, carried out process improvement in their own units, and were integral to the phased implementation of an array of changes. Ongoing multimedia communication was carried on throughout the company. Trained middle managers and professionals selectively educated and trained others through a systematic involvement pattern. Great effort was made to prevent the inhibition of bottom-up efforts across the company. As the frames and coordination were put in place, the required linkage and alignment of the workflows and relationships to avoid suboptimization was provided.

Strategic Change Analysis:

Guideline II—Competitive Foresight

Before any reengineering effort begins, the critical question asked is: Competitively, how much change is enough? At Dow Corning this strategic change analysis was often referred to as "searching for the smoking gun."

There are three fundamental types of competitive situations to be considered—ongoing, challenged, and lost. In an on-going competitive situation, no significant impacts are likely in the competitive environment from either competitors, customers or external events. This is business as usual. Ten to 15 years ago 50 percent of American companies were in this situation, while today there are less than 20 percent.

As a company in an ongoing competitive situation faces the future, it has surface-level issues that tend to be individual or discrete. The required analysis is superficial. What is the symptom? What is the problem? What is the solution? Let's implement! TQM tools are particularly helpful here in working through the activity breakdown analysis and finding value-added activities for a revised workflow. This is a tactical approach that requires issue-by-issue investment to achieve incremental change.

At the other extreme is the predictable lost future competitive situation in which competitors encroach or results falter. Customers have changed expectations, and/or external impacts have turned hostile to products, services, and profitability. This requires looking deeper for the causes of this predicament. Prevailing values and mindsets must be examined, since most of the issues in this situation are pervasive, cutting across and through the entire organization.

In a challenged competitive situation, products, services and/or profitability will be impacted in the coming years by competitors, customer's rising expectations, and/or regulatory requirements, without dramatic change. The analysis must be moderately deep to address problems and their causes. While the issues are not pervasive, they are interrelated across the organization. Even though much is working well, innovative principles and processes must be developed and put in place.

The challenged competitive situation may involve selective areas and high priority processes that need to be focused on first, starting at the core process or management decision-making level. Step change is the desired result from the required double hump investment—first recognizing the need for change, then developing and implementing the change. Today 50 percent of American companies fall into this situation.

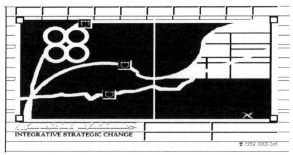

Figure 1

The WorkFrames Solution includes an interactive Strategic Change MAP (see *figure 1*) to help a client make this competitive assessment. Unless the level and type of analysis and change are matched with the competitive situation, progress is unlikely.

Renewal Foresight:

Guideline II—Competitive Analysis

Given their past success, Dow Corning showed great foresight in acknowledging their challenged competitive situation. The executive committee, the renewal leadership team and the core process teams, along with middle management and key professionals, struggled to recognize that Dow Corning faced a challenged position. This necessitated the core process approach, discussed next, to achieve the step change.

Using a scale of one to ten, (one being totally ongoing and ten being totally lost), Dow Corning placed itself just above six. A few operations and the commercialization process were in the eight plus range, necessitating selective radical reengineering. Most operations and processes were between five and seven. This smoking gun analysis was further verified when they learned that their Japanese competitors, with better quality in some product, but no operations in the United States, were planning to produce in America.

The first question asked by many at Dow Corning was, "Why didn't the renewal leadership team start by changing the structure of the company?" To some people, changing structure solves everything.

In the lost competitive situation, most of the changes involve principles, large processes, and mindsets. In the challenged competitive situation, the emphasis is on principles and processes, and infrastructure and/or mindsets that support them. The goal is to fit the appropriate level and type of required change to the competitive situation.

Renewal Depth:

Guideline III—Iceberg Analogy

Observing an iceberg, symptoms are the ice on the surface and the problems are the reflection of ice in the water. Causes are the just faintly seen ice, apparent only upon looking directly into the water. Root causes form the underlying mass of an iceberg that is far below the surface and beyond the ability to view directly. Delving deep enough to understand the full extent and implication of an issue increases the likelihood of change leading to lasting issue resolution.

At Dow Corning, as elsewhere, it was easier to stop at symptoms. Those with responsibility to improve New Product Market Sales (NPMS), for instance, could have merely changed the indicator. However, when the problem was really a lack of market penetration that leads to insufficient NPMS, then the cause needed to be pursued. Another problem that surfaced was a lack of prioritization. An obvious solution would have been to apply a criteria matrix for more effective prioritization. However, the real problem was not lack of prioritization, but failure to take priorities seriously. Further analysis uncovered that this was caused by a deep-seated belief in stretch resourcing.

Sufficiently deep analysis is required to understand the reason the organization does not have or cannot sustain a competitive advantage into the future. The WorkFrames CreativeSolveMAP software provides a systematic framework for thinking about and delving deeper to uncover such causes and root causes. This is also the realm of breakthrough thinking and competitive advantage. Very few breakthroughs are achieved by dealing with symptoms or even solving problems.

The paradox, in terms of depth, is that the some characteristics that have made Dow Corning successful are the very factors that were most in the way of ongoing success. At Dow Corning, strengths, pushed so far that they had started to become weaknesses, were:

Dominance of rational, logical, must-lead top executives, based on chemical engineering backgrounds and related personality preferences

Emphasis on sequential and activity/event based work patterns, including relationships with customers

Reliance on solving known problems analytically, primarily with proven technological solutions using the framework for change, now built into the WorkFrames CreativeSolveMAP, these characteristics are evident in many of the causal factors.

Renewal Depth:

Guideline III—Causal Analysis

Among the categorized causal factors uncovered in the Causal Analysis at Dow Corning were the following:

External view
Inadequate connection with customers and the marketplace
Internal view
Individually focused, boundary-conscious, results-oriented and internally competitive
Differentiation by doing things the Dow Corning way.
Approach to work
Work viewed as a series of independent events
Time not valued
Avoidance of problems without knowing the solutions
Dualistic thinking with difficulty in handling open conflict

Deeper analysis uncovered these causes and root causes, so that related changes could afford lasting resolution. At Dow Corning, there were a series of issues related to gridlock and additiveness—creating additional work for individuals. The Creative SolveFRAME prompt or question at this point in the analysis was, "If these problems are so obvious and long standing, why have they not been resolved?"

The responses were:

> we tend to make changes, and consistently confuse this with changing

A few key people are consistently tapped for assignments, especially those who can get the system to work for them.

No framework for addressing the gridlock and additiveness issues.

Everything is treated as unique and novel.

The Matrix is often an excuse for gridlock.

Systems are designed for the average, lacking both discipline and flexibility.

At Dow Corning using time as a driver for process innovation was resisted. The reasons were:

We tend to make changes, and consistently confuse this with changing

We are also not clear, nor do we seem to want to know the when (long lead time for meaningful improvement)

Without a crisis, it's necessary to have a significant emotional event or a role model rise to lead the change with time as a driver

We do not know how to change fundamentally the way and pace at which we work internally, as if time and timing are not important; we even run meetings that way.

Therefore, the underlying cause, time is not valued, had to be addressed, or substantial amounts of energy would have been wasted using a driver that did not fit the culture.

Within Dow Corning, most of the people were trying to improve, but either did not see what was in the way or understand that there was something different on which to work. There workflow was invisible because it went across organizational boundaries, so optical illusions were often helpful in getting this point across. Workflow was outside of job definitions. The cause—they viewed work as a series of independent events.

This Causal Analysis was expedited by frameworks and tools that provided a creative, yet systematic methodology for understanding troublesome mindsets.

At Dow Corning, the causal analysis, related to dualistic thinking, emerged in this way:

We are excessively polite, to the point of not confronting critical issues, which we tend to deny.

Duality (emphasizing the extremes) gets in the way.

We have difficulty handling conflict, especially open—even if it is healthy.

There are few mechanisms for prioritizing and solving critical issues

Our strong personal risk avoidance is most evident in our not being willing to allow ourselves or others to make and learn from our mistakes.

The underlying root cause was found to be a composite; dualistic thinking with difficulty handling open conflict.

Addressing the causes or shifting the mindsets implied by the root causes usually makes the problems and symptoms fall away, or at least isolates them for direct resolution.

> deeper analysis uncovered these causes and root causes, so that related changes could afford lasting resolution

The WorkFrames Solution was also used to recognize and foster developing managerial judgment that balances the analytical with the intuitive. Several WorkFrames expert system MODELs take personality preferences and approaches to problem solving and decision making into account, with specific FRAMEs to expedite and document this balanced judgment.

Renewal Breadth:

Guideline IV—Change Puzzle

In Dow Corning, as in most corporations, people primarily work on jobs with task-focused activities, activities that one can touch and feel and work on for business as usual. To improve, systems are developed to support these activities. These systems are started for one purpose, something is added to it, and then something else. This may or may not help get work done.

Disconnected top-down direction and bottom-up activities result in being disorganized competitively, not in how the organization is structured, but how it functions. Dow Corning's matrix structure, for example, was set for positive checks and balances. Many believe it would make sure that the big mistake would never be made. However, this checking slows decision making, and becomes a competitive disadvantage as customers expect quicker responses to their concerns.

For example, a survey showed that instead of only eight competitors in a particular market, there were actually 208 niche players. Those 208 did not care about Dow Corning's matrix. When their customers wanted something, they just figured out how to do it. This was particularly evident in Dow Corning's cumbersome commercialization process. Sometimes it took as long to change merely the color of a product as it did to enhance it significantly.

The answer is to focus on quality. However, an approach is only successful when people are committed to and follow through on implementation.

The typical quality approach is very positive in generating incremental change in an ongoing competitive situation. However, in a more competitive situation, it ultimately leads back to being competitively disorganized. The issues become interrelated and cross-organizational. The work is not being framed and middle managers most still determining how to manage it. Dow Corning had to look at large, cross-organizational processes, not because they wanted to, but because of their challenged competitive situation.

Renewal Breadth:

Guideline IV—Core Process Strategy

What is a core process strategy? It is a way to systematically organize management decision making and related workflows across the organization. The top-down workflow view of the organization is quite different from bottom-up additive systems.

Strategy and coordination, which are aligned and moving in the same direction, are put in place first. The cross-functional, cross-unit workflows of what is going on in the company are macro processes. These are approximations, rather than the one right answer. The purpose is to understand them so that the workflows at the next level, the core processes, can be analyzed, prioritized, and redesigned.

What is largely missing in corporate America, what was missing at Dow Corning, is this core process level of management decision making. Instead of middle managers struggling to manage change, work is framed by strategy and coordinated through core processes that link and align the other workflows, sub- and micro processes.

A top-down approach is no better than a bottom-up approach.

The highest priority core process at Dow Corning was New Product Commercialization Process (NPCP). The core process team that was formed was the fifth team in six years to look at commercialization. They initially had a beautiful flow chart drawn by a consultant on a computer. The problem was that the process did not work, and the chart implied that it did. What really existed in Dow Corning for commercialization was a disjointed series of hand-offs with breakdowns at almost every step, or an additive system. Given the extended cycle time, customer dissatisfaction, and myriad of other symptoms and problems, a root cause analysis and workflow redesign were in order.

People were working on disjointed efforts. Tools and techniques abounded. The key questions to answer were:

How do you design these micro processes?

How do you fit them into the sub-process so there's a workflow?

How can these sub-processes be coordinated in a core process?

Does this reflect the overall strategy?

The only way to ensure satisfactory results is to have change at all levels. A top-down approach is no better than a bottom-up approach. The two working together create the synergy for change. This requires framing sub-processes in core processes with milestones, while the macro process helps define the previously non-existent core processes. Core process strategy frames from the top-down, and builds on this bottom-up activity-driven approach, ensuring that everything happens with middle management involvement and commitment throughout the company, across all the processes.

> the problem was that the process did not work, and the chart implied that it did

The president of a Dow Corning's joint venture with the Japanese once observed: The Japanese see the Americans with their big ideas and inventions and smile. To them, this amounts to only 10 percent of the required work. The other 90 percent is the innovation required to deliver high quality products to customers that delight them. To Americans the invention and ideas are 90 percent, followed by plan, plan, plan.

In summary, overall macro processes help define core processes, which have imbedded within them linked and aligned sub-processes made up of micro processes. All the effort and energy becomes linked and aligned. The commercial operations unit documented five pages worth of improvement efforts.

The questions were: If you add it all up, is it going in the same direction? Is it leading to the results and deliverables that customers expect.? Does this lead to a competitive advantage?

Renewal Breadth:

Guideline IV—Apple "Core" Analogy

An apple analogy ties together the iceberg and the change puzzle, thus illustrating how to interrelate the depth of issues, the level of change required for lasting resolution, and the related process improvement and/or innovation.

In the apple analogy, a symptom could be a skin bruise, indicating that something happened to the apple. Polishing the apple might be a temporary fix. The necessary information, however, is whether the bruise indicates an external impact or something deeper, like the tip versus the base of the iceberg.

At this level of analysis, when the commercialization team completed an overview analysis of workflow breakdowns and related problems, several members asked, "Why don't we go into further detail on each of these breakdowns and solve them?" While such work might have been invigorating at first, frustration would have set in when solutions prove insufficient for lasting resolution, because the underlying causes were not addressed.

The deepest level of analysis can be threatening. With the apple analogy, this means that the seeds are discovered to be rotten. If the seeds are disintegrating, then the apple cannot be reproduced. This deeper analysis uncovered the mindsets to shift, the principles to change, and cross-organizational processes to reengineer.

> the rumor within the company was that renewal was a failure because the macro processes did not work

Understanding the depth of issues and the related level of change required for lasting resolution revealed the level of process improvement and/or innovation required. Dow Corning was not in a lost competitive situation. Therefore, the purpose of their macro process step was not to fully develop the macro processes, spending time figuring them out in detail, but to frame the work required to deal with their set of underlying causes.

Interestingly, after the macro process teams had served this framing purpose and core process teams were formed, the rumor within the company was that renewal was a failure because the macro processes did not work. This highlights the crucial need for vision and direction coupled with ongoing communication.

Renewal Breadth:

Guideline IV—Workflow Redesign

The core process strategy led to defining ten core processes. The renewal leadership team completed a competitive analysis and the macro process teams framed these workflows and the related issues and causes. After establishing and applying a set of success criteria, the highest priority was to redesign the coordination level commercialization core process.

Framing this core process, and related to other competitive priorities, was redesign of the three key management decision-making core processes, those involving vision, strategy and people capabilities. While the linkage and alignment issues were handled by a core process leaders team, the other core processes continued to be improved through less intensive, ongoing bottom-up sub-process work.

> the simplicity of these principles belies the mindset shifts required

The five RKB WorkFlow Design Principles were utilized in each of the core and sub-process reengineering work. The WorkFlow design Principle;

1. Focus on Workflow Analysis, based on an agreement to manage on the basis of the optimum movement of ideas and resources.

2. Emphasize Workflow Milestones, ensuring agreement to use the high level decision points to frame the results expected in the workflow.

3. Involve Simultaneous Workflows, where one workflow runs partially concurrent with the following workflow.

4. Require waterfalling information, built upon a commitment to pass on an agreed-upon certain percent accuracy and a specified complete percentage information in the workflow.

5. Looks like mushy and interlocking ends that sequentially connect micro processes so that the beginning of the next process starts somewhat before the end of the preceding process.

The simplicity of these principles belies the mindset shifts required and the power for reengineering unleashed with their application.

There are two major types of core processes, calendar-driven management decision-making processes, such as strategic planning, and customer-driven process, like commercialization. The priority for workflow redesign involved several of these, and offered a means of explaining and showing the application of the five principles.

A redesigned workflow resulted from this workflow analysis.

For each team, applying the first workflow principle required analyzing the existing flow of work by documenting the activities, events, decisions, linkages, and roles, and then identifying all existing workflow breakdowns. These breakdowns were then analyzed as critical issues with causes, along with looking for potential burning solutions and spin-offs. At that point, the ideal future opportunities and desired results were envisioned. This was standard Total Quality Management (TQM) work, although the more in-depth causal analysis surfaced the underlying causes.

A redesigned workflow resulted from this workflow analysis. The cautions surfaced by applying the first principle by not being too detailed or taking the initial redesign too seriously. This was a minor step for ensuring that process reengineering does not lead to suboptimization across processes or solve the same issues over and over again. The team's tendency for too much detailed flow charting and problem analysis has already been described. They filled the walls with the overview workflows, including breakdowns, recognizing at least 35 variations across the company.

The most profound observation, reinforced by the causal analysis, was that the constant hand-offs of responsibility between functions required the immediate implementing of putting cross-functional commercialization teams in place. This was presented to the leadership team who agreed to work on the solution themselves and carry its implementation to the line organization. In summary, this first principle is best applied at an overview level that highlights the breakdowns and the opportunity for change.

The second principle of setting workflow milestones—disciplined, time-valued, prioritized, and customer-focused decision points—is quite different from TQM and other reengineering approaches. The shift here is away from decisions based on unenforced, untimely, nonprioritized and internally focused requirements. Critical problems, their causes, and potential opportunities and desired results for the workflow are analyzed and agreed to. The prioritized solutions are implemented. Spin-offs, changes required now, but not necessarily part of the ultimate workflow, were set up. At this point at least 50 percent of the breakdowns should be eliminated. Finally, there is a reshuffle of all workflow events, activities, linkages and realigned functional roles and responsibilities in support of the milestones.

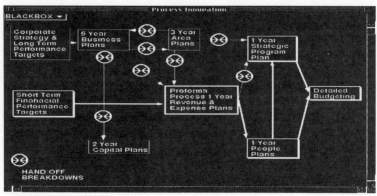

Figure 3

At Dow Corning, several spin-offs had to be put in place. The statement made at the time, "Waiting for the future Medivac helicopter (a redesigned New Product Commercialization Process) to be bought does not help those bleeding on the highway now," highlighted how people felt about handling customer complaints about the existing commercialization. These spin-offs included computer programs to enhance and simplify documentation, while others expedited tracking of commercialization requests. They also gave the longer-term effort credibility as the broader redesign was completed.

The Proforma Process (see *figure 3*), when put into perspective by being related to processes, demonstrated the significance of reframing. As the accompanying diagram shows, there are linkage or transition breakdowns between both the prior vision and subsequent strategy planning processes. The executive committee may well have received better information in a more timely manner by redesigning the Proforma process itself. However, in light of the payoff from redesigning the whole series of interrelated processes, the broader effort was achieved.

The third principle, establishing simultaneous workflows, counters the typical approach of starting a process after the preceding process is completed with a buffer for "redo"s. Redesigning simultaneous workflows is accomplished by repositioning processes that can happen concurrently, from top to bottom, between the workflow milestones. This involves reorienting the workflow by sequentially aligning processes across workflow milestones. Implementable changes need to be developed and evaluated based upon success criteria for each pilots.

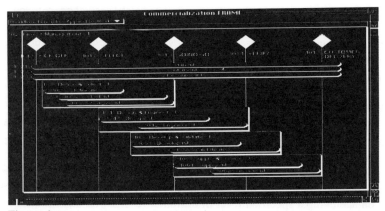

Figure 4

The manufacturing area was ahead of the company in terms of some quality, teamwork and systems improvements. Early in the new product commercialization effort, the cross-functional commercialization teams had only tacit manufacturing representation and the improvement efforts were consistently treated as outside the commercialization effort (see *Figure 4*). The change needed required that heads of both the manufacturing and quality improvement efforts participate on the core process leader's team. This not only refocused the energy on a joint effort, but the bottom-up work could be properly linked and aligned within the overall milestones and sub-processes.

At the strategic level, the work on milestones bogged down in determining whether the frame should be around strategy or operations or strategy/operations. By separating the milestones that had requirements for each, concurrent strategic and operational workflows could be designed and aligned. They also found that the calendar-driven planning processes could be linked through milestones to the customer-driven processes for assessment and resourcing.

Potential impacts and barriers were identified and removed, in support of full implementation.

The fourth principle, waterfalling information, runs counter to people's desires to withhold information, at least until it was almost 100 percent accurate and 100 percent complete. Time-valued waterfalling of information enables the simultaneous workflows to be closely linked, assuring further concurrence. At Dow Corning, the milestones were recalibrated based on meeting of customer expectations, and more detailed sub-milestones were added. The implementable changes were evaluated and chosen on the basis of the success criteria implementation of larger and more comprehensive pilots. Potential impacts and barriers were identified and removed, in support of full implementation.

The fifth principle, mushy and interlocking ends, involves sequential connections between micro processes at Dow Corning, rather than discrete and sepa-

211

rate ending and starting points for interrelated activities. The sub-and micro process workflows were further defined with these mushy and interlocking ends. Implementation changes were monitored, variances assessed, and further adaptations were made for continuous improvement.

Renewal Balance:

Guideline V—Internalizing Capabilities

Dow Corning started running meetings as a reengineered process. A balanced leadership approach reflected the five WorkFlow Design Principles applied in a facilitative, yet disciplined way for meetings and team sessions.

First, a meeting was recognized as a process. There was a defined context, a legitimate purpose, and an agreed-upon decision-making process. The focus was on achieving a specified level of customer results with stakeholders in designated roles, following a preset process agenda.

> the executives had to demonstrate changing the way they ran meetings; planning, being consistent and following through was hard work

Second, milestones were set to ensure meeting work was properly framed, measured, monitored, and adjusted. Third, simultaneous workflows were set up for proactive leadership before a meeting, principled teamwork during the meeting, and targeted action following the meeting. Fourth, information was waterfalled between stakeholders across these simultaneous workflows. Fifth, the mushy ends or tightly sequenced steps within the workflows were evident in the process agenda. The leader or facilitator monitored progress toward achieving results in light of this process agenda, strategically preparing for the next transition.

Previously within Dow Corning, meetings were typically done on the run. People were not raising critical issues. Open conflict was avoided. Harmonizers, those who lighten up tense moments, were everywhere. The executives had to demonstrate a change. Changing the way they ran meetings; planning, being consistent and following through was hard work.

Renewal Balance:

Guideline V—WorkFrames Solution Applied

The new president of the Japan and Pacific areas had an opportunity to accelerate further the process reengineering through computer-augmented sessions. This extensive effort encompassed a full range of reengineering changes. He acted on the belief that electronic meetings were the only time-effective way to handle multi-cultural, high level, and complex tasks. The president also found that, if a leader positions computer augmentation properly, it works well down in the organization.

Workflow design sessions have been expedited. The process design has become seamless with WorkFrames. Information is input only once. The analysis is automatically formatted from the initial input of breakdowns through the application of the five WorkFlow Design Principles. A project with actual dates for cost and quality milestones has been formed.

> Dow Corning's renewal led to dramatic results, including a 74 percent cycle time reduction

Dow Corning Case Study—A Summary

Dow Corning executives the five guidelines for integrative strategic change to provide the blueprint for cost effectively resolving critical strategic issues and competitive dilemmas, bolstered by the WorkFrames Solution with computerized road maps, behavioral guidelines, expert systems, and integrative tools. Leaders, teams and others learned to dramatically improve work relationships and processes, build knowledge capital and develop the capabilities required for implementing integrative strategic change to achieve competitive results and internalize capabilities. Dow Corning's renewal led to dramatic results, including a 74 percent cycle time reduction to commercialize across all of their new products. The average cycle time was reduced from over 48 months to 12.3 months over 1,000 new products. Quality was increased and customer satisfaction significantly improved while costs were reduced.

REFERENCES

Clark, Kim B. and Wheelwright. *Managing New Product and Process Development, Text and Cases*; New York, NY: Free Press, A Division of Macmillan, 1993.

Colson, Chuck and Jack Eckerd. *Why America Doesn't Work: How the Decline of the Work Ethic Is Hurting Your Family and Future- and What You Can Do*; Dallas, TX: Word Publishing, 1991.

Davenport, Thomas H. *Process Innovation: Reengineering Work through Information Technology*; Boston, MA: Harvard Business School Press, 1993

Dimancescu, Dan. *The Seamless Enterprise: Making Cross Functional Management Work*; New York, NY: Harper Business A Division of Harper Collins Publishers, 1992.

Hammer, Michael and James Champy, *Reengineering the Corporation: A Manifesto For Business Revolution*; New York, NY: Harper Business, Division of Harper Collins Publishers, 1993.

Harrington, H. James. *Business Process Improvement: The Breakthrough Strategy For Total Quality, Productivity, and Competitiveness,* New York, NY: McGraw-Hill, Inc., 1991.

Hickman, Craig R. *Mind of a Manager, Soul of a Leader*, New York, NY. John Wiley and Sons, Inc., 1990

Kanter, Rosabeth, Moss Barry A., Stein, and Todd D., *The Challenge of Organizational Change: How Companies Experience It And Leaders Guide It.* New York, NY. The Free Press A Division of Macmillan, Inc., 1992.

Kochan, Thomas A. and Michael Useem, ed. *Transforming Organizations*; New York. NY: Oxford University Press, 1992.

Meyer, Christopher. *Fast Cycle Time: How to Align Purpose, Strategy, and Structure for Speed.* New York, NY. The Free Press, Division of Macmillan, Inc., 1993.

Pascale, Richard Tanner. *Managing on the Edge: How the Smartest Companies Use Conflict to Stay Ahead*; New York, NY: Simon and Schuster, 1990.

Senge, Peter M. *The Fifth Discipline: The Art and Practice of The Learning Organization*; New York, NY. Doubleday/ Currency, 1990

Smalley, Gary and John Trent. *The Two Sides of Love. Colorado Springs, CO.* Focus on the Family Publishing, 1990, 1992.

Stalk, George Jr. and Thomas M. Hout. *Competing Against Time: How Time-Based Competition is Reshaping Global Markets;* New York, NY. The Free Press Division of Macmillan, Inc., 1990.

Tichy Noel M. and Startford Sherman. *Control Your Destiny or Someone Else Will: How Jack Welch is Making General Electric the World's Most Competitive Company*; New York, NY Currency/Doubleday, 1993.

Higgins, Thomas. "Secret Plan is Blueprint for Ford's future" in the *Detroit News* April 24, 1988.

Kirkpatrick, David "Groupware Goes Boom" in *Fortune*, December 27, 1993.

Schrage, Michael, "Robert's Electronic Rules of Order, in *Wall Street Journal*, November 29, 1993.

Thomas A. Stewart. "Reengineering: The hot new managing tool" *Fortune*, August 23, 1993.

Therrien, Lois. "Consultant, Reengineer Thyself" in *Business Week*, April 12, 1993.

Case Study: Grampian Regional Council

Dean Cruse, Vice-President, Marketing
Recognition International

Grampian Regional Council (GRC), Scotland's third largest regional council, is responsible for administration services for northeast Scotland. With a population of 508,000, the Revenues section of GRC services a tax base of 217,000 Council taxpayers and handles 108,000 Council tax benefit cases a year.

The Business Problem

Community Charge, a local taxation system, has been producing 1.2 million pieces of paper annually for billing and related activities. It is expected that Council Tax, which has replaced Community Charge, will produce approximately 600,000 pieces of paper annually. Not only must the Council keep track of the incoming paper, it is also responsible for tracking about 108,000 benefits case files for those individuals who are in lower income households and cannot afford their portion of taxes.

> it became apparent that customer service levels would continue to decrease over time

These benefits case files contain 15 to 20 supporting documents that must be kept on file for a number of years. This means that a staggering amount of paper must be processed, filed, and tracked each year by the Revenues section of GRC.

As part of Community Charge, 135 employees of the Revenues section were divided into four groups responsible for different tax processing functions. Each group maintained its own unique filing system, operated as a specialist function, and was not cross-trained. Therefore, for a taxpayer to receive an answer to an inquiry, it sometimes was necessary for the taxpayer to work with one or more individuals in different groups in order to get the information needed. This was inefficient and time consuming. More importantly, this structure did not provide an adequate level of customer service.

With the inception of Council Tax, the Revenues section workload increased significantly for two reasons. First, they took over administration functions that had been carried out by other sections of the council under Community Charge.

Second, there is an ongoing need to administer the Community Charge system to ensure that all back taxes are collected. The Revenues section, therefore, increased in size from 135 to about 200 employees. Even with more employees, however, they could not provide the level of customer service to which they were committed.

The old structure of the system was becoming more and more difficult to manage and control. It was time for a system solution that created a greater level of employee productivity, office efficiency and customer service.

Analyzing Business Processes

The first step GRC's Revenue section took to improve the management of their system was to analyze their business processes. Considering their old method of doing business, it became apparent that customer service levels would continue to decrease over time.

The Revenues section needed to reengineer their business and have the capability to track the work through all four functional groups to provide a "one-door" approach to its customers. This meant a major upheaval within the section and an effort was needed to cross-train the staff.

Plexus Software Solution

> GRC recognized that the only way was to implement a system solution that used the latest technology

GRC recognized that the only way to achieve greater levels of employee productivity, office efficiency and customer service, was to implement a system solution that used the latest technology. They chose Recognition's Plexus line of software products for their software solution.

Bull Systems Integration group from Livingston, Scotland, was chosen as the integrator. The software solution, known as the Workflow and Imaging Revenues Development (WIReD) application, was designed by the Revenues section and programmed by the Bull team using Recognition's workflow-enabled imaging application software called Plexus CMA (Case Management Application).

CMA software provides the core functionality needed to process, manage and route folder-based information through a series of workflow steps by using Plexus FloWare workflow software and XDP imaging software together in an integrated application.

The new WIReD application provides a series of solutions for individual applications within the Revenues section. It combines information collected and processed throughout all four functional groups, allowing each user on the system immediate access to any information required. The system founded a new business process that solved the paper problem and the coordination of workflow between groups. The first application GRC tackled was benefits claims processing system, a folder-based application, which was designed by GRC Revenues and implemented by Bull. The next application will be written in-house and will be change-of-address processing.

Based on a client/server architecture, the solution runs on 486 PC workstations networked to a Sun 1030 Sparcstation. The Sun server connects the workstations to a Cygnet 1602 optical jukebox providing 271 gigabytes of on-line optical storage.

This equates to approximately two million pieces of paper being available to any person in any group at any given time. Today, any telephone call or visit from a customer is serviced by one Customer Care Assistant.

Perspectives on Workflow

Ronni T. Marshak, Editor-in-Chief
Patricia Seybold Group

The following is a series of editorials on workflow written by Ronni Marshak in the Workgroup Computing Report, *a Patricia Seybold Group publication. Marshak, who is editor-in-chief of the* Workgroup Computing Report, *is a leading analyst of workflow technologies and applications.*

Introduction to Workflow—June, 1991

Definition of workflow

Workflow is the sequence of actions or steps used in business processes. Automated workflow applies technology to the process, though not necessarily to every action. Workflow, by our definition, also implies that more than one person is involved in the process. Most workflows have both sequential steps (steps that happen in a prescribed order) and parallel steps (steps that can occur concurrently with other steps).

Workflow is part of business

I'm very hot on the promise of workflow. In fact, I believe that, eventually, almost all business computing applications will fall into the workflow category. Let me explain. Very few of us work in a vacuum, where no one else depends on our work to complete theirs, and where we are responsible for every step in a process, from conceiving of the need for the process to putting away the final related documents. To those few individuals who are completely autonomous, you have my awe (you must work very hard) and my sympathy (it must be very lonely).

Most of us depend on information from colleagues to complete our tasks, just as they are dependent upon us. In this environment, we create processes and procedures to ensure that the right information gets to the right people at the right time. Unfortunately, although most of us are pretty darn good at doing the individual tasks that make up a process, too many of us are pretty bad at monitoring the process itself. How often have you been asked the status of a certain project only to be stymied for an answer? All you know is that the project is somewhere in the process, just not at your step.

Workflow systems do more than report status

Computers are good at keeping track of things. Once the process is explained (programmed), the system will remember it forever (or until you change it), making sure the proper information is sent to the proper person or application. If asked nicely, the system will also give you status information when you need it. But workflow systems should do more than monitor and report status. They should also facilitate the process itself. By "facilitating the process," I mean several things:

- Notifying the user that he or she has a step or action on his or her plate
- Providing the user with the proper tool(s) to complete each task (right spreadsheet, right analysis tool, right document template)
- Providing the tool with the proper data to complete the task (appropriate data already flowing through the tools)
- Allowing the users to see where their tasks fit in the complete process.

Notifying The User: Notification to the user, ideally, should be able to be integrated with the user's standard e-mail package. Users should not have to go looking through multiple messaging systems to find out what is going on in the organization. Today, electronic mail is used primarily to send messages from person to person. Increasingly, the same e-mail systems will be used to send messages from application to person and vice versa.

> I'm very hot on the promise of workflow

Workflow messages can be identified by a special icon or subject category. They can be placed in a separate "in box." But the key is that the user is familiar with the mail environment and interface, and does not have to check in several different places throughout the day.

Providing The Proper Tools With The Proper Data: A scenario; a regular customer places an order. Ordinarily, in the workflow, the order form would go to the assistant credit manager for approval. However, because the customer is already at the top of his credit limit, the form is sent to you, the credit manager (the workflow application automatically determined this). In addition to the order form, the system brings up the customers credit history, latest Dun and Bradstreet (D&B) rating, and a 1-2-3 worksheet already loaded with the appropriate formulae for calculating the interest on the extension of credit. All of this is part of the workflow application as it was designed.

Of course, every factor in making the decision cannot be anticipated. You may want to check the inventory database to see if your company is overstocked with the item and just wants to get rid of it. Or you may want to talk to the sales representative to see how much business this customer might give you in the future. But, having the basic tools you need to access credit history in an internal database, spreadsheet template on your local desktop, appropriate data, credit information and D&B rating on that specific customer, and the correct loan amount loaded into the spreadsheet would make your task much easier. You can spend your time making decisions and looking for mitigating circumstances rather than searching for tools and data.

Allowing The Users To See Where Their Tasks Fit: I believe that it is very important for you as a user to see exactly where in the process your actions fit. Although this does not necessarily help you complete a task, it does help you understand the importance of your role and the consequences of a task poorly, or well, done. In addition, by looking at the process as a whole, you are more likely to discover modifications that could significantly improve the procedure. Too often, workflow applications are merely on-line versions of old, perhaps antiquated, paper systems. Seeing them in their entirety on-line helps you recognize the problems and bottlenecks.

Workflow applications are unique to your organization

Your processes and procedures are unique to your organization. They are the way you do business. My excitement about workflow is that it helps groups of people do their jobs, facilitating both the individual tasks as well as the flow of information between tasks. And it lets you know what is going on! Look at how macros have caught on. What used to be a technology only for spreadsheet junkies now is a tool for the most naive word processing user. (You mean, all I have to do is say, "Learn this," and I can run the process again and again? Wow!) Macros automate individual tasks. Workflow automates the flow or sequence of these tasks throughout an organization. It makes your job easier and, hopefully, makes you and your processes more productive. Isn't that what workgroup computing should do?

Characteristics of a Workflow System—May, 1993

Mind your Rs and Ps

How did we get into this workflow stuff in the first place? Well, for decades, computer scientists have looked at the work we do, the order it needs to be done in, and the information we needed to get out of it, and they have designed systems to try to provide this information—in other words, to automate our business processes. In the last few years, these automation systems have become more flexible, allowing the business users, who truly understand exactly what the process is intended to do, to take a more active role in the design of the automated process. Although we have yet to reach the point where non-technical business people can fully automate complex applications (that is, without support from IS), we do now have tools that allow us "real users" to develop relatively straightforward applications by ourselves. A lot of theories about workflow have been thrown around in the past few months. Exactly what is it? What makes up a workflow system? How do you design a business process? Well, just to add to the abundance of theories, here's mine: The Rs and Ps of workflow.

The Rs

The three Rs of workflow are:

- Routes
- Rules
- Roles

To qualify in my book as a true workflow development tool, the product must offer a way to define and automate these three things.

Routes: Routing is probably the first area of business processes that was automated. In the imaging world, the first workflow products from such companies as FileNet and Recognition allowed vendors or resellers (and, later, the customers) to define the order in which images were to flow. In today's world, you need to be able to specify the flow of any sort of object. These objects should be able to be routed sequentially (one after another), in parallel routes with rendezvous points (an object can go off on any number of different sequential routes and then reconcile into a single route at a specified point), and to be sent in a broadcast mode (the e-mail model, where everyone gets the object at once) or in any ad hoc order (as described by the user at the time of processing).

> your processes and procedures are unique to your organization

Routing needs to take into account more than just the person (or process) to whom the work is routed. It must also include what objects—document, forms, data, applications—are to be routed.

Rules: A more advanced feature of workflow automation is defining rules that determine the information to be routed to whom. This is sometimes called *conditional routing* or *exception-handling*. Most workflow builders have mechanisms for defining rules. Unfortunately, at this point, rule definition is often accomplished by scripting or other programmer-like activities. Products in other areas, especially in e-mail, as evidenced by BeyondMail have delivered user-defined rules engines that allow business users, without any technical capabilities, to write relatively complex rules by selecting options from drop-down lists and from menus.

Roles are also vital when a number of different people have the authorization to do the same work

I understand that defining the rules of workflow can be very difficult and that rules can be very complex and convoluted, with multiple options, variations, and exceptions. And I realize that trained programmers and application developers, who can be sure to think through the entire set of possibilities that can result from a single rule, are necessary for sophisticated, multipath, exception-laden processes. But I am also convinced that business users can think through the more obvious (and more commonly used) rules: for example, if amount is greater than $5,000, send it to the supervisor; otherwise, send it to purchasing. A few of the workflow products on the market, such as WorkMAN from Reach Software, allow the end user to define simple rules using Boolean logic operations. And this is a very good start.

Roles: This leads us to roles. In the example above, I did not route the request to Sue or to Max, but rather to a supervisor or to Purchasing. The ability to define roles independent of the specific people—or processes—that happen to fill that role is very important to ensure flexibility of a workflow application. For example, if I did route the "amount greater than $5,000" to Sue and if Sue left the company, I would have to re-specify the recipient under the new conditions. If I send it to the role, I will add the new person's name to the role of supervisor. Now, agreed, it takes the same amount of work to add a name to a role as to change the name in a single workflow step. But consider what happens if Sue is involved in multiple steps in dozens of workflows. The change could be indicated once—in a role table, say—and any workflow that needed to route something to supervisor (Sue) would now route the information to her replacement.

Roles are also vital when a number of different people have the authorization to do the same work, such as claims adjusters. Any one of them will do; just assign the task to the next available. Finally, a process or agent can assume a role. It does not need to be a person.

Okay. Now you have the three Rs, all of which can be considered objects that must be defined in the workflow application. Let's look at the Ps of workflow, which encompass the softer-side--the people's issues.

The Ps

The three Ps of workflow are:

- Processes
- Policies
- Practices

Processes: The processes (a.k.a. procedures—yet another P) that we have established to run our businesses are as varied and as personal to our companies and the people who take part in them. Often, processes are not "designed" but are identified after the fact, extracted from common usage. "We've always done it this way," is a common cry when people try to examine and evaluate processes. One of the biggest areas of potential and pain (two more Ps) is in redesigning existing processes, eliminating the redundancies, identifying the bottlenecks, and understanding why it is you do what you do.

Policies: Policies are more than just the formal written statements of how certain processes are handled; they are the actual reasons for doing the work—the guidelines that explain how the decision was made to do things a certain way. Formal policies rarely capture this information. Most of it is anecdotal at best. "Oh, the reason that everything must go through Charlotte in quality control is that we want to deliver working product. Before Charlotte came on board, Henry in packaging did the final check, and he missed so much!" And, even more, practices are the "breaking of the rules" of the process.

Practices: Finally, we come to the practices, which are an organization's reflections of its corporate culture and values. The practices we put in place in our companies are based on not only the work we have to do, but also the way we perceive the actual work experience should feel. Practices include issues such as democratic access to information, responsibility versus authority to take risks.

Falling in Love with Distinctions—July, 1993

A dangerous route on the road to groupware

International Data Corporation (IDC, Framingham, Massachusetts) has proposed three separate categories for types of workflow applications:

- Ad hoc
- Administrative
- Production

These are very useful categories, and they have helped customers get their minds around a very complex and diverse set of products and methodologies. But I am concerned that vendors have taken these categories too literally and are, therefore, ignoring what really needs to happen in the workflow world.

> distinctions are useful in the area of image versus document management

The very nature of groupware often suggests fuzzy distinctions

I believe that IDC offered these distinctions as guidelines—general category buckets where people can look at the processes used in their businesses and figure out where to start looking at technology solutions to automate them. What I do not believe is that IDC meant these as static categories with impenetrable boundaries.

Why do I bring this up? Recently, I have met with a variety of companies that have chosen a workflow category and have positioned software products that address only that category (or two of the three categories). The problem is that these vendors do not have adequate solutions for what happens when the solutions they propose need to scale up or down.

In my view, IDC'ss workflow categories represent a continuum of automated processes, not mutually exclusive arenas. Workflow solutions often start at the ad hoc level, developed by business users without a lot of preliminary planning, and are very flexible within predefined rules and structure. But these same Ad Hoc Workflows quickly grow into more well-defined administrative workflows. And, once administrative workflows—such as purchase order requests and expense reporting—are used extensively and have the bugs worked out, they often identify areas that can and should be rigorously structured and automated, thus becoming production workflows.

Another area where distinctions are useful but have become too rigidly defined is the area of image versus document management. Solutions targeting the imaging market usually do not adequately address the management of electronically generated documents, and vice versa.

The very nature of groupware often suggests fuzzy distinctions, where one type of application can suddenly become invaluable in a totally unexpected solution. For example, scheduling systems are obviously an aid to arranging meetings of groups of people, but when you look at scheduling software as a service available to workflow, you can begin to develop applications where a step of the workflow automatically schedules a meeting of team members and runs a query against relevant data immediately before that meeting. The proper reports would be provided at the proper time to the proper people. Is this a workflow application or a database application or a scheduling application? I propose that it is all three. The distinctions are fuzzy.

So, vendors, beware. Using understandable distinctions can be the best way to initially position your product, but, useful as these categories can be, restricting your vision of your product to a single category can be counterproductive and limiting. Do not fall into the trap of one vendor, who, at a trade show, explained how it provided a mail-enabled workflow solution where integration with all popular mail clients was the primary focus. Unfortunately, one customer wanted a workflow system that captured all information in a robust underlying database, so he took note of the presentation, thanked the vendor, and walked on to the next booth. The sad thing is that the product in question does use a robust underlying database structure, but the product had been positioned and touted as a mail-enabled application. By falling in love with the distinctions rather than promoting the multiple capabilities of the product, the company lost a potential sale.

What Users Want from Workflow—September, 1993

Are we asking for too much? I think not!

I just returned from *Groupware '93* and the *Workflow Conference*, where I spent a great deal of time discussing what exactly is going on in the workflow market. This subject seems to fascinate users and vendors alike, though we still sometimes find ourselves using the same words to mean totally different things words—like "process" and "application" and "workflow." For purposes of clarity, here are my definitions for these terms (in reverse order):

- Workflow: applying technology to business processes—in other words, using computers to help groups of people get their work done
- Application: an automated process developed to help your business (the results of using workflow tools and methodologies)
- Process: a series of specific steps that need to be done to accomplish a specific goal. Typically, more than one person is involved, and the order and nature of the steps change according to conditions.

At the San Jose Workflow Conference, I was asked to speak on a panel, representing the users' point of view regarding workflow. So I put on my user hat (after all, I am a user of this stuff), stood at podium, and gave my wish list for workflow software. I want:

- Software that runs in my current environment, for example, desktop platform, LANs, e-mail backbone, and provide scalability, software tools that support development from business-user prototyping up to enterprise process reengineering
- Modularity, that is, putting together workflows developed separately, creating reusable steps, rules, roles, groups
- Corporate data sources, corporate directories, and repositories access
- Integration with desktop applications of choice as well as legacy systems
- Choice of access points for workflow task assignments (e-mail inbox, to-do list, calendar) and multiple views and features (did I design the workflow, do I participate in it, am I the manager?)
- Management tools and reports, that is, access to the aggregate data I capture from the multiple instances of a workflow
- Customizability, to let me design workflows that reflect my business
- Flexibility, to let me change my workflows as my business changes

I want customiz-ability, to let me design workflows that reflect my business

The list received general approval, but one audience member asked whether I wasn't asking for too much. How could a single vendor deliver all of this?

My response was that a single vendor did not necessarily have to deliver it all; there is a need for standards that support interoperability of workflow products so that a single product does not have to do it all. I also suggested, since no one product satisfies everything on my list, that you have to separate the "I needs" from the "I wants."

> work
> processes
> change —
> sometimes
> overnight

Upon further reflection, I am even more committed to the list. Why should users lower their expectations to make life easier for technology vendors? If we demand less, the products we are offered will never exceed our demands. And if our demands do not reflect our requirements, we are not going to buy the technology.

Users and vendors should not be adversaries. They should work in partnership to come up with software and tools that are truly useful and can thus be cost-justified. Then, and only then, will this industry lift off its sandbar and continue its advance.

Workflow-Enablement—November, 1993

I may have been wrong—at least partially—in my view of workflow. For the past three years, I have been telling you that workflow is the umbrella application under which sit services such as document management, time management, and messaging. I advocated using workflow application builders as you design new applications. And, while I have stressed that the workflow tools you use interoperate with and leverage existing installed software, I have always viewed the workflow software as the development and execution environment.

It is now approaching the end of 1993, and workflow still has not taken off. There are dozens of products on the market, but no clear winners. Users are reluctant to invest the time, effort, and expense in technology that has no proven longevity and is not particularly well understood.

Workflow is poorly defined

At last count, over 140 software companies claim that they provide workflow software. The functionality and focus of these products run the gamut from distribution lists in electronic mail to completely automated phone/fax sales response systems to complete business process modeling systems. In the current market, these are all workflow. No wonder users, not to mention vendors, are confused.

Workflow takes planning

You don't just go design a workflow prototype (or, at least, most people think you can't—we actually encourage rolling up your sleeves and doing some rapid prototyping sooner rather than later in the application definition process, but that's fodder for another editorial). Most companies contemplating implementing workflow solutions are mired in the business process reengineering stage, employing high-priced consultants to draw flow charts on white boards. These charts will, ultimately, turn into applications, perhaps even using workflow tools, but the up-front work cycle is long and intimidating. Workflow can fail in many ways.

Workflow might not work

Technologically. Too often, new systems, especially group or enterprise systems that depend on networked communication, actually bring the network to its knees. Sudden increased traffic, incompatible commands, unexpected glitches—these happen when new systems are put into place. Heck, they happen when you load a new word processor!

Design

Work processes change—sometimes overnight. Workflow applications, especially those with long planning cycles, are often so complex and so difficult to modify that they are out of date before they have a chance. Another classic workflow design problem is that of efficiently automating an inefficient process.

Even long and painful business design sessions sometimes yield poorly designed processes.

Cultural resistance to change

If a workgroup is not properly prepared or motivated to use a new workflow application, the application will not succeed. Too many good applications have failed because they were basically sabotaged by users who liked the way things were done before automation.

Workflow-enabled software

I have been thinking about Microsoft's view of groupware: Group-enable all software by providing group functionality in the operating system rather than in specialized products. Mail-enablement has definitely taken off. Well, why not workflow-enabled software? Take, for example, a document management application. Your users are familiar with their document manager, using it to save and locate documents, to check in and out of documents, and for version control. Now, you want to start routing these documents based on certain rules and/or conditions. Rather than building a workflow application in a new paradigm, you want to be able to add these workflow capabilities to the existing document management application. You want to workflow-enable the document manager. Nobody is intimidated, and, even if not everyone takes advantage of the functionality, the entire application is not thrown away as a failure.

> I still want MIS to build complex, production, mission-critical applications

I still believe that almost every business application written is a workflow application—automating business processes to get work done by a group of people. And, eventually, as a result of this ubiquity, the term, workflow, will disappear. It will simply be synonymous with application development. But, until we are ready for that day, let's try implementing manageable chunks of workflow functionality by augmenting our familiar and comfortable personal and group applications with workflow capabilities.

Lotus Notes—December, 1993

The best thing to happen to the workflow market

almost every business application written is a workflow application

Now, before all the vendors of workflow products start screaming, let me say that I do not believe that Lotus Notes is the best workflow product on the market. Indeed, I do not classify Notes as workflow software. But I do believe that the Notes phenomenon has played a significant role in bringing the all-too-invisible workflow market into the public eye.

But isn't notes workflow?

Many people believe that Notes is, indeed, a workflow product. And the Notes platform does offer quite a few workflow features, such as serial routing, action buttons, and status-tracking. You can also write Notes macros, which, when combined with other Notes features, simulate rule-based workflow routing and management. But the product is not optimized to create workflow applications; it is optimized for developing document database and tracking applications.

A workflow builder provides specific tools and interfaces for defining the flow of tasks in the process to be automated, for defining the roles of the people doing those tasks, for defining the rules by which the flow is determined. And workflow management engines provide specific information on where each instance of a process is at any one point. Although this type of application can be, and often is, developed in the Notes environment, the application developer has to jury-rig the Notes features to come up with the results that a workflow builder (if it is well designed) will guide you through.

A testament to the value of partnership

One of the most intriguing elements of the Notes marketplace is the cottage industry that it has spawned. Dozens of companies have sprung up to build companion products to Notes, some of which are completely Notes-based and some of which add functionality to the Notes environment. The workflow industry is very visible in this arena.

Companies such as Quality Decision Management Incorporated with its Quality *At Work* product and API/Crossroad with its Workflow Engine have built tools on top of Lotus Notes to automate and manage processes. Other companies, such as Action Technologies with its recently shipping ActionWorkflow Builder for Notes, and Reach Software with its newly announced WorkMAN for Notes, have built versions of their existing workflow products that integrate with Notes as the deployment environment.

I still want MIS to build complex, production, mission-critical applications.

Even those workflow vendors that do not have specific Notes versions of their products, such as XSoft Corporation with InConcert, and NCR Corporation with ProcessIT, have all articulated (or are about to reveal) a "Notes strategy" indicating how their products work with Notes. No one, but *no one,* in the workflow marketplace is stressing a purely competitive positioning against Notes.

Lotus Notes has become proof of the concept that users want to develop, and are eminently capable of developing group applications that reflect how their businesses run. Workflow applications fit neatly into this arena—they are applications that reflect the group processes that run businesses. The visibility that Notes has given to the concept of desktop-based group applications has brought into the sunlight other tools that were too often overshadowed by the entrenched MIS-focused tools, such as 4GL, and relational database application builders.

There is a valuable place for MIS tools. I still want MIS to build complex, production, mission-critical applications. I do not believe that us desktop jockeys are ready for that. But the tools aimed at sophisticated business users and LAN administrator/IT types have been gaining more and more acceptance and support. I think we can thank Notes for much of that.

The Work Management Market

Michael Howard, Vice-President, Marketing
Xerox Corporation

Management Overview

Workflow software was once the secret ingredient of document imaging systems, which used it to expedite and codify the movement of document-based information across an organization. With it, imaging vendors could radically transform data processing, document processing, and customer service operations. By 1991, workflow software clearly had ramifications outside the fairly tightly bounded space of document imaging. In fact, it fit perfectly the description of emerging middleware—software wrapped into specific applications now, but destined to become a platform service called by many applications.

In the past two years, new workflow products and approaches have emerged, coming from companies like Action Technologies, Beyond, Digital Equipment, Hewlett-Packard, Keyfile, NCR, Reach Software, and Verimation. Their workflow ideas fit into today's generalized computing environments for offices and work groups, targeting such simple concepts as electronic forms routing. The workflow vision thus begins to unfold not as a single layer of middleware for the enterprise, but as multiple layers packaged differently.

> workflow applications understand that users are not "dumb terminals"

The essential workflow principles remain the same. Workflow software takes business problems and translates them into technical solutions that streamline work processes and make them more efficient. Designed for a networked computing environment, workflow software boosts the number of work processes that can pass through the intelligent workstation. Office work can be assigned, routed, activated, and managed through system parameters that mirror actual business operations and decision processes. Workflow applications understand that users are not "dumb terminals"; the work of each user differs in content, intensity, time, and exception conditions.

End users and IS organizations are now driving workflow vendors harder than ever in an attempt to reengineer business processes. Business process reengineering aims at replacing old and outdated work methods with new or streamlined methods that focus on core business principles—end-user empowerment, customer service, product quality, and fast product design. Workflow, more accurately called work management, turns the abstract themes and expectations of business process reengineering into a practical and concrete method to implement that reengineering.

The past year has seen changes in the work management market:

- New generations of systems are emerging based on familiar imaging technologies. The imaging vendors provide a visual approach to workflow, complementing it with workflow libraries that reflect horizontal and vertical tasks and processes.
- At the same time, work management is teaming up tightly with electronic mail systems. Packages bundle workflow, electronic forms, and electronic mail.
- System integrators, database and tool providers, and traditional system players all are beefing up their involvement in work management. These parties promise a sophisticated knowledge- or object-based approach to workflow, one that is not tied to image plumbing or e-mail interfaces.

The work management offerings will gradually get richer, but at the expense of complexity in buying decisions. We urge users not to forget the fact that workflow will be application-dependent for a few more years; thus multiple approaches may make sense. Moreover, users must insist on vendors providing explicit responses to questions of business benefits, function points, application design, support assumptions, budgets, and hardware and network configuration dependencies.

The most compelling implementations of workflow over the next two years will solve well-understood business and paper processing situations. Mail-enabled forms and document routing and approval applications will likely mushroom from the bottom up; in other words, from the desktop. By 1997, workflow will become a series of interlocking workflow designs rather than any single workflow repository (0.7 probability).

work management streamlines and transforms crucial business processes

Strategic Planning Assumption: Work management systems will translate the knowledge and principles of business process reengineering into usable software code by the end of 1995 (0.8 probability).

The Gartner Group Office Information Systems service has analyzed the workflow market for the past three years. In the first year, workflow was considered relatively new, pioneered by the imaging market and expanding beyond it. Last year, it was discussed in terms of document management. This year workflow is branching off on its own. The narrow focus of imaging-oriented workflow has broadened to a new notion called work management, which encompasses various types of workflow software and services.

As a reference point, we define work management in this fashion: Work management is a set of software products and services that apply workflow structure to the movement of information and to the interaction of business processes that generate the information. Work management streamlines and transforms crucial business processes and thus can improve results and performance.

In many senses, work management goes hand in hand with business process reengineering and business process automation, both of which similarly capture the spirit of change. However, though discussions of business process reengineering and business process automation are intellectually appealing, they often are too abstract. Work management, on the other hand, takes a close look at end-user work habits, especially at the real-life bits of work that consume so much time and money. Work management systems aim to automate and monitor as many office tasks and functions as feasible, including keyboarding, faxing, filing, scheduling, accessing, updating, communicating, and approving. The systems will grow more complex as we move from work-group processes to enterprise-wide processes.

1.0 The Connection to Business Process Reengineering

The principles and systems behind work management are the most powerful and practical way for information technology professionals to satisfy boardroom reengineering mandates. Work management can transform reengineering goals into run-time systems that strengthen service quality, shorten product development time, accelerate customer service transactions, empower line decision-making, raise revenues, and lower labor costs. Work management focuses on automating and measuring organizational work processes without the constraints of departmental boundaries.

Work management can help an organization in three distinct ways:

- Work management can "mirror" how organizations operate, illuminating not only what works but also what does not work. At this minimum level of benefit from workflow, users can expect to reduce costs, improve productivity, and avoid potential new costs.
- Work management can add to the incremental reengineering of businesses, as with platform transition strategies. There, workflow can link legacy applications to new client/server functions, empowering users by adding new data and simpler processes to the business.
- Workflow can be used to reengineer business processes completely, not just fixing processes, but quite literally changing the way in which the organization does business. To reach this target, organizations must have enough foresight to anticipate what will be needed in the future need and then set up a flexible infrastructure for changing conditions.

Not surprisingly, a huge gap frequently separates the abstract goals invoked in the boardroom from the real actions and steps required to fulfill the mandates. In a real sense, work management bridges the gap between executive-level reengineering mandates and the hands-on work that makes mandates a reality. It adds weight to the mandates by making the abstract concepts concrete.

For example, here we list a series of business goals and add suggestions for focused work management initiatives:

- To increase revenues, work management should focus on sales leads, responses to proposals, new product introduction
- To generate more working capital, work management should focus on accounts receivable, item processing throughput, and accounts payable
- To improve customer satisfaction, work management should focus on customer correspondence, preventive maintenance schedules, and customer service tracking
- To reduce costs, work management should focus on plant maintenance schedules, and development project management
- To improve morale, work management should focus on eliminating clerical routines
- To improve quality, work management should focus on measuring organizational performance against goals.

1.1 The Glue that Binds the New and the Old

Strategic Planning Assumption: Work management software will emerge first as a means of integrating disparate applications. In its earliest incarnations, it will envelop applications and mimic the useful processes of the physical office (0.8 probability).

Strategic Planning Assumption: By 1996, work management software will play a crucial role in weaving together sophisticated desktop applications and objects, and that role will open new application frontiers (0.7 probability).

Before applying any new technology to a reengineering project, we recommend that users examine the installed systems and procedures, and fix what ails them. Abandoning old but still useful systems is a foolhardy proposition. More than 70 percent of the time, information technology is applied to well-understood business processes, many of which suffer simply from being paper-bound, tethered to an outdated system, or poorly connected to other business systems. In some cases, more than half the benefits expected of a reengineering process come from actions taken before new technology is introduced.

Work management systems act as the glue that binds legacy applications to new systems, client/server functions, and document and folder management schemes. Generally, work management pulls together departmental functions that mesh poorly with the conventional data center. Order entry and purchasing are prime examples of host-based applications that can benefit from work management's addition of processing logic and data to the systems and the human processes.

2.0 Inside Work Management

Work management will push applications out beyond the confines of traditional boundaries of the accounting, administration, or legal departments. The new class of applications will be logical extensions of today's production-class work management, which generally focuses on back-office and front-office applications.

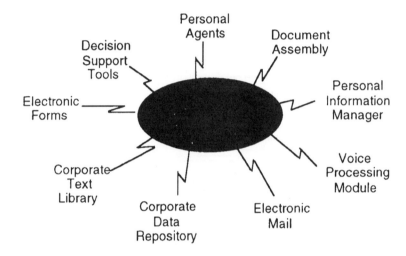

Figure 1. A Web of Electronic Processes. Source: The Gartner Group

However, the new applications will be tuned to the needs and work habits of business professionals and knowledge workers, who typically rely on paper, telephones, PC-centric applications, and electronic mail. Those extraneous tasks lend themselves well to the idea of automation, but poorly to the practical implementation of automation, largely because of their ad hoc nature.

As technology draws users into an electronic web of organizational processes, work management software will provide the means of joining the modules or results of diverse office applications (see Figure 1).

2.1 How Does a Work Management System Work?

Work management systems are leading-edge implementations of client/server technology, and their power comes from the sophisticated interaction of server and client software mechanisms. At the core are four unique components: intelligent work packets (comprising work items, work tasks, and role tools), transaction couriers, work queues, and work processing engines (see Figure 2). Over the next few years, vendors that concentrate on those four components will create sustainable competitive differentiators in the workflow market.

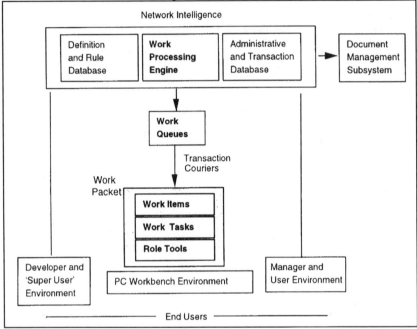

Figure 2. The Basic Components of a Work Management System.
Source: The Gartner Group.

Users invoke queued work items through a graphical depiction of the workflow. Once the work queues are invoked, the system dynamically assembles the environment, the data, and the task logic, which invokes the next related task within a larger process. The systems apply considerable processing logic to the work-item instantiations to determine priorities, wait states, rendezvous arrangements, and timing monitors.

2.2 The Four Components of Work Management Systems

The ideal work management system of which there are very few encompasses four environments: 1) method and analysis services, 2) prototyping and development, 3) execution and end-user, and 4) management control, administration, and simulation (see Figure 3). Most commercial workflow systems today cover both the prototyping and development environment and the execution and end-user environment; the remaining two are handled either by system integrators or through custom software. As work management grows, vendors will concentrate first on the management, control and simulation environment for their systems, and then on method and analysis.

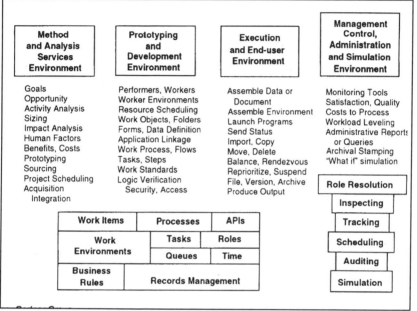

Figure 3. Four local Work Management Functions.
Source: The Gartner Group

2.3 Work Management Application Categories

Work management applications generally fall into four categories:

- Production and core business applications are host-oriented and typically deal with clerical work processes, most likely those found in the back office or in the front office. These systems are robust, structured, and expensive—few systems in this class go for less than $200,000—and they require system integration of one kind or another.

- Electronic forms and work-group applications are relatively new, driven as they are by desktop and work-group computing vendors. These applications generally take a simple, incremental approach to process automation by focusing on structured communication between business professionals (for example, travel and expense forms) and on the day-to-day paper forms of the business. They require few services, are relatively cheap to adopt, and are packaged to link easily into work-group office systems.

- Groupware communication applications, like the previous class of applications, are desktop-oriented. They add workflow management logic to such off-line activities as managing meetings or brainstorming with teams of people. Here the software is designed to capture and encourage unstructured, or ad hoc, communication among people.

- Document manufacturing applications add workflow management to document publishing and engineering change systems. Though the workflow portion tends to be permanently embedded in the bigger document manufacturing application, it will gradually be extracted and adapted for other systems and purposes.

3.0 Adoption Of Work Management Software

Key Issue: How will work management software be absorbed by user organizations?

Tactical Recommendation: Adoption strategies for the near future must take a portfolio approach that explicitly recognizes some variation in work and workers.

	Back Office	Front Office	Knowledge Development
Focus	Internal	External	Solution
Processing Styles	Batch	Transaction	Project
Objectives	Produce	Respond	Change
Examples	Administrators Accountants	Salespeople Purchasing	Managers Professionals

Figure 4. White Collar Employment Categories.
Source: The Gartner Group

Opportunities for work management applications are closely related to the composition of an organization's white-collar employees (see Figure 4). Generally the work force has three types of workers: back-office workers, such as claims processors in an insurance company; front-office workers, such as people who handle customer inquiries; and knowledge workers, such as advertising executives or lawyers. A company with a big population of claims processors, for example, should invest in technology particularly suited to the back office (for example, imaging, micrographics replacements, structured approaches).

On the other hand, companies with a high percentage of front-office or knowledge workers will likely get the greatest productivity benefits through technologies that encourage creativity and brainstorming (for example, electronic mail, document management, electronic forms, groupware). In any case, the notion of adding some degree of process structure to applications is important. The daily work life of professionals and knowledge workers usually reflects an unbearable percentage of mundane clerical processes, many of which could at least be off loaded, if not eliminated entirely, through structured work management.

3.1 Barriers to Adoption

Strategic Planning Assumption: Through 1996, work management will penetrate slowly, impeded by the lack of a client/server infrastructure and the lack of such universal middleware services as databases, messaging, and document management (0.8 probability).

3.1.1 Slow Penetration of Client/Server

In many senses, the notion of work management depends on the notion of client/server computing. Unfortunately, IS specialists and end users alike have a hard time believing that client/server computing is real and economically feasible. Convincing them is the major challenge facing software vendors. Then too, even if the vendors fulfill that evangelical mission, they still must create a foundation for client/server computing—even to the extent of repairing flawed local-area networks and desktop operating systems to make client/server workable. The evolution of client/server—and hence of work management software—will proceed along two paths: infrastructure and application (see Figure 5).

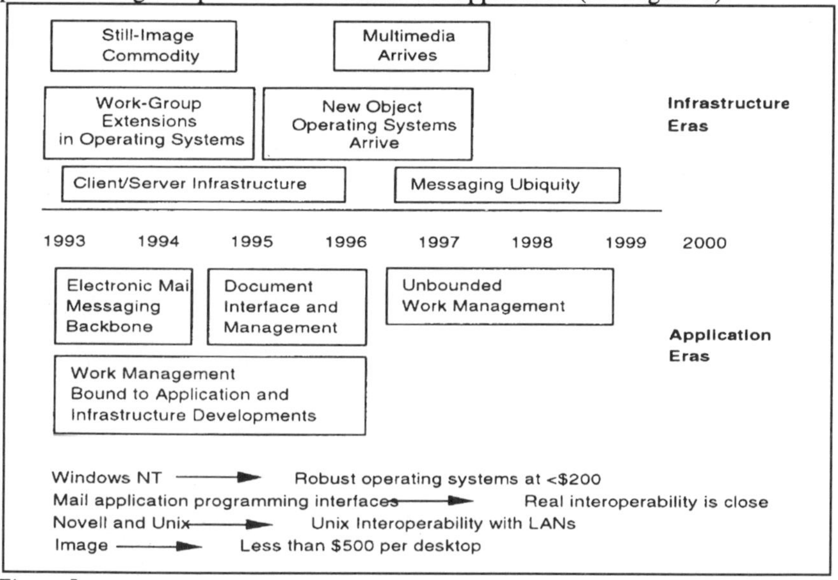

Figure 5
Source: The Gartner Group

239

3.1.2 Absence of Standard Services

During the next three years, work management will be bound tightly to client/server infrastructures and to specific middleware services, such as databases, mail transports, user interfaces, and object and folder models.

Finally, by 1997 interfaces will exist across various architectures, leading us into an era of unbounded work management. Unbounded, here, means an environment in which document management and object management are implemented not on the host computer alone but rather in all computing environments, including the network, the server, and the client.

3.1.3 Poor Attention to Human Factors

Strategic Planning Assumption: The penetration of work management systems will be slow because of steep learning curves in dealing with human factors and organizational change management (0.8 probability).

Work management systems cut right to the heart of how individuals and work groups operate, yet many vendors and users are implementing work management without considering its impact on the labor force. Huge reallocations and dislocations of people are expected during the next five years, and information technology cannot bear the brunt of reapportioning jobs.

3.2 Separating Myth from Reality

When a work management project dovetails with reengineering, myths abound. For instance, consider four myths:
* Management always knows best
* All computer systems simplify jobs and reduce costs
* Electronic information is always better than paper
* Virtually all work processes should be translated into electronic processes.

The organizational realities are difficult to stomach:
* Management does not always understand life in the trenches
* Systems are hard and costly to support
* People must see an immediate two-to-one improvement in information processing capabilities to justify disruptive transition costs away from paper
* Some processes should not be codified given their innate complexity.

4.0 The Office Technologies Beneath Work management

Key Issue: What is the impact of the key office technologies on work management?

Whether labeled process coordination, workflow, or work management, the concept of designing systems and applications that mirror human and task interaction has its roots in the office environment. Over the past three or four years, work management has drawn on a handful of office technologies, some relatively mature and others just surfacing.

4.1 Imaging

Strategic Planning Assumption: Imaging software and hardware technology will drive 50 percent of work management installations during the next three years, given rapidly declining price points and imaging's power to replicate and improve everyday office processes (0.7 probability).

The imaging marketplace is where many work management vendors cut their teeth, yet the market has changed forever. Imaging is no longer a dedicated market; vendors cannot survive based solely on handling imaging peripherals and image data types. Instead they must open their architectures and focus on applications, software, and service expertise. Moreover, we see an explosion of providers offering imaging technologies at low to midrange price points, both for high-end and low-end applications. Imaging technologies directly substitute capital for human labor with almost overwhelming increases in efficiency. The fundamental design model of the imaging application market is appealing and viable, including its notions of folders, mixed objects, client/sever computing, host system integration, and work management.

> the electronic forms market will be a hot segment of the work management market

4.2 Electronic Forms

Strategic Planning Assumption: Electronic forms automation is a Trojan horse brought into the production application arena by work-group vendors. The latter vendors will put pricing pressure on production-class work management specialists (0.7 probability).

The electronic forms market will be a hot segment of the work management market during the next three years, as corporations seek to eliminate paper and as work-group computing vendors expand in influence and size. Though the reasoning behind electronic forms is sound, the product functions and channel support required to satisfy the need for electronic forms must evolve more before the market really takes off.

Electronic forms vendors must start to address such user objectives as host system updates, document management integration, and integration of key development tools. Ultimately automated electronic forms will force convergence of those objectives in work management software, where applications deal with host updates, end-user work environments, queuing, work items, in-boxes, and process logic.

4.3 Hybrid Frameworks

Strategic Planning Assumption: The most savvy users will build a work management framework that leverages PC and host architectures, builds corporate knowledge about work processes, and smoothes the technology adoption process as business and technology conditions permit (0.7 probability).

Users are starting to demand work management systems that incorporate the robust features and qualities of production-class applications—queue management, forms management, fast prototyping, host and PC integration—but without the historical dependency on image. Hybrid systems like these will enable users to automate such key electronic office procedures as credit checks, host updates and reviews, and correspondence, while gradually bringing such off-line procedures as records management on line. In this picture, a work management framework provides moderate to high payback while avoiding massive up-front costs for new technologies (for example, EDI, image, voice). The framework does, in addition, allow for integration.

One of the chief reasons for the image-independent hybrid approach is the quest for real data about the business process—an important part of reengineering.

4.4 Work-Group Computing

Strategic Planning Assumption: Work-group technologies, coupled with electronic mail, will lay the foundation for an entirely new computing paradigm built on messaging and intelligent objects (0.7 probability).

Strategic Planning Assumption: By 1997 work-group and production approaches will converge on managing objects and providing work management function points, rendering the approaches indistinguishable (0.7 probability).

Applications based on the production model emphasize host-oriented conventions and databases that use SQL and remote procedure calls; as such, the applications tend to have technical underpinnings different from the electronic forms and work-group applications, which are network-oriented. Applications based on the model of electronic forms and work-group computing take maximum advantage of local-area networks, PC software, applications and services, such as Microsoft's Object Linking and Embedding (OLE) facilities, transport agents, mail directories, and now Notes databases. Here, vendor leverage lies in reusing inexpensive work-group facilities.

4.5   Technology Convergence

By 1996 all work management approaches will converge, an advantage for users. Application developers will design systems that facilitate either high-speed database technology or low-speed messaging technology (see Figure 6). Work management tailored to electronic mail will be used for widespread geographic reach. Databases will focus on highly targeted work groups and department functions.

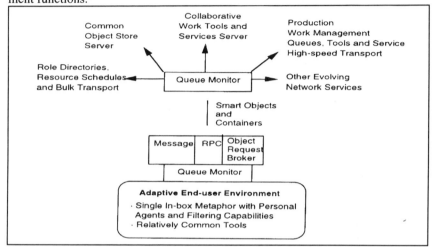

Figure 6. The Convergence of Production and Work-Group Approaches.
Source: The Gartner Group

5.0 Evaluating Work Management Software And Services

Key Issue: How should users evaluate work management software and services?

Strategic Planning Assumption: Production systems will deliver up to three times more power than work-group systems, but will cost five times as much and demonstrate less flexibility in dealing with front-office workers and knowledge workers.

Strategic Planning Assumption: Work management acquisition decisions through 1995 will force users to determine a comfortable entry point into the fast-paced world of client/server application development (0.8 probability).

Production-class work management systems are built to solve more complex problems than either electronic forms or work-group applications; thus they generally have more functional strength, though they also are more rigid and less flexible—a drawback for the unstructured work and communication patterns of electronic forms and work-group computing (see Figure 7).

> electronic forms and work-group systems excel at distributed worker support

While production systems are too inflexible and rigid for most distributed environments, electronic forms and work-group systems excel at distributed worker support and thus are destined to ride on top of LAN and PC work-group extensions. Price points will fall dramatically, but the forms and work-group systems will not include many functions of the production model. In most cases, service will be handled by value-added resellers and integrators, channels that are not fully formed for work management. Early players are building in-house capabilities to address channel deficiencies. Users must decide if they need functions immediately, or if they can build it later.

Evaluation Category	Production	Electronic Forms and Work Group
Work Manipulation	•••••	••
Host Integration	•••••	••
Scalability in Documents	•••••	••
Sophistication of Process and Queue Management	•••••	•
Power of Work Management Tools	•••••	••
Intuitiveness of Work Management Tools	••••	•••
Platform Flexibility	••••	••
Openness to Client/Server Tools	••••	•••
Leverage of Work-Group Tools	•	•••••
User Environment Power	••••	••
Scalability to Users	•••	•••••
Distributed Worker Support	••	••••
Detached Worker Support	•	••••
Pricing and Packaging Flexibility	••	•••••
Related Services	••••	••

••••• Highest Ranking • Lowest Ranking

Figure 7
Source: The Gartner Group

6.0 Work Management Summary

The following summarizes the key principles and ideas presented in this Strategic Analysis Report:

- Reengineering a business without understanding the real user world context and without a pragmatic and incremental approach to introducing new technology introduction is a flawed process. IS organizations must gain some control over the meaning and pace of reengineering, or they will constantly be on the defensive.

- Until 1996, workflow will remain a service tightly wedded to key application environments, given today's dependencies on user infrastructure, client infrastructure, and middleware requirements. By 1996 workflow vendors will differentiate themselves through specific implementations of workflow objects.

- Production and database approaches to workflow will be the most popular way to introduce work management. Implementations will address concentrated departmental applications. Imaging is foundation work for work management in back-office operations where benefits are quite demonstrable today. Imaging is at the forefront of work management since so much work is embodied in paper processes.

- Electronic forms will show explosive growth during the next five years, with the technology at the crossroads of different workflow models. Work management applications based on electronic forms or work-group computing will incorporate messaging models that excel at distributed worker support but will lack sophisticated functions.

- Leadership in work management will vary by application class and by user views of proper design models and deployment platforms. Though many work management technologies exist today, vendors are constantly pushed off balance by the churn of middleware and platform. In their place, value-added service providers prosper.

The following summarizes the strategic planning assumptions presented in this Strategic Analysis Report:

- Work management systems will translate the knowledge and principles of business process reengineering into usable software code by the end of 1995 (0.8 probability).

- Work management software will emerge first as a means of integrating disparate applications. In its earliest incarnations, it will envelop applications and mimic the useful processes of the physical office (0.8 probability).

- By 1996 work management software will play a crucial role in weaving together sophisticated desktop applications and objects, and that role will open new application frontiers (0.7 probability).

- The work management market will be driven to production applications through 1995 as users surround well-understood business processes and as they protect previous information technology investments. The untapped market of professional and knowledge workers is at least as big a potential market as the production market, though it will grow comparatively slowly (0.8 probability).
- Through 1996, work management will penetrate slowly, impeded by the lack of a client/server infrastructure and the lack of such universal middleware services as databases, messaging, and document management (0.8 probability).
- The penetration of work management systems will be slow because of steep learning curves in dealing with human factors and organizational change management (0.8 probability).
- Imaging software and hardware technology will drive 50 percent of work management installations during the next three years, given rapidly declining price points and imaging's power to replicate and improve everyday office processes (0.7 probability).
- Electronic forms automation is a Trojan horse brought into the production application arena by work-group vendors. The latter vendors will put pricing pressure on production-class work management specialists (0.7 probability).
- The most savvy users will build a work management framework that leverages PC and host architectures, builds corporate knowledge about work processes, and smoothes the technology adoption process as business and technology conditions permit (0.7 probability).
- Work-group technologies, coupled with electronic mail, will lay the foundation for an entirely new computing paradigm built on messaging and intelligent objects (0.7 probability). Users must strike a balance between message and database approaches based on user class and application requirements.
- By 1997 work-group and production approaches will converge on managing objects and providing work management function points, rendering the approaches indistinguishable (0.7 probability).
- Production systems will deliver up to three times more power than work-group systems, but will cost five times as much and demonstrate less flexibility in dealing with front-office workers and knowledge workers.
- Work management acquisition decisions through 1995 will force users to determine a comfortable entry point into the fast-paced world of client/server application development (0.8 probability).
- To achieve leadership in production-class work management, visionaries must solve customer problems in a fast and pragmatic manner—without onerous schemes for hardware and software pricing and packaging (0.8 probability).

- Work management success in the electronic forms and work-group arena will reflect user decisions either to grow the LAN or to drive "open office" solutions (UNIX, X.400). The "grow the LAN" scenario will be the more popular and will create a longer market ramp (0.6 probability).
- Value-added service providers will be the most efficient sources of work management products and services (0.6 probability

Groupware and Workflow: The European Perspective

Rose Lockwood, Director
ITALICS, **United Kingdom**

1. Introduction: A Workgroup System Architecture

The forces driving the market for workflow tools and workgroup applications are pervasive in the industrial economies of the world. Companies and administrations, wherever they are located, face the same kinds of problems that call for new methods and new tools to build solutions. Despite massive investments in Information Technology (IT), white collar productivity has not improved significantly. Competitive pressures force retrenchment and cost-cutting, while simultaneously demanding higher levels of service and more targeted product positioning. A new generation of IT tools is emerging to meet these goals, geared to process-oriented workgroups.

Business process reengineering occurs at a crossover point between two powerful trends. One trend we might call sociological—the flattening of hierarchies, dispersal of decision-making and responsibility, and the dissolving of rigid departmental boundaries that are characteristic of cross-functional teams. The other trend is technical—reaping the benefits of vastly improved price/performance ratios in electronic equipment, right-sizing IT systems to exploit these cost improvements, and extending information access more widely through networking technologies.

> business process reengineering occurs at a cross-over point between two powerful trends

The group-oriented solutions resulting from this convergence are based on an emerging "workgroup architecture" for IT products. It is multi-vendor, multi-platform and multi-protocol, and it contains the building blocks on which business process reengineering is based. These include operating systems and services, process automation workflow engines, messaging transport, packaged workgroup applications, and "team productivity" as well as personal productivity tools. Most solutions built on this architecture will eventually be delivered within a single user environment which I have called a Groupware Suite.

Workflow is a part of this new architecture. The workflow paradigm and the tools that build workgroup solutions are part of a new set of products and resources for solving business problems. Even more significantly, perhaps, they are the tools that will enable businesses to re-invent themselves.

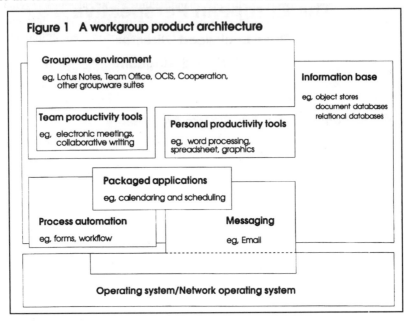

Figure 1   A workgroup product architecture

2. Profiling European users

In the course of research on a recent Ovum report on the groupware market, it became clear that European users are driven by the same needs and aspirations as those in the U.S. They can be summarized as the need to improve operational effectiveness, the desire to achieve strategic business goals through innovative use of technology, and the need to improve IT systems development methods. These broad goals are being pursued in a surprising variety of ways using workgroup and workflow products.

2.1 Goal: More effective operations

The need to improve operational effectiveness is a priority among the documented users of workgroup and workflow technologies. Companies and public administrations in Europe, as in the U.S., are looking for ways to improve performance and service output, or the value added by office workers. This involves addressing both the quality of the work being done, and the cost of doing that work.

Improving quality

Quality goals are achieved through improving the accuracy, consistency, and timeliness of operational work. Improving the processes supporting product documentation, for example, was a goal at ABB Stromberg Drives (a subsidiary of the ASEA Brown Boveri group) that manufactures electrical motors, generators and frequency converters in Helsinki, Finland. Although ABB Stromberg Drives is an industrial company, half its staff of 1,400 people are employed in office jobs.

The experience at Stromberg Drives typifies how a medium-sized industrial company can approach the decision to downsize its IT infrastructure and tackle the white-collar productivity problem at the same time. The company's strategy has largely been to replace legacy systems, but to do so with careful planning, reengineering and user training. They have chosen a Groupware Suite as the platform for future developments of their office IT. In the long run, they expect this platform to carry them forward to paperless documentation, multimedia communications, and richer electronic links to outside companies.

The company runs its IT operations on an outsourcing model, though another ABB subsidiary is a significant supplier, handling the company's mainframe operations. It runs a dedicated IBM mainframe in the Helsinki area and shares the use of a second larger mainframe located in Vaasa, on the west coast of Finland. Currently all manufacturing systems are running on mainframes, including production planning, scheduling and control, and MRP. For the last two years, however, Stromberg Drives has been working to decentralize its IT operations and replace host systems with client/server systems.

Stromberg Drives has implemented a document management workflow solution as part of its installation of ICL's TeamOffice product, to address the time-consuming and expensive tasks associated with developing, distributing and maintaining their technical product documentation. Besides conforming to rigorous technical specifications (and compliance with ISO 9001), the documentation must be developed and managed in six different languages. The automated solution is based on a manual reengineering project that had already taken place as a result of quality programs driven by engineering.

Like many pioneer workflow users, Stromberg Drives needed functionality that was not yet available in the product suite at the time of implementation. Creating a customized workflow feature proved to be a relatively viable enhancement, however, because TeamOffice is well designed to take advantage of its native e-mail features. Documentation is now retained centrally in the Team-Library, and users involved in development, reviewing and distribution of documentation receive their work packages based on distribution codes built into the library function. The implementation will affect several key areas of the company, including R&D, sales and customer service in addition to the operational staff who manage development of product documentation.

Consistency in the information base from which employees work is a significant problem for many companies, and often stands in the way of improved quality. This is the operational face of "corporate memory"; the knowledge base of an organization should be available in consistent form to the employees who rely on information to perform their jobs. At Banque Hervet, a medium-sized French bank headquartered in Paris, the risk management group formerly relied on manual systems to maintain and share the information on which daily risk assessments were made. By installing a small peer-to-peer network they were able to implement an automated solution based on a combination of database, spreadsheet, on-line information and press feeds, in-house reports and a document management system. Analysts use and share around 50 different information sources, all of which are now available electronically, and updated consistently. Since the risk-assessment report is the result of a team effort, where the contributions of different team members are developed in parallel, the reengineered solution is both more timely and more accurate.

Bureaucratic organizations are particularly vulnerable to the delays imposed by cumbersome paper workflows, and, in many public administrations, this is the critical barrier to improving the quality of their services. This problem is being tackled particularly effectively in the administrative operations of Stadt Bochum, a northern German town of 400,000 inhabitants. Stadt Bochum is a typical administrative organization with typical problems—complex procedures, multiple information sources, dispersed geographic installations, an expensive legacy IT system and limited resources for IT development. Nevertheless, the city has developed a networking and workflow strategy that both accommodates its intrastructural and budgetary constraints, and has vastly improved its flow of "paperwork."

> bureaucratic organizations are particularly vulnerable to the delays imposed by cumbersome paper workflows

Stadt Bochum employs 7,500 people, about a third of whom work in their various administrative centers spread out over eight city offices, and an additional 50 rented sites scattered throughout the city. Activities include the usual local council functions as well as responsibility for administering social welfare payments to the unemployed. The fundamental problem within the city administration has been that processing cases have been slow in both processing and elapsed time because it requires collecting information and approvals from multiple sources. Whether for benefit payments, building permits or any other area over which the city has jurisdiction, workers faced the problem that every stage of their work involved delay. Case processing that could take as long as three or four months consisted principally of waiting to receive information from many sources within the administration. Inefficiency at any point in the complex network of information exchange would ramify throughout the organization, resulting in stereotypic bureaucratic ineffectiveness.

Although the city had some successful experience with host-based office systems, they realized that a true solution would only be achieved when they had extended their communications environment to cover all office workers and to capture the personal productivity of the PC within a team environment. Because the city had already tandardized their document production on WordPerfect, they chose WP Office as a platform for implementing workflow among their many different sites. In the first phase of their project, Stadt Bochum implemented basic infrastructure tools (mail, scheduling, database access) as well as a simple mail-enabled document routing system; phase two will add forms and more robust workflow capabilities, and the long run goal is to achieve full text archival and retrieval.

The city has experienced a problem not uncommon in Europe—while the forms and workflow features they needed had been released in the U.S. English versions of WP Office, the German version was not yet available at the time of their implementation. Nevertheless, even with a partial implementation of a case-processing workflow, the city is saving money. They are able to lose one job—through attrition—for every five workers they add to the LAN-based system.

> user surveys show that cost containment is not a primary goal

These examples are typical of the sorts of quality problems that are being solved with workgroup and workflow solutions in Europe. Further examples are summarized in Table 1.

User surveys show that cost containment is not a primary goal for companies who are developing workgroup and workflow solutions, either in the U.S. or in Europe.

Nevertheless, cost control is a clear—and quantifiable—benefit that is achieved by many users implementing these systems. In Stadt Bochum, for example, controlling the cost of infrastructure development was a given constraint; thus the cost benefits of the workflow implementation are written off against the expansion of the network and networked resources across the city.

In Europe, many organizations are achieving cost benefits precisely because of the transition to client/server and desktop solutions. This trend is more pronounced in Europe because the desktop infrastructure is less mature than in the U.S. (For more detail on this issue, see section 4.)

Because the proportion of in-house e-mail running on host-based systems is higher in Europe, companies can often reap the benefits of LAN-based messaging transport at the same time that they implement workflow solutions on top of that transport. Stromberg Drives, for example, is abandoning its expensive host-based mail system—a move that will recoup one-fifth of their entire groupware investment in the first year alone.

253

Table 1. Improving operational effectiveness through improved quality

Quality Goal	Sector	Problem	Workgroup solution
Accuracy	Utility company	Poor project control; details "falling through the cracks"	Project Tracking System for work process, stages, deliverables and resources; implemented in workflow
	Healthcare products manufacturing	Lost requests for materials; poor stock requirements planning	Inventory tracking system with notification workflow and request database
	Advertising agency	Missing documentation in the creative process	Document tracking system to assure necessary information is collected at the beginning of a project
Consistency and corporate memory	Utility company	Inconsistent information supplied by an internal help desk	Database of technical manuals and previous technical solutions
	Government agency	Inconsistent and inaccurate responses to public enquiries	Central database of information available on inter-networked LANs available to all offices.
	Insurance company	Inconsistent information supplied to brokers	Database of product information available to field sales staff using laptops and modems
	Equipment manufacturing company	Inconsistent application of company policies by line managers	Policy and procedures database, giving all managers access to the same information
Timeliness	Auditors	Slow and inefficient auditing procedures	Shared procedures and resources (financial and tax information) and participation of expert personnel reduce audit cycle-times
	Cosmetics manufacturer	Members of project teams slow-up team progress when they travel	Remote access to project conferences (via email) and immediate input from absent personnel

Cost savings come in many forms. Saving time also saves costs in many implementations; this is true at Banque Hervet, where routine data collection and collation have been automated, and the professional time (and cost) devoted to these tasks drastically reduced. At another French company, Amadeus, the use of workgroup solutions has reduced problem-solving cycles from days to hours with a similar result. Amadeus was founded in 1987 by Air France, Iberia, Lufthansa and Scandinavian Airlines to supply booking services to travel agencies, air carriers, hotels and car-hire companies on its European-wide booking network. The company has offices in Madrid (Spain), Sophia-Antipolis (France) and Munich (Germany). The product development division is at Sophia-Antipolis, where the R&D staff responsible for Travel Agency Management Systems (TAMS) develops end-user installations to provide customers with pre-configured PCs and connection to the Amadeus network and mainframe systems.

A workgroup system based on Lotus Notes has been developed for the TAMS staff to improve the problem-tracking and bug-fixing procedures in the group, who are responsible for carrying out as many as 1,000 tests on new products. Prior to implementing the Notes system, problem-tracking was paper-based; problem diagnosis, correction and re-test took three to four days. Using the workflow and database system, problems are now routinely corrected within three to four hours. While these time-saving benefits are measurable, Amadeus has not done a systematic cost/benefit analysis. Other benefits are not so easily measured, in any event, and are considered equally important—such as the value created by discussion databases that enable the R&D team to design better products.

The company could no longer operate without the problem-tracking system; currently maintaining a repository of 5,000 items, the system would not be manageable using paper and simple e-mail. The availability of Notes for other applications has, moreover, created the opportunity to expand the benefits of the initial implementation. Project reporting, which was also a manual process, required a weekly consolidation of input from five project managers; reports were never on time or completely up-to-date.

Using a Notes project reporting system, project leaders and managers enter project information into templates that are automatically consolidated for the departmental report. In short, Amadeus has found a number of different ways to improve the efficiency of their project control and reporting procedures, all of which help control costs and improve the quality of the department's output.

Other cost benefits of workgroup and workflow systems include reducing paper workflows and eliminating redundant work, improving staffing efficiency, exerting better business control over operational processes and reducing the amount of time spent in face-to-face meetings or other direct interaction.

Table 2 summarizes examples of cost-control benefits achieved through workgroup and workflow implementations.

2.2 Goal: Supporting Strategic Business Goals

Many early adopters of workgroup and workflow technologies have taken a more strategic view of the significance of these new tools. While operational benefits may (and indeed, almost always do) follow, the driving force behind the use of the technologies is the pursuit of a strategic corporate goal that would otherwise be unattainable. These strategic approaches to workgroup systems fall roughly into two types: those enabling organizational innovation, and those which supporting new strategies for revenue generation.

Organizational innovation

An increasingly common goal for implementing of workflow solutions is to provide technical support for existing projects, such as quality programs.

Table 2. Improving operational effectiveness through cost control

Cost Goal	Sector	Problem	Workgroup solution
Save time (and therefore cost)	Investment company	Need to upgrade a host-based customer-tracking system which was underutilised	LAN based replacement (with data feeds from the host) with much shorter development time and lower maintenance costs
	Government agency	Hand tabulation of a required annual report was time-consuming and therefore expensive	Generation of report from LAN-based inquiry database (linking multiple offices)
Reduce or eliminate paper workflows	Healthcare products	Paper-based tracking of expired inventory was too slow	Workflow-based system reduces cycle time from weeks to days (with goal of hours)
	Construction company	Printed procedures were cumbersome to update and distribute	Procedures database eliminates paper copies
	City government	Requests for information were passed manually from office to office	A requests database has replaced the paper workflow
Improve staffing efficiency	Financial services	Need professional staff to generate more proposals	A document production workflow enables professionals to generate more and better quality proposals
	Insurance company	Ineffective field sales staff leads to reduced profitability	Remote access to sales management and information databases increases the coverage of each field staff person
Direct cost reduction	Electrical equipment manufacturing	Persistent lot rejections in the manufacturing process	Quality control database enables component level reject identification
	Financial services	Heavy use of fax in proposal development was slow and costly	Automated data and document management are linked among multiple offices
	High-risk insurance company	Costly host-based e-mail poorly integrated with PCs	LAN-based e-mail adds teamwork features and reduces system costs
Eliminate redundant work	Diversified services company	Inefficient document production leads to constant duplication of effort	Networked document/proposal production system eliminates redundant professional work
	Specialty insurer	Legacy time-tracking system on the host was duplicated in PC environment	Link between legacy system and PC-LAN eliminates manual entry of data
Better business control	Pharmaceutical company	Major account sales needs to track team members in multiple technical environments	An inter-LAN system links all mail clients and provides integration of project databases

This was the case at Stromberg Drives, where a long-term reengineering program had been in place for nearly two years before the decision was made to implement a workflow solution. Indeed, the reengineering process had itself revealed that significant bottlenecks occurred when systems crossed from engineering into "front-office" functions, such as sales and customer service, which were the targets of the workgroup solution.

A similar example is a large multinational manufacturing organization (who wishes to remain anonymous) with production facilities in several European locations. The company has been developing quality teams at various sites within its organization for several years. A manager at corporate level was interested in piloting a workflow solution for the purchasing function. He chose a site in the U.K. to develop the pilot because this installation had a mature and smooth-functioning quality program in place, providing a sympathetic culture to develop a workflow solution.

Table 2. Improving operational effectiveness through cost control

Cost Goal	Sector	Problem	Workgroup solution
Save time (and therefore cost)	Investment company	Need to upgrade a host-based customer-tracking system which was underutilised	LAN based replacement (with data feeds from the host) with much shorter development time and lower maintenance costs
	Government agency	Hand tabulation of a required annual report was time-consuming and therefore expensive	Generation of report from LAN-based inquiry database (linking multiple offices)
Reduce or eliminate paper workflows	Healthcare products	Paper-based tracking of expired inventory was too slow	Workflow-based system reduces cycle time from weeks to days (with goal of hours)
	Construction company	Printed procedures were cumbersome to update and distribute	Procedures database eliminates paper copies
	City government	Requests for information were passed manually from office to office	A requests database has replaced the paper workflow
Improve staffing efficiency	Financial services	Need professional staff to generate more proposals	A document production workflow enables professionals to generate more and better quality proposals
	Insurance company	Ineffective field sales staff leads to reduced profitability	Remote access to sales management and information databases increases the coverage of each field staff person
Direct cost reduction	Electrical equipment manufacturing	Persistent lot rejections in the manufacturing process	Quality control database enables component level reject identification
	Financial services	Heavy use of fax in proposal development was slow and costly	Automated data and document management are linked among multiple offices
	High-risk insurance company	Costly host-based e-mail poorly integrated with PCs	LAN-based e-mail adds teamwork features and reduces system costs
Eliminate redundant work	Diversified services company	Inefficient document production leads to constant duplication of effort	Networked document/proposal production system eliminates redundant professional work
	Specialty insurer	Legacy time-tracking system on the host was duplicated in PC environment	Link between legacy system and PC-LAN eliminates manual entry of data
Better business control	Pharmaceutical company	Major account sales needs to track team members in multiple technical environments	An inter-LAN system links all mail clients and provides integration of project databases

The project team assigned to the pilot included an analyst from the central purchasing group, a senior buyer from the purchasing department at the pilot site, a representative from MIS, and two consultants from Action Technologies, whose workflow engine was used to develop the workflow system, based on Lotus Notes. As a result of the project, substantial improvements in the interaction of staff across departments were achieved particularly by defining roles and identifying undocumented rules and procedures.

Table 3. Supporting strategic goals through organisational innovation

Goal	Sector	Problem	Workgroup solution
Support quality programmes	Electronics company	Needs to support a TQM programme	Developed in-house TQM support in a LAN conference database
	Equipment manufacturing company	Drowning in paper as a result of introducing TQ programme	Used document management groupware to control quality programme
Create a customer culture	Utility company	Poor support of in-house system after acquisition	Establish in-house help desk and facilities to support internal users
	Government agency	Civil servants unable to provide adequate response to the public	Database of information available to all workers who interact with the public
	Chemical company	Problems with customer returns and complaints	Complaints tracking system improves customer service
	Network integration supplier	Response to service calls not adequate	Compound document contains detailed specifications of customer configurations
Improve regulatory compliance	Utility company	Inadequate data to support requests for rate changes	Up-to-date database of customer and cost information
	Government agency	Consistent failure to meet legal requirements to supply information	Request logging database and networked information services bring the agency into compliance
	Construction equipment company	Exposure to random department of transport inspections; fined for inadequate records	Distributed database of activity logs will eliminate the risk of non-compliance
Market integration	Building products manufacturer	Poor methods for advising customers of supply status	Link customers to manufacturing project databases
	Equipment manufacturer	Difficulty keeping up-to-date records on replacements and defective parts	Acquiring machine - readable parts notices from suppliers to feed service bulletin database
Cross-functional integration	Insurance company	Legacy systems could no longer support business	Cross-functional teams replace assembly-line process
	Airline company	Difficulty organising charter flights	Cross-function flight planning system services multiple departments
Geographic integration	Healthclub chain	Need to support geographically distributed franchises	Inter-networked LANs support standard customer health analysis and planning
	Consumer products manufacturer	Problem coordinating the work of managers worldwide	Creating "virtual teams" through the use of online meetings conference tools
	Oil company	Coordinating scheduling systems at multiple sites	Implementing synchronised directories to support multi-site scheduling

The redesigned process reduced errors and cycle times, created a cross-functional workgroup identity in the purchasing process, promoted a "customer culture" (by clarifying roles in the process), eliminated obsolete and redundant worksteps, and highlighted other areas for improvement. The project was, to quote the team, a "phenomenal success," particularly for transforming the goals of the quality program into concrete business processes.

Other strategic goals may also be promoted and supported through workgroup solutions. Cross-functional integration in support of team-focused work may be undertaken in conjunction with workflow implementations. Regulatory compliance—including compliance with quality and process standards such as ISO 9000—is an increasingly important strategic goal, and is often supported (as at Stromberg Drives) through workflow and workgroup systems. Market integration, where suppliers and customers create trading domains, is virtually impossible without electronic integration, and is greatly enhanced through systematic work process support. Indeed, this is one of the major strategic goals at Amadeus, where they have plans to extend their workgroup systems to clients and trading partners.

A synopsis of various user approaches to organizational innovation is included in Table 3.

> cross-functional integration in support of team-focused work may be undertaken in conjunction with workflow implementations

Revenue generation

Some aspects of workgroup and workflow solutions are not related specifically to reengineering, but are targeted directly at improving the revenue stream. These benefits are achieved by supporting knowledge workers and professionals, by differentiating a service offering and by enhancing the systems that underpin marketing activities.

Workgroup systems can be used to develop USPs (unique selling positions) in the market. This approach carries the operational benefits of EDI (or purely administrative structured data interchange) a level higher, providing informal, ad hoc links to customers and greatly enhancing the quality of the sales communication channel. Even where workgroup links extend only as far as the sales team, the integration of mobile staff into the information resources and systems of the company can have a dramatic impact on the bottom line.

The other significant contribution to revenues that workflow solutions can bring is through the support of the work of professionals and knowledge workers. At the same time that information-based work has become increasingly significant, organizational support of that work (through clerical, research and secretarial staff) has diminished. Workgroup systems can replicate the skills of the vanishing (and expensive) support staff, leaving the growing (and even more expensive) base of knowledge workers free to maximize their value to the company.

Table 4 summarizes examples of revenue-generating uses of workgroup systems

Table 4. Supporting strategic goals for revenue generation

Goal	Sector	Problem	Workgroup solution
Establish USPs	Construction materials	Differentiation with developers	Give customers access to online project management databases and conferences
	Specialist publisher	Differentiate an information service	Give readers electronic access, and ability to provide direct feedback
	Brokerage consortium	Secure loyalty of institutional investors	Provide client access to trading desk systems and trading decision tools
	International bank	Need to boost sales performance	Provide analysts and sales persons with competitively significant information
Professional revenue generation	Equipment manufacturer	Provide tools for senior manager tasks	Train senior managers to use team coordination tools
	Financial services company	Need for better proposal system	Proposal development and tracking system to generate more proposals per principal; 5 - 25% case load increase
Improve marketing support	Oil drilling company	Support sales promotion	Use rig-status tracking system to demonstrate business effectiveness
	Utility company	Need for competitive information on natural gas	Gas procurement system to support cost-effective acquisition
	Insurance company	Need for more field intelligence	Supply sales staff with database of information about brokers and major accounts

Source: Groupware Market Strategies, Ovum Ltd, 1993

2.3 Goal: Solving Systems Development Problems

Workgroup systems will have a significant impact on the evolution of technical support for office functions. The transition to LAN-based solutions (the characteristic platform for workgroup and workflow systems) has several effects. One is the increasing importance of technical network-support staff in the development of office solutions; increasingly IT and network support managers must work together in developing implementations. Another effect is the enlargement of departmental—and increasingly of cross-functional team—responsibility for designing and developing systems. A third effect is the integration of a business perspective into the IT function.

Table 5. Solving systems development problems

Goal	Sector	Problem	Workgroup solution
Rapid SW prototyping and development	Cosmetic manufacturer	Develop travel tracking systems	Groupware system developed in three days
	Diversified services company	Develop tracking systems	Two to three day development cycles
	Building products company	Develop incremental applications	One to two week development cycles
	Investment company	Client tracking system	Budget for nine months; took one month
Effective use of pilots	Financial services company	Implement change without disruption	Implement pilot applications and add process incrementally
	Professional services	Add control within existing systems	Combine tools in improvised pilot applications
	Construction products company	Introduce change gradually	Use "small is beautiful" approach by starting with pilots
	Cosmetic manufacturer	Needs to measure results during implementation	By gradually expanding pilot applications, success is monitored and controlled
Integrate resources and applications	Oil company	Enhance existing groupware application	Experimenting with pre-commercial academic systems to improve use of
	Space agency	Need to support multiple sources and applications	Piloting the integration of mail, scheduling and forms based products
	Real estate agency	Need to view different types of data about properties	Compound-document database gives access to maps, images, plans, etc.
	Machinery manufacturer	Need to streamline budget planning	Integration of host system databases with desktop spreadsheets, templates and automated workflow
	Utility company	Need general access to information about resources	Incorporate pipeline maps into LAN document databases
	Investment company	Need better integration information resources	Incorporate external information-service feeds into in-house shared information systems
Improve coordination between MIS and end users	Government agency	Long delays in IS development	Train end user to develop ad-hoc applications

Workgroup solutions are posing new challenges to MIS/IT staff, who are not familiar with the new paradigms and/or architectures of the products and tools, and who often have a vested interest in more traditional approaches. Yet these new paradigms offer rich opportunities for improving the development processes within systems departments as well as throughout the organization.

One of the most startling effects is the rapid ability to prototype operational systems. The purchasing workflow system described above, for example, was developed in just three weeks. And because workflow and workgroup systems tend to be modular and LAN-based, pilots can be implemented incrementally, and enhancements built smoothly into operational systems.

Other advantages from the systems development perspective include the ability to integrate resources and applications in ways that would have been unthinkable (or at least impracticable) under older paradigms.

This is particularly important where new workflow systems are integrated with legacy resources, and conversely where the massive investment in personal productivity tools can be retained within new workgroup applications. Workgroup systems also tend to improve the coordination between technical and end-user staff that, in the past, has been either absent or mediated by layers of systems analysis. And finally, workgroup and workflow systems are the ideal vehicles for successfully downsizing those applications that need to be brought into desktop, LAN and client/server environments.

Table 5 gives examples of improved systems development processes.

3. European workflow suppliers

With a few exceptions, such as accounting software, the European software market is overwhelmingly dominated by U.S. Suppliers, particularly for packaged products. Consequently, the European supply stream shares many characteristics with those in the U.S., and many of the most innovative American products (as we have seen in the case studies previously cited) are making an early impact in Europe.

That said, there is an indigenous computer industry in Europe, and the major suppliers have recognized the potential significance of workflow and workgroup systems, and have developed strategies for the market. There are four principal European systems suppliers: Bull (France), Olivetti (Italy), Siemens-Nixdorf (Germany) and ICL (that, though largely owned by Fujitsu, is operated as a U.K.-based company). Each of these suppliers has developed products and strategies to meet the need for workgroup and workflow products in Europe. In addition, the leading supplier of workflow software in Europe, Staffware, is a U.K.-based company. Several of the European computer systems companies OEM Staffware as the workflow element of their workgroup product suites.

3.1 Staffware (U.K.)

The first version of Staffware was released by London-based FCMC in 1988, the first customers were OEMs Unisys (1988), ICL (1989), IBM U.K. and Bull. The product runs a wide variety of UNIX operating systems (around 30). In 1993, Staffware was re-architected to run under a UNIX server with Windows clients. Since then the company has expanded its partnership arrangements to include leading LAN software suppliers such as Lotus, Novell and Uniplex.

Staffware is highly configurable with other software packages, as evidenced by the large number of products to which it currently supplies workflow support. The latest version permits users to employ third-party forms products. Reflecting its European roots, Staffware handles multilingual issues well; clients may employ any one of eight available languages regardless of the natural language version used by the server or other participants in a workflow implementation.

Tasks are automated by implementing procedures specified in a flowchart; process actors are defined in the directory. Routing can also be programmed for multiply defined roles, which can also have a network address. The system generates to-do menus, and presents only actionable items to a process actor. It also includes deadlines and notifications. While the original UNIX version was designed to be used by non-programmers, the addition of a GUI in the Windows client has greatly enhanced the usability of the product, both for the development of workflow procedures and for end-user actions.

Table 6. ICL's workgroup products

ICL Product	Product description
OfficePower	Client-server office automation suite for DRS/NX, RS 6000, SCO Unix, Sun
OfficePower XPress	X.400 mail facility
PowerFile	Text database management
PowerFlow	ICL enhancement to FCMC Staffware for workflow applications
PowerSearch	Text retrieval system
PowerVision	Document image processing for standalone PC, small workgroup, DRS 6000 server, or enterprise-wide configurations
PowerKit	API for OfficePower
ProcessWise Integrator	Workflow management generator
ProcessWise WorkBench	Process/workflow design and development tool
ProcessWise Guide	Methodology tool
TeamOffice	Scalable PC/LAN based groupware: TeamMail, TeamLibrary, TeamCalendar, TeamForum, TeamFlow

3.2 ICL (U.K.)

ICL supplies computer systems and software in more than 70 countries, though nearly 90 percent of its revenues is primarily in Europe and the U.K. Less than 20 percent of revenues is from software sales, but the company is still the eighth largest packaged software supplier in Europe (according to estimates by Ovum Ltd.). The following table summarizes ICL's office product offerings, including workflow and workgroup applications.

ICL's workflow and workgroup application offerings are neatly divided between the UNIX-based suite, the components of which are largely (though not exclusively) native ICL products, and the TeamOffice suite, a set of PC-based products that were originally acquired as a part of Finland-based Nokia Data

Systems in 1991. The Nokia product line, which has become ICL Personal Systems, is now the core of the desktop line of business.

OfficePower is a multi-language, multi-user office system that presents a core range of services in a consistent user interface. Although OfficePower can be used for small workgroups, it fits more logically at the higher end of workgroup products, and can support up to 500 users on a single server. The system is X/OPEN conferment and has core services including word processing, X.400 e-mail, scheduling, databases, spreadsheets and graphics. PowerFlow, a procedure processor, is an add-on to OfficePower and is OEM'd from Staffware. The principal difference from the Staffware product is that PowerFlow has been given the OfficePower look and feel and employs the ICL X.400 message transport.

TeamOffice, on the other hand, is essentially a set of PC products that were acquired with Nokia Data Systems, although the suite has been enhanced and repackaged since then. Server platforms are SCO UNIX and OS/2, with DOS, Windows and OS/2 clients. In addition to mail, scheduling, bulletin board and library services, TeamOffice can be enhanced in various ways. In addition to imaging and workflow extensions, the product line offers a shell system, macro-based integration of third-party applications with native services, support for sub-sets of VIM and MAPI and a set of application development tools including TeamOffice APIs and a SQL Windows link. Although a full-fledged workflow module is promised, the first release of TeamOffice offered a "platform" of tools and services on which custom workflow applications could be built (originally only available for OS/2 servers).

ICL's two parallel groupware suites are not clearly differentiated in the market, though generally OfficePower is thought of as high-end, and TeamOffice as low-end. As functionality and platforms converge, it is not clear how the two product lines will coexist. The picture is further complicated by the development of a set of business process reengineering tools known as ProcessWise. The ProcessWise Workbench is a graphical, rules-based tool for defining business processes using action (task or activity) role and flow objects. The workbench provides a library of process objects, a forms designer and alternative views of the process being designed. ProcessWise Integrator complies the results of a process design into a "workflow manager." ProcessWise Guide is a management framework based on research at Sloan School of Management at MIT.

3.3   Olivetti (Italy)

Olivetti has evolved from a typewriter manufacturer (founded in 1908) to a worldwide provider of information systems and office equipment operating in more than 30 countries. Olivetti sells a full range of hardware products; software products include operating systems, development tools, desktop applications, vertical applications, and the Integrated Business Information System, known as IBIsys. The major components of IBIsys are summarized in the following Table 7.

Table 7. Olivetti's workgroup products

IBIsys product	Product description
X_Manager	Environment manager, coordinating activities of the user
X_Index	File management system
X_Mail	Email system
X_Edit	Access to native and third-party word processing programs
X_Text	Word Processing
X_Note	Notepad
X_Diary	Shared calendar system
X_Admin	Administration utilities
X_Workflow	Workflow development tool / workflow environment
X_Image	Document image processing

X_Workflow is an optional component of IBIsys and was developed internally by Olivetti. (In the past Olivetti was a reseller of Filenet.) X_Workflow contains four modules. An authoring environment is used for defining procedures. The maintenance module installs the previously defined procedures and defines the user directory and roles. The user module is the environment in which users initiate and execute steps of the procedure, and the auditing module monitors, audits and reports on process activities. A recently introduced graphical interface to the scripting language (called Coplan/S) has improved the friendliness of the authoring environment.

3.4   SNI (Siemens-Nixdorf, Germany)

SNI is the second largest computer systems vendor in Germany (after IBM). It also has a growing business in packaged software products. The company operates in 25 countries, but two-thirds of revenues are still generated in Germany. SNI's groupware suite comprises the Office Communication and Information Systems (OCIS) product line, which is configured on three platforms: OCIS/PC (DOS/Windows), OCIS/A (character-based UNIX UI), and OCIS/X (X-Windows, /Motif UNIX UI). The applications environment is called ComfoDesk, an object-oriented graphical user interface (GUI) that is the core of OCIS/PC. Some of the components of OCIS are summarized in the Table 8.

SNI has followed the same path as most other traditional computer systems suppliers in building a basic suite of workgroup applications, on which enhanced functions can be added or developed. WorkParty is a relatively new (and optional) component of the OCIS suite. Workflow folders contain work process definitions. A graphical editor supports the interactive generation of workflow procedures that are developed from an outline of activities. Workflow folders are

Table 8. SNI workgroup products

OCIS Products	Product description
ComfoTex	Word processing
ComfoForm	Graphical forms editor
ComfoMerge	Macro language for integration applications
ComfoTalk/Fax	Drag-and-drop fax gateway
File.D	File management system
Mail.D	Email
DBA.D	Interface to relational databases
WorkParty	Workflow development and execution environment

linked to the Organization and Resource Manager (ORM) that defines "organization units," roles, and resources used during the workflow process. Process actions can be assigned to an entire unit (such as a department), a role or a specific person. While the structure and methods of WorkParty are very CASE-like, the highly graphical quality of the interface makes the tools case easy to understand and use.

4.   Prospects for the European market

The emerging workgroup architecture (see section 1) is client/server and LAN-based. Consequently, the size of the market for workgroup and workflow products will be driven, in part, by the existence of an appropriate infrastructure on which to build new solutions. The only significant difference between the European and U.S. markets is the extent to which that infrastructure is already in place.

The user base for workgroup and workflow requires desktop workstations (PC, Mac, and UNIX clients), LANs connecting these workstations and messaging transport over which applications and users communicate. The U.S. infrastructure is currently more developed in each of these areas. Although the number of white-collar workers in Western Europe is somewhat higher than the U.S., the number of installed desktop workstation seats is (and will continue to be) higher in the U.S. (note that all European statistics used here refer to Western Europe only.) Table 9 shows a forecast for desktop seats. The proportion of these desktop seats that are networked on LANs is considerably lower in Europe than in the U.S. is shown in Table 10.

Table 9. Forecast growth of desktop installed base, US and Europe

Desktop seats (millions)	1993	1994	1995	1996	1997	1998
United States	24	28	32	38	43	47
Western Europe	20	24	28	33	38	44

source: Inteco

Table 10. Forecast growth of seats on LANs, US and Europe

Seats on LANs (millions)	1993	1994	1995	1996	1997	1998
Seats on LANs, US	17	21	25	31	37	43
LAN penetration, US	71%	75%	79%	83%	87%	91%
Seats on LANs, Western Europe	8	11	14	19	24	31
LAN penetration, Western Europe	40%	46%	52%	58%	64%	71%

source: Rose Lockwood, Ovum Ltd

These forecasts show the number of potential workgroup and workflow users, and the population into which these products will be sold. Despite the fact that the largest market for these products will be in the U.S. for the next few years, the European market will be strong. Sales will be distributed in Europe roughly by the size of software markets in general, with the largest share going to Germany, the U.K. and France.

Table 11. Forecast growth of LAN email users, US and Europe

LAN email users (millions)	1993	1994	1995	1996	1997	1998
United States	11	15	20	26	33	40
Western Europe	3	5	8	13	18	25

source: Rose Lockwood, Ovum Ltd.

Table 12. Groupware and workflow forecast - Western Europe

($US millions)

Product/service category	1993	1994	1995	1996	1997	1998
Intelligent messaging products	44	60	77	91	96	107
Workflow products	72	99	129	168	217	279
Team productivity application products	17	21	26	32	36	40
Groupware suites	83	161	234	318	388	505
Training and implementation services	323	512	699	911	1107	1386
Total groupware and workflow market	538	853	1166	1520	1845	2326

source: Groupware Market Strategies. Ovum Ltd. 1993

Forecasting the actual market for workflow and business process reengineering is fraught with ambiguity—primarily because there are no consistent and agreed definitions of what are included in these markets. The Ovum forecast is based on product categories and the training and implementation costs associated with those products.

It is clear from the previous discussion of users and products that buying patterns for workgroup and workflow products will be varied. While there will continue to be a market for "dedicated" workflow products, users will increasingly purchase workflow (and other workgroup functionality) within product suites. Furthermore, the cost of products is a minor part of the investment in workgroup solutions. The largest proportion of expenditure will be on training and development services in connection with groupware implementations.

A Three-Step Process to Workflow Automation

By Nina Burns, President and CEO

Creative Networks, Inc.

Not every process or business practice warrants reengineering

The terms, *Workflow Automation* and *Business Process Reengineering* have become almost as pervasive as *Total Quality Management*. Yet it is difficult to tell what workflow automation actually means and what it has to do with business process reengineering. Not every process or business practice warrants reengineering, and workflow automation can provide incremental improvement that makes a magnitude difference in productivity, efficiencies and competitiveness without undergoing costly and often wrenching business process reengineering. The trick is to correctly characterize the processes and to map the business need to the myriad technologies and products available for workflow automation. These range from simple electronic forms routing to sophisticated workflow systems that will enable your business process reengineering efforts.

This chapter presents a methodology for characterizing your applications, allowing you to identify potential workflow automation targets and requirements for specific applications, map these requirements to the technologies and products that are available today (and in the future) and to choose products that deliver the solution.

Workflow defined

Workflow automation is the structure that is applied to the movement of information in order to improve the results of a business process. Workflow automation software actively manages the coordination of activities among people in general business processes. The three key concepts are active, coordination and people. Workflow automation software makes decisions based on conditions of flow set during design, notifies people involved in the process of work to be performed, status, etc. It can be active in sending alerts, notifying people of late work and so forth. Secondly, workflow automation also facilitates the coordination of work, relieving people from coordination overhead. This is not simply providing information sharing capabilities. For example, let's say you are creating a company background document for your marketing kit. You simply create the document in your favorite desktop publishing or word processing application.

The workflow process then knows who to send the document to, checks to make sure the recipients review and comment on the document, and returns it to you upon completion. The workflow process also notifies you immediately if someone is late or has not approved the project and it relieves you entirely from calling people to make sure the document is routed to the correct individuals and from tracking the progress to the schedule.

The third key aspect of workflow is that it is people oriented. To be successful it needs to focus on the people doing the work, not just the information. It needs to incorporate the concepts of work from the perspective of how people work, not just the tasks they perform. Two differentiating factors of this are commitment and time. For example, Action Technologies' Workflow model identifies a customer and performer of the workflow. Within each action in the workflow there is a performer that agrees to complete the action to the satisfaction of the customer. They further identify all work into four phases: proposal, agreement, performance and satisfaction. This approach shifts the structure of work from tasks to be performed to work to be accomplished—a subtle but powerful concept. Once this shift takes place, quality is inherent in the process and you achieve controlled quality (as an active, integral part of your business) rather than quality control that happens after the fact.

That is not to say that all workflow automation requires business process reengineering to achieve significant/measurable results. In fact, workflow can be used in conjunction with reengineering and/or to automate processes not in need of reengineering. In both cases workflow automation should enable continuous incremental improvement.

Workflow automation products and technologies

The concepts discussed below provide a framework for understanding the broad scope of possibilities for implementing workflow automation systems.

Workflow solutions are not a technology or product. Rather, a number of technologies, methodologies and tools make up a workflow automation system. These include infrastructure, some common implementation elements and architectural components. For example, infrastructure elements that enable workflow automation include local and wide area communications, database storage, graphical desktops, store-and-forward messaging, user and resource directories, and process definition techniques. Elements that seem to be common among all workflow implementations include the ability to specify the process, connect the user interface to elements in the process, the ability to take actions, status reporting, process monitoring, simulation tools and measurement of incremental improvement.

You need to analyze each application and your business objectives

Different workflow solutions take various architectural approaches relative to user interface, process specification, transport and storage. For example, the user interface can be forms or images. Some workflow solutions allow the user to use any existing application rather than a proprietary user interface. The process can be specified using a rules language, programmatic interface or graphical design tools. Likewise, the specification process can be proprietary as in Lotus Notes, or use a common tool such as Visual Basic. In terms of the transport, some workflow solutions use the underlying messaging system (such as Reach's) or a database system, or both (such as Action Technologies'). Storage may be mail folders or database and be supplied by the workflow vendor or use existing systems.

Vendors provide a myriad of products and technologies, not all of which meet the needs of every application. To really do it right, you need to analyze each application and your business objectives according to specific criteria rather than in an ad hoc fashion.

A three-step process for successful workflow automation

Many companies have a variety of processes they would like to automate. Often automation begins in an ad hoc fashion without coordination with IS/IT and without the left hand knowing what the right hand is doing. For example the purchase order department may start a project to automate the processing of the thousands of forms used by the department. It isn't until they go to evaluate the various options for electronic forms that they realize that it is not just a forms issue but an infrastructure issue as well. Many forms routing packages today use the underlying e-mail system for store-and-forward transport.

Therefore, a prerequisite for the process is that all participants can be reached through the e-mail system and that they can all be accessed through a common directory service. Furthermore, unless you analyze the process to determine the degree of automation and the technology you will need to apply to that process, you may find that you have spent lots of money on a solution that will not meet your short-term or long-term needs and may actually do more harm than good. Or that the benefits and cost savings do not justify the investment. In short, you will save a lot of time and expense if you:

1. **Identify the need:**

    What problem are you trying to solve?

    How does the workflow automation effort fit in with company reengineering projects?

2. **Map technology to the application and the business need:**

    First characterize the application and identify the business need
    Then map that need to the technology that will solve the problem.

3. **Choose products that deliver the solution.**

Workflow and reengineering

Workflow can be used in conjunction with reengineering or for processes not in need of reengineering. It is important to correctly distinguish between the two. The goal of reengineering is to invent new processes and look for dramatic increases in productivity (hundreds of percent). In the words of Michael Hammer, president of Hammer and Company, Inc., one of the originator's and leading proponents of the concept of reengineering, reengineering is "starting over." It is "fundamental rethinking and radical redesign of business processes to achieve dramatic improvements in critical, contemporary measures of performance, such as cost, quality, service, and speed."

Workflow automation is a critical enabler of this type of reengineering effort. But reengineering where it is unnecessary can be a disaster. Reengineering may take years to implement and usually requires significant, major changes within organizations from a management, cultural, information and computing standpoint .

The second category of workflow automation is much more pervasive. It provides incremental improvements of existing processes. Even with incremental improvements, businesses save millions. For example, how much would you save if you reduced your missed shipments by just a fraction of a percent? Peter Van Dyke, Manager of Information Systems at Boehringer Mannheim, presented the following statistics at the Workflow Conference in August, 1993: one workflow-enhanced system increased call capability by 50% and keeps the information infrastructure running smoother than ever.

> how important is it to enable users to work within their current desktop applications?

In a cost/benefit analysis of electronic forms in a company of 3000 employees that use an average of three forms per week, JetForm Corporation (Waltham, MA) reports ROI (return on investment) of 812% in 1.32 months just by going from paper-based forms to electronic forms without any major changes in the process. Most of these savings are in processing costs such as the time to fill in, verify and route forms.

How to get the most out of workflow automation

The dramatic paybacks described above are possible only if the workflow is successful and the solution matches the problem in the first place. To help characterize applications and map technology to the application, we distinguish three categories of applications: Unstructured; Structured; and Complex (often enterprise-wide applications).

Unstructured workflow automation solutions supply the greatest benefit to the individual versus the company, tend to have lower business value and also cost less to implement. Complex workflow automation solutions on the other hand, tend to provide very high benefit to the company versus the individual, have high value to the business and are more costly to implement. Structured workflow automation solutions benefit the workgroup most, have value to the business overall and are somewhere in the middle in terms of cost.

Incidentally, the same application, (e.g. purchase order processing) may fall into the structured workflow category in one organization and the complex workflow category in another.

Unstructured workflows are usually project-oriented applications such as document development which are difficult to automate in a standard way. They typically change frequently and the participants or the roles they play in the workflow may also change frequently. Consequently, users need a lot of control over the process as it occurs, and over the design of the process itself.

Integration with desktop applications such as word processors and page layout software is important. Typically workflow automation solutions need to offer sequential routing of workflow instances, simple management reporting back to the initiator of a workflow and conditional rules. Unstructured workflow automation provides significant improvements to the individual but generally not to the organization or process as a whole. For example, the process may be very similar to the non-automated

how much would you save if you reduced your missed shipments by just a fraction of a percent?

process, but will be done much more effectively than before automation because it provides automatic routing, coordination and feedback mechanisms.

Structured workflows are typically simple, well defined processes such as administrative processes like expense reports, time sheets and check requests. Automating these processes improves them and their individual efficiencies but are not necessarily part of a reengineering effort. In these applications, processes and participants don't change frequently.

Solutions often require parallel workflow coordination, conditional routing and desktop management with alerts, reminders and management aids. Instance tracking and reporting are required, as well as process management information. Integration with external electronic information from sources such as legacy databases is important. These types of solutions are often mail-based and provide a high degree of value to the individual.

Complex work flows are processes that span entire organizations, are often mission critical and frequently extend to external organizations. Examples include purchase order processing, litigation support and loan processing. Automation improves processes and efficiencies and is often part of reengineering efforts. The processes change infrequently, require extensive management information and tracking and require sophisticated development capabilities, typically from an IT organization. These processes are often database-based and require integration with external databases, paper processes and applications. Automation provides a high degree of value to the enterprise.

Characteristics to look at

We have defined at least six categories of characteristics against which you can analyze your application requirements to determine whether they fall into the unstructured, structured or complex workflow segmentation. They are:

- Integration
- Routing
- Robustness
- Frequency of Change
- Degree of Reengineering Potential
- Business Value

Rate the degree to which the application requires each of the characteristics described below to identify if the application falls into the Unstructured, Structured or Complex category, then map the identified requirements to what is offered in products.

Integration

Analyze the application to understand the degree to which it must be integrated in four areas:

- Other desktop applications
- External data sources
- Paper-based information
- Platforms

To successfully meet the needs of the application, how important is it to enable users to work within their current desktop applications and not impose a special workflow environment? This is very important in unstructured work flows but probably less important in complex work flows.

You must also understand if the application needs access to external data sources or paper-based information. For example, it will be very important for a purchase order processing application to automatically access electronic databases that hold pricing and part number information. Litigation support applications will have a high degree of need to incorporate paper-based information.

In general, unstructured applications have a low requirement for integration overall while Enterprise workflow has a high degree of need, and Workgroup is somewhere in between.

Routing

The second category is routing. How sophisticated are the routing requirements of the application in the following areas:

- Parallelism
- Conditionals
- Need for exception handling
- Degree of computer control versus user control

Is there a need for multiple processes and instances to occur simultaneously and then be reconciled at some point, or is sequential routing sufficient? How sophisticated do the conditions of flow need to be, or are simple if-then statements enough? How much of the workflow can be accomplished without user intervention like grabbing data from external sources, spawning processes, and making decisions based on conditionals? How much control does the user need to change the process on an ad hoc basis?

Unstructured work flows typically have less sophisticated routing needs while Enterprise will require a great deal of robustness and computer control.

Robustness

Robustness is a catch-all category that includes:

- Services
  - *management*
  - *administration*
  - *security*
  - *audit trail*

  The need to simulate the workflow as it is developed
- Scalability
- Error recovery

You should examine the extent to which the application needs management tracking, reporting of instances and reporting of the process overall. This information is critical to enabling incremental improvement and process management. Security is also a very important factor. In general, the more mission critical the application the greater the need for security and manageability. The more complex the application the greater the requirement for simulation software so you can anticipate problems and bottlenecks during design.

Frequency of change

How frequently the application changes in terms of:

- The process itself
- User requirements
- Participants and Roles

Typically Ad Hoc work flows have a high degree of change while Enterprise work flows are characterized by infrequent change.

Degree of reengineering potential

Again, it is important to understand the investment that will be required and when and how to incorporate workflow automation with business process reengineering. Looking at the application from the standpoint of process improvement and improvements in both business and individual improvements will help make the distinction.

Business value

The degree to which you invest in workflow automation technology and process should be determined for each application in terms of its value to your business from a variety of standpoints including:
- Financial Competitiveness
- Total Quality Management
- Customer Satisfaction
- Is this one of the key processes of the company?

every application needs to be examined for workflow automation potential

The higher the value, the more investment that can be made. For example, in processes that have a lower business value, you do not want to go through a reengineering effort but may choose off-the-shelf solutions to gain substantial incremental improvements.

> the more mission critical the application the greater the need for security and manageability

How do you choose?

Workflow Automation is the first true blending of technology and business practices that will revolutionize the way we do business. Over time as technology and products improve, users, administrators and IS/IT will have a role in developing and implementing workflow systems.

Every business and every application needs to be examined for workflow automation potential. There are tools available today that will significantly improve your business systems. Here, finally, is a technology that will begin to pay back the huge investment that has been made in the network infrastructure.

Next to electronic mail, it is one of the easiest application categories to cost justify. At the same time, unlike e-mai, it captures the imagination, and provides intuitively obvious benefits both in terms of the business and in terms of individuals. Quite concretely, these include the elimination of redundancy, accountability, increases in personal productivity, increases in jobs completed on time, a high degree of customer satisfaction, the empowerment of personnel, a reduction in overtime and improvements in management reporting.

A note (or two) of caution

Although we expect many more products and vendors to emerge over the next 12 to 18 months, most workflow automation products available today are still first generation. Products are immature, incomplete, incompatible and often difficult to implement. There are no standards for interoperability and each vendor is taking a different approach to solving the problem, e.g. forms routing, mail based, data based, etc. Furthermore, the market is small, with few vendors and even fewer complete solutions.

But those that experiment with the technology now and implement solutions that meet a specific need will gain extraordinary benefits to their companies as long as the technology is matched closely to the problem they are trying to solve. There are many methodologies to choose from for process analysis and implementation. The important thing is to understand your requirements, choose the right products and technologies that meet your business needs and don't over-or-under-engineer the solution.

Workflow and Electronic Commerce

Torrey Byles, Director, Electronic Commerce
BIS Strategic Decisions

A Look at Combining Paperless Offices with Paperless Trade

Abstract

Two distinctly different information technologies are creating the paperless business environment. Workflow automation technology eliminates paper inside companies, such as memos, requisition slips, reports, and the myriad internal business forms completed for various tasks. Electronic commerce aims at eliminating paper transmitted between companies such as purchase orders, invoices, ship notices, checks and currency, and other tokens associated with trade.

They are the two information technologies exclusively focused on streamlining business processes through use of information technology (IT) A company's internal processes (sales, marketing, production, accounting, service and support) are now integrating its external processes (suppliers, customers, and other trading partners). Workflow and electronic commerce are also the IT foundations for a company's business process reengineering efforts.

Early Electronic Commerce

From the 1960s until about five years ago, the only forms of electronic commerce were electronic data interchange (EDI), adhering to a standard format, and proprietary order entry systems. These were developed in the context of the old generation of IT technology. The cost of old technology made electronic commerce affordable to only the largest companies. Equipment and software were expensive; Implementation and operations required specialists. Thus, few companies really conducted trade electronically. Also, the old technology didn't take advantage of the efficiencies inherent in electronic systems. In the past five years several alternatives to EDI have emerged including World Wide Web, electronic catalogs, electronic mail, and intercompany workflow platforms (such as Lotus Notes).

Initially, these EDI systems were mainframe based. One mainframe sent a batch of files to another mainframe. This was a major barrier to small and medium-sized non-mainframe companies to adopting EDI.

Second, the systems typically focused on a single application st a time. An order entry system received EDI purchase orders. An accounts receivable system sent EDI invoices. The applications were independent of each other in operation, even though they may have used a common EDI translation software package. There was no connection between the two unless an order entry software application updated accounts receivable. Any scheduling, routing, automatic creation of an invoice, etc. was hard-coded in the application. There was seldom integration of the company's entire workflow so that sales, shipping, manufacturing, and accounting were notified and triggered into action.

Third, EDI focused on the paper document that it replaced. To develop a format for the data fields in an electronic purchase order, engineers simply took existing paper documents and standardized them. Only in the last five years have companies begun to see redundancies in this approach. Companies are now experimenting with evaluated receipts settlement where payment to the supplier is triggered with the receipt of goods, not sending an invoice. Automatic replenishment systems have the retailer sending raw point-of-sale data to the vendor who then determines reorder amounts (no purchase orders are sent).

In the early days of electronic commerce, networking within a company and between companies was a complicated undertaking. To do EDI required the user to build a lot of "lower level" transport protocols in the data standard. It also required the user to build the lower level physical transport network within the company. And, the few wide-area, "value-added" service operators available charged dearly for protocol support.

As a consequence, a huge industry in EDI outsourcing grew up. In the USA, during 1994, half a billion dollars was spent on outsourcing EDI software and network services. Because of the expense, only about 70,000 companies are using it out of a potential six million. There are several vendors of software, network services (and now the Internet is being readied for EDI) and scores of systems integration/professional services firms. EDI is big business, but, it doesn't have to be the only game in town. The currently available enabling tools of workflow, network operating systems and client/server software herald the day when companies and consumers will touch a key and have immediate electronic commerce capability.

Workflow and Electronic Commerce

Corporations are now integrating their internal workflow systems with external electronic commerce systems. This takes many forms: EDI messages routed to and from computer applications by internal company mail networks; Lotus Notes software used for inter-company information transfers and coordination; and corporate "homepages," an electronic storefront on the World Wide Web that accepts purchase electronic orders. Projects that begin as strictly a workflow implementation often lead to an electronic commerce implementation — and vice versa.

Functions that were once conceivable only as a department within a larger organization — such as sales, telemarketing, design and development, manufacturing, customer support, payment collection, distribution — are now viable stand-alone businesses. As workflow and electronic commerce technologies merge, the infrastructure for virtual organizations will be in place.

Workflow automation's natural synergies to electronic commerce are seen by recognizing that commerce is inherently workflow extended beyond the boundaries of the corporation. Nevertheless, the extended workflow ties directly into and is a part of the internal workflow of a company. This is seen in the nature of the commercial transaction.

Electronic Commerce

All commercial transactions (between businesses, consumers, and government) have a set of common features. There are always two fundamental roles: a buyer and a seller. There are always two things being exchanged: funds for goods and services. See figure 1.

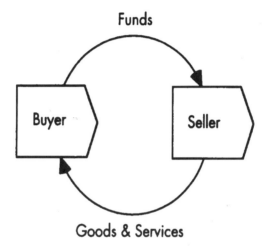

Figure 1

The Commercial Transaction

When buyers and sellers meet to exchange funds for goods and services, a dialogue ensues which often involves each party checking information sources on the other. For example, buyers may consult catalogs before they meet a seller. A seller may conduct a credit check before it agrees to accept a buyer's order. And the seller may consult with a record of past sales to help it plan what it should do in response to a changing market place. This dialogue and associated information checks is illustrated in figure 2.

281

The Messages of Trade

These constituent roles, dialogues and information needs of commerce apply to all commercial transactions, even before networked computers, paper documents and associated institutions and processes supported the players of a commercial transaction and their actions. Computers and telecommunications now replace these paper processes and bring a new level of efficiency and speed to commerce.

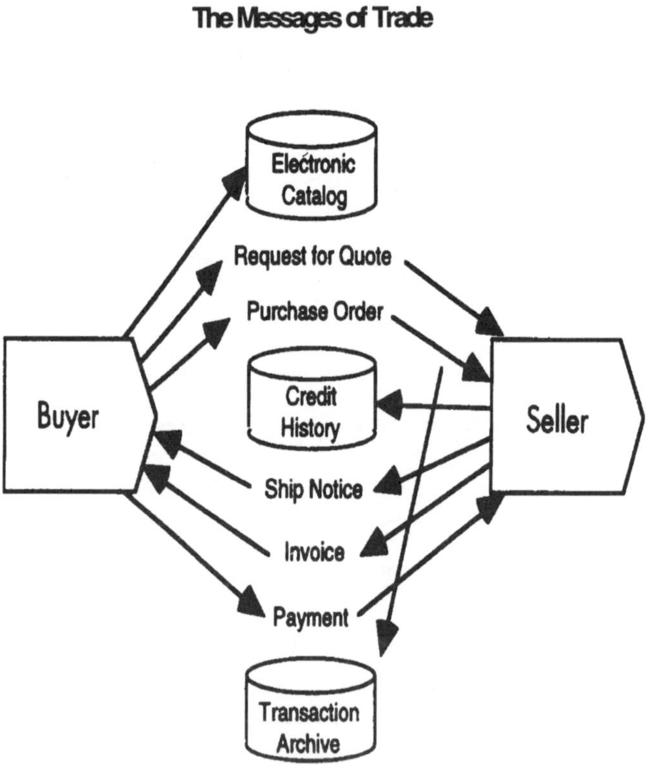

The Messages of Trade

Figure 2

The Workflow of Commerce

Companies are buying and selling value chains. They buy things and services, add value to them, and then sell them. The manner in which a company buys and sells is wholly dependent on communicating with suppliers and customers outside of the company. The steps by which companies engage in trade are depicted in figure 3.

Figure 3 employs Michael Porter's characterization of companies as value chains. It shows the relationship between the internal business functions (value chains) of buying and selling companies. The figure also shows today's representative applications of electronic, paperless execution of these business functions. The applications are categorized according to their relation to the actual transaction.

Thus, there are a "pre-" and "post-" transaction applications in addition to the transaction component itself. These categories of electronic commerce underscore the point that no longer is EDI the only kind of electronic commerce, but one of several alternatives (including electronic catalogs, file transfers via the Internet and other carriers, and electronic mail).

Note: While this diagram is aimed at explicating corporate electronic commerce, it also applies to consumer electronic commerce. In a consumer context, the buyer value chain is the consumer. The seller value chain is the retail merchant, utility, credit card issuer, or with whomever the consumer is conducting the transaction (whether at a retail outlet or through an online, "homebank/shopping" connection).

Electronic Commerce Applications and the Cycle of Commerce

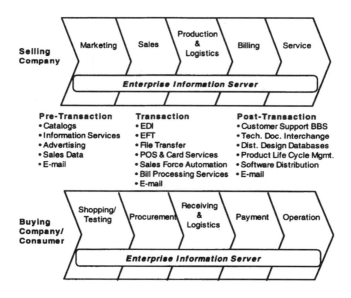

Source: Torrey Byles
Figure 3

Within each company, value-adding functions are performed by various corporate departments (sales and marketing, engineering, manufacturing, accounting, etc.). Depending on whether a company is buying or selling determines which value adding activities are invoked. The buyer company's value chains are different to the seller company's value chain. Having all communications contained within a single electronic medium greatly facilitates this correspondence. A typical commercial transaction using an integrated electronic medium may occur as follows:

(1) A design engineer peruses online news, business information and electronic catalogs for a desired component.

(2) Once the engineer finds what she wants, she e-mails the procurement department to buy the part in quantity.

(3) The procurement officer sends an electronic purchase order to the selling company. At the selling company, the enterprise message server routes the electronic order to the order-entry application. The component is physically shipped to the buyer. If the component were software, this could have been downloaded over the network.

(4) After shipping the component, the accounts receivable clerk in the selling company sends an electronic invoice.

(5) The accounts payable clerk in the buying company initiates an electronic funds transfer (EFT) to the seller.

(6) The design engineer and colleagues in the production arm of the company continue to correspond with the selling company for support in using the component. Network-based support includes communicating through e-mail, bulletin boards, the distribution of software, and other similar kinds of communications.

Tying Internal to External Processes

Key to tying internal processes of a company with its external, commercial processes is the enterprise information server. This is a generic name given to any device (e-mail server/gateway, company mail room, mainframe) where messages and information are routed into, out from, and within a company. Today's workflow software — with a few enhancements — is tomorrow's electronic commerce software. Lotus' next version of Notes and Microsoft's Exchange Server will be fully-functioning internal and external workflow-enabled messaging platforms.

Increasingly, companies are building messaging servers that connect desktop workstations and application servers within the company as well as gateways to public e-mail and EDI networks, including World Wide Web sites. It is at this intersection of the enterprise information server that workflow meets electronic commerce. Workflow — the software that monitors the movement of information through systems — is intrinsically valuable to the architects of electronic commerce systems.

Electronic Commerce at Work

Companies are experimenting with workflow-enabled networks to build links with their trading partners. This shows that EDI is not the only way to conduct electronic commerce. More importantly, it shows that companies are beginning to recognize that a commercial transaction is a workflow.

- Retailer Egghead Software is using Lotus Notes with its largest corporate customers. The customer's employees can peruse an electronic Egghead catalog (in Lotus Notes), make a selection, and route the purchase (via AT&T) to a manager for approval before placing the order.

- Texas Commerce Bank is using Delrina FormFlow to service corporations who have a retirement plan with the bank. Employees of the customer company can sit at a terminal within their own organization, enroll in a retirement plan, or make changes to an existing plan (allocations of money to securities). The system is programmed to dial out nightly to the bank and at the same time uploads the bank's customer system (which itself is a workflow product)

- A Canadian insurance company permits its employees to make small purchases of office and computer equipment. Using a product from Fischer International, which is also an EDI vendor, it created a workflow product that sends POs to suppliers. The system links to catalogs of preapproved items as well as routes to appropriate managers for approval.

Today's Technology Supports Integration

We have moved into the era of distributed computing. This means that the corporate IS environment is no longer just mainframe (if that at all) but a network of servers and desktop PCs. Network operating systems (NOS), such as NT, Unix, Netware, and OS/2, are setting the stage for the next phase of IT and are distinguished from earlier OSs by their rich features in moving files and interconnecting applications across machines.

Why is this new environment so supportive of electronic commerce? My research team performed 15 case studies of companies that switched EDI software from an earlier either mainframe or PC product to a Unix product or other NOS. Although not a statistical sample, all fifteen cited the following features as reasons and/or benefits of having switched.

- Integration with applications in a Unix environment was superior to integration in the older, non-NOS environments. Scripting features, multitasking, and distributed processsing of Unix allowed for tighter, more streamlined linkages between translation server functions and specific applications. Also, manual initiation of processes and several data preparation routines could be automated.

285

- The communication features of Unix provided greater flexibility. Unix has robust features, moving files easily from one computer to another. Some companies found that it was now easy to log directly onto their trading partners' computers to send EDI data. This eliminated the need and the expense of using a third party VAN. Also, several companies especially in engineering and manufacturing companies said that their trading partners were also Unix envionments and having the same underlying OS facilitated file transactions.

- Unix allows event driven processing, multitasking and on-the-fly invoking of applications. It eliminates the batch processing of mainframes and even PC EDI software. These abilities allowed users to be more responsive to their trading partners. It allowed them to have a more fluid workflow between companies. As soon as an electronic purchase order is received, it is immediately processed by the order entry system. As soon as the accounts receivable system creates an invoice, it is immediately translated and sent to the trading partner. Processing of data occurred at the time of need, not according to a set schedule. This major benefit cited by Unix users would apply to any network operating system today.

- A Unix environment is easily scalable. EDI, as well as any system that supports the company's commerce, is open-ended in terms of volume throughput. In other words, as the company's business expands, so must its capacity for processing commercial trade data. Building EDI/EC systems that are easily scalable according to the level of transaction flow is a key benefit of network operating systems. As the EDI volumes increase, users can upgrade from low end RS/6000s to higher end IBMs to Sequent 2000s to HP and AT&T high capacity Unix boxes. The software remains the same; it just gets faster.

- The Unix operating system (as well as NT and the other network operating systems) allows the user to expand incrementally as the number of electronic trading partners and transaction sets increase. The user can buy faster processors and more hardware to keep up with volumes, yet the software remains the same.

The result of the new IT technologies, particularly the move to networks, client/server, and workflow, is that we now have several alternatives to traditional EDI for electronic commerce. This includes e-mail between companies; electronic catalogs — everything from Internet home pages to service bureaus who put a company's products online; bulletin boards that have become essential customer support forums; and shared databases which are standard procedure where sub-contractors work together with a major contractor. There are enormous expansions in specialized activities such as processing services including bill payment services, medical claims processing, freight bill processing, and others.

Changes to Come

As file translation is integrated with standard workflow servers, we will see the following trends in the next five years:

- EDI as we know it today (X12 and EDIFACT) will be used proportionately less because companies will have more alternatives from which to choose in communicating documents with trading partners.
- The ability to translate between file formats will be built into either the operating system (such as Microsoft NT or UNIX) or it will be built into a multipurpose message server (such as Microsoft's Exchange or Lotus' enterprise email platform). In this way, translation between files will be a readily-invoked utility any time a new format is needed.
- Workflow software will have capabilities to route messages to trading partners around the world just as easily as routing to your manager down the hall.
- We will surpass the critical mass where it is more acceptable to send purchase orders, invoices, and payments electronically than by paper. Most companies in the US with revenues over one million dollars will have some sort of EC capability.

This merging of electronic commerce with workflow will accelerate the move toward outsourcing. Companies will be able to focus on core competencies and rely on other companies to take care of non-core business functions such as sales and marketing, design and development, manufacturing, customer support, payments, and distribution.

As value-adding activities are more closely circumscribed and managed through information technology, the ability to modularize company practices increases. Not only will companies restructure themselves, but whole industries as well. The "process reengineering" of the world economy has only just begun.

References:

Porter, Michael. Competitive Advantage: Creating and Sustaining Superior Performance. 1985. The Free Press. New York, New York.

Identifying Emerging Technologies

Amy D. Wohl, President
Wohl Associates

Workflow technology is likely to become a "bread and butter" application by the end of the nineties, with many levels of automation, formality, and structure available depending on the volume and duration of a workflow, as well as its complexity. As we move into the future, constantly expanding technology will enable higher levels of task and process support and permit the automated processing of more complex tasks.

Many types of technology could be applicable to the workflow application. Our job here is to identify the ones that are most likely to appear over the next five to ten years, and those that will have the greatest potential for changing how workflow, and office workers, operate.

We will focus on the problems of:

- Identifying the technologies that are likely to intersect and impact workflow
- Validating these technologies as ready for operational use, as opposed to experiments and demonstration projects

Deconstructing the workflow concept into its constituent parts is a good way to help identify the likely areas for useful technology. In this article we are going to explore six areas, each encompassing many technologies. Of particular interest are technologies that affect multiple parts of the workflow model, because of the potential for greater impact. And, of interest are technologies that will be assisted in widespread proliferation by other technology and usage trends, because they will provide a more robust infrastructure for workflow at little or no perceived incremental cost.

The process of building infrastructures

In the 1980s, we tried to sell companies on the idea of installing electronic mail to improve the communications infrastructure and decrease the time it takes to make and implement decisions. But to do this, companies had to install terminals or other workstations on almost every desk, plus host computers, software, and interconnecting wiring. The cost was enormous and difficult to justify. By the late 1980s, when 70 percent or more of the desktops in large companies were equipped with personal computers, the incremental cost of running a local area network, adding low-cost servers, and electronic mail software, was small enough, compared to the value of enhanced communication, that it was easy to sell; users who needed computers only to read their electronic mail could be justified (or equipped with recycled, low function equipment) on the basis of "completing the system."

In much the same way, organizational plans to move from aging PCs to new robust platforms (which they must do to run the latest personal productivity environments and applications) will also equip users to handle workflow software, with graphical user interfaces, imaging, and eventually multimedia.)

The technologies we will address in this chapter include:

Interfaces: New interface technologies, hardware (pen, voice) and software (agents, natural language, animation, voice recognition) are sure to be useful in managing complex interactions.

Process Models: Object-oriented tools that allow a process to be modeled and code, which reflects that process to be automatically generated; visualization tools, including virtual reality tools, which allow workflow processes to be simulated or visualized in one place as they occur in multiple physical locations.

> geographical
> boundaries will be
> meaningless

Databases: New database techniques, including friendly interfaces and query tools that provide the ability to work with multiple large and possibly remote databases simultaneously (without the need to possess any substantial information system skills). A single natural language query interface that accesses information from any database, no matter its style or age.

Communication: Faster, transparent network technologies will permit any type of data to be stored anywhere and immediately accessed. Geographical boundaries will be meaningless. New wireless communications infrastructures will support the increasing numbers of workers who will operate in a mobile fashion, using small, hand-held computers that communicate and exchange information with office-based systems. In this way, data input and expertise to a workflow will be much less constrained by the limits of time or space.

Storage: New high-volume storage technologies, beyond optical disk, and new indexing and retrieval methodologies, particularly associative logic software based on neural networks.

Display of Information: Many new visualization techniques, including animation and visual reality, that may be suitable for helping to construct and revise process models, particularly where they are complex and involve crossing functional or geographic boundaries.

Now, let us examine each of these technologies in a more rich and detailed fashion, looking for examples of their potential to change how we work or the work itself.

Interfaces

Imagine the ability to build an auditing workflow for a multinational manufacturer.

Pen-based interfaces offer an intuitive and familiar way to interact with the computer. Nearly everyone already knows how to use a pen or pencil to write, draw, and select (by checking boxes). We can choose between passive pens (the pen itself is inert; the preciseness of its tip and pressure exerted creates the interface) and active pens (a button or other device on the pen and/or the pen's ability to recognize variations in exerted pressure).

Useful pen interfaces require real-time, accurate recognition of a broad range of handwriting styles with unlimited vocabularies.

Useful pen interfaces require real-time, accurate recognition of a broad range of handwriting styles with unlimited vocabularies. Today, we must have limits in speed, vocabulary, or style in order to get even somewhat acceptable levels of accuracy. But it is likely that continuing work in this area, together with increases in processing power, will eventually permit users to simply write on the pad-like object in their hand (or on any computer display) with any firm object, including a finger, and be readily understood. That includes more difficult issues than the ones we are currently working on like sentences that span multiple languages, drawings with handwritten labels, and recognizing existing handwriting (including the annotations or revisions you have made).

> new interfaces will increase the participation of the business user (who owns the workflows) in the design process

None of this will keep pen-based systems from seeming much less exciting when Voice Recognition, especially voice recognition enhanced with artificial intelligence, becomes available in commercial products. This is the Star Trek model come to life. You talk to the computer in ordinary English (or French or Chinese). The computer hears you, recognizes the words (continuous speech voice recognition), understands their meaning (natural language processing), and then replies in idiomatic language. The computer offers rapid access to all types of knowledge, so it can answer questions with complete authority. Since it speaks all known languages, it can also serve as a kind of interpreter between people who wish to communicate, but who do not share a common language (machine translation).

This is not fantasy, but simply the integration of a number of different technologies into a smooth and seamless whole. Pieces of this model have already begun to appear; getting it all may take as much as another 50 years, especially in terms of doing it in real-time on systems that are small enough to be readily portable and cheap enough to be distributed to every potential user.

Software agents are already beginning to arrive as part of the computing environment. They permit users to delegate work to the software, rather than doing it themselves. Originally, agents were part of individual applications and had expertise about the application itself (such as word processing, electronic mail, or workflow). Now we are getting system- level agents, such as the agent facility in General Magic's Telescript, which exist for the purpose of sending messages and the ability to do work (carry out programs) from one application to another and from one environment to another. This will obviously be very useful in complex workflows and global environments.

> it is likely that we will continue to build highly customized, complex custom models that are entirely unique to a particular application

New interfaces will increase the participation of the business user (who owns the workflows) in the design process, rather than requiring that the business user explain business processes to system analysts and designers who then create the workflow processing program. In that sense, new interfaces are all about enhancing and increasing accessibility.

They are also about making accessibility available in situations where conventional computing is inconvenient or simply inappropriate. (I would not mind approving something back in my office while I am at the opera or dining in a restaurant in another city, but I am not taking a laptop computer with me in the pocket of my evening gown. A palmtop with a pen interface and wireless interconnectivity, on the other hand, extends the possibility of including my participation (rather than delegating the decision or simply waiting and increasing the average turnaround time). We already have the physical tools. Now we need the software to let us connect multi-platform workflows in an elaborate client/server hierarchy securely together.

Imagine the ability to build an auditing workflow for a multinational manufacturer. It can be sent to a particular location and audit specific processes or check for accuracy. Is the inventory correct, as reported? Does the work in process plus the work shipped tally with the report to headquarters two days ago? Conditional logic in the agent would permit it to adapt to local situations and unique customs; machine translation would allow it to read and translate labels to create visual reports for human review.

Animation will be used both to make the interface more personable and also to make complex workflow processes more understandable and accessible.

Image recognition will be used in the interface incorporating richness. For instance, a workflow might include input from a meeting, with visual scanning of the participants, image recognition, voice recognition, processing of the results, and incorporation of the meeting decision into the workflow. This is a far cry from the kinds of simple, mechanistic workflow models we think of today, but entirely possible within the technology we can already imagine.

Process models

Workflows are collections of tasks, often complex and conditional, which may occur simultaneously, sequentially, or both. Understanding the order and logic of the workflow is an important part of making it rational and being able to optimize its *efficiency*.

Fortunately for workflow processing, it flowered in the marketplace just as the personal computer revolution began and was able to take advantage of the highly distributed architecture enabled by the PC, culminating in the client/server model. Just as important, was the appearance of *object-oriented tools*, allowing processes to be modeled and code to be automatically generated that reflects those processes.

We are still in the infancy of object-oriented tools and software; many developers are still in the learning process, getting ready to convert to these new development techniques that are particularly well suited to modeling a world in which tasks (discrete modules) will be combined and recombined in multiple workflows. In the second half of the nineties we will see more object-oriented tools; the appearance of object-oriented operating systems; and the availability of a new kind of software. This new software, built from object modules, will permit developers to create their own custom environments, combine off-the-shelf components (for word processing, calculation, graphics) with custom components for in-house tasks (budgeting, payroll, sales lead management) and workflow objects to combine them all.

It is likely that we will continue to build both highly customized, complex custom models that are entirely unique to a particular application (and which are only appropriate to a high volume application that will endure for a long period of time). But, at the same time, object oriented technology is going to enable a kind of mass customization, based on the ability to take existing code and reuse it at a highly granular level.

The high-end applications will still be the realm of the custom systems integrators

It's as if you were being offered the opportunity to design your own car, with every component fully interchangeable with all of the other components in its category—some, of course, with price or performance penalties—and you could just sit at a giant real-time palette instructing the assembly line robots how to put it all together. But, in this case, you are putting together any application you can imagine, from administrative services to manufacturing, from something within a two-man benefits administration department in your smallest site to a global workflow that includes all your customers and your entire distribution channel.

The high-end applications will still be the realm of the custom systems integrators, but the smaller applications, the ones you need right away that affect 14 people this week and for the next three months, will be very much like our robot assembly plant where we'll put together the parts using process models, object-oriented programming, and highly granular applications that can be taken apart and put together in any way we please.

This means that when Jean D'Arc becomes the supervisor of the Mission Impossible Team on the first Mars Mission and she needs a project management tool suitable for her group's needs, which includes supporting an intergalactic workflow, but which is otherwise rather ordinary, she'll sit down with the 21st century version of Word, Project, Excel and a few communication robots. She will look at them through a process modeling filter to visualize the workflow, ask her virtual team (separated by a galaxy or two) to agree to the plan, and let the code coalesce.

Or you could request (using that natural language voice recognition interface) that your computer find some suitable illustrations for requests for tours to Frank Lloyd Wright's residential structures and that, further, this group is only interested in those that included steeply pitched roofs and large gardens. Header information, stored in an index, would likely get you to the Frank Lloyd Wright section of your architectural photographs, but image recognition and workflow software would then recognize and insert the appropriate pictures and plan the tour.

> high-end applications will still be the realm of the custom systems integrators

Databases

We will add to the friendly interfaces we have described natural language query tools plus the ability to work with multiple large and possibly remote databases simultaneously (without the need to possess any substantial information system skills). The goal is to permit the user to employ a single natural language query interface that is comfortable and familiar to access any information that might be required, from any database, no matter its style or age.

We are moving to very distributed database models where the user accesses data under programmatic control without knowing or caring where the location of the database—or its platform—might be. This can lead to very interesting potential models. Some argue for the continuation of host storage of data for its economy(?), performance, and security. The host becomes a kind of giant data server. A workflow, of course, does not care what kind of server data resides on, as long as its software knows how to access it, but it seems unlikely that host economics will not continue on their long slide out of the market. Many data sets are, in fact, owned by users in departments and simply stored for them on the central host. As we move toward a more distributed computing environment, with secure and robust database technology available everywhere in the architecture, it seems likely that data will be stored based on convenience and cost, rather than on history. In the cyber-centered information structures of the future, data may become a valuable commodity, bought and sold by canny corporate managers, much like cash managers rent their overnight funds for the interest as they rest between two transactions.

Imagine your corporate information broker realizing that he could sell various kinds of demographic data to research houses (with real-time data, of course, being infinitely more valuable and higher priced). You would think you were collecting information on the sales of cornflakes in Ohio. Your information broker might be aggregating all the information queries this morning about cereal sales in the U.S. and selling them to a grain futures broker. In fact, he could create a workflow where the queries would create their own reports and send the data to the appropriate clients using intelligent agents. In high performance, completely networked environments, we would never even notice—and we probably would not care.

> data may become a valuable commodity, bought and sold by canny corporate managers

Communication

We are at the edge of the information superhighway. Soon, as fast as transparent network technologies permit any type of data to be stored anywhere, geographical boundaries will become meaningless. Anyone will be able to choose to work anywhere (making the morning rush hour a thing of the past). Since wireless communications infrastructures will support the increasing numbers of workers who operate in a mobile fashion, using small, hand-held computers that communicate with and exchange information with office-based systems, anyone will be able to contribute data or expertise to a workflow. Our notion of workflows as activities that mainly occur within a single department or location will seem as quaint as morning traffic jams.

The availability of high bandwidth interconnection will mean that anything—a video, a real-time image, laboratory data, an on-line audio and video conference—could be part of a workflow, with its results incorporated into the ongoing process.

Coordination workflows would oversee scheduling and deadlines as well as billing and customer satisfaction.

Imagine then a secretary of the year 2050. A human, not an electronic agent. This independent contractor would work out of her home or personal office, providing a variety of support services to her clients. They might think of her as sharing a virtual office with each of them, but they are not necessarily known to each other at all. Much of the work will be accomplished by established workflows that pass work between various workers, wherever they happen to be. Our secretary, for instance, might provide the writing or editing of documents and presentations, the creation of travel arrangements and documents, the handling of client relationships, or the management of special events. Work assignments would often arrive as part of clients' ad hoc workflows. Much of the work would occur as part of a workflow designed to handle a particular task. Coordination workflows would oversee scheduling and deadlines as well as billing and customer satisfaction. The secretary (human) could create an agent-clone animation of herself, who spoke in her voice and style and carried her greetings and instructions to clients as part of a normal workflow.

> we need to move in the direction of highly automated tools and templates

Storage

If workflows are going to contain all sorts of data types, including such storage-intensive objects as images, video, and voice, high volume storage technologies, beyond optical disk, and new indexing and retrieval methodologies, particularly associative logic software based on neural networks, seem especially well suited to managing the storage in a workflow environment. We particularly need to consider rewritable CD-ROM, the ability to manage large numbers of CDs (through changers, jukeboxes, and other devices, both desktop and shared), and the notion of storing data and images in database machines (image is, after all, simply another data type) at the end of a high-speed communication "line."

No one cares, after all, if the information is stored, only that it is utterly seamless to request the information and to display it instantly. In fact, given the weight penalty for carrying information (or, more accurately, the storage devices which hold the information and the power supplies to enable them), keeping the information elsewhere and transparently piping it to the user sounds quite seductive.

In fact, with combinations of technology—such as wireless connectivity, highly portable small devices, and distributed storage—new computing models spring into being. Some of them seem to fit the pages of a science fiction novel better than the offices we work in today. For instance, given the human propensity to quickly outgrow whatever amount of storage we incorporate into personal devices—and the human desire to carry around as little as possible, we will never be able to carry all our information around in our hand or our breast pocket. With a wireless device, however, there is no need to do that. Today's wireless devices are not very interesting yet; messages are short and generally limited in richness. But as that changes and bandwidth increases we will cease to care where things are stored. We will only care how easy it is to access them and what it costs.

A scenario: Harold is sitting in a meeting. He has his palmtop computer Einstein in his hand. He is invisibly made seven stock transactions while his boss gave an incredibly boring motivational speech that he has already heard three times. Now he is going to attach to his main research database and write his presentation for his meeting next week; that means he can take Nanette to dinner tonight instead of working late to get the presentation done. Later, in yet another meeting, Harold realizes he has forgotten to tell his secretary he needs to be in New York Friday morning for an 8:00 a.m. meeting. He sends her an e-mail.

> visualization tools, including virtual reality tools, allow workflow processes to be simulated or visualized

While he is on line, an agent intercepts him and points out that this meeting requires that he present a report that is not finished yet. He quickly checks into a data base stored in another country (he can tell because his response time is great; it's midnight there) and downloads the data he needs to prepare his charts. The agent will nag him occasionally (it's set on a nag cycle every four hours) until the chart preparation workflow is completed. He has never been attached physically to anything, but he has accessed a half dozen different systems and his work is done. He does not care where in cyberspace things are stored as long as they are safe—and always available.

Display of information

We are all children of the television age. When the 500 channels of the age of the information superhighway arrive, our expectations are likely to increase, not diminish. Our idea of a nice visual was established not by looking at tables of number and pie charts, but by being seduced to spend big dollars for cars and vacations by watching million dollar minutes: the commercial on TV. You are not going to become a TV producer, but there is no reason why the material presented to you on a desktop or portable display—or the material you present to others—should not reach toward this high standard. We need to move in the direction of highly automated tools and templates so that when we specify a workflow and an end result with recipients, that combination will cause the system to alter the way information is displayed to suit the combination of information and audience.

Complex information for a technical audience might be presented in a fairly straightforward way. Complex information for senior executives would be abstracted and beautified so that it would be simple, understandable, and very pleasing. This also means that you could write a document once and create many documents automatically by asking that it be republished for specific audiences—children, teenagers, consumers, elderly and visually handicapped shoppers, professional athletes—you name it. The document would change not only in the complexity of its sentences and the size of its vocabulary, but also in its format—type and type size, use of white space and graphics, and in the electronic world, use of animation, visualization, and voice.

This takes us right to Star Trek and the Enterprise—or Apple's vision of a Knowledge Navigator. Ask for the information you need (through voice recognition, natural language processing, unformatted data) and the computer instantly (incredible processing and communication performance) finds what you are looking for (fuzzy search engines attached to all the knowledge in the world through indexing schemes yet undreamed of) and speaks the answer in idiomatic language constructions—English or Martian.

In a workflow context, this could mean that the decision-maker can access any needed additional information and that the workflow would then adjust depending on the content of the reply supplied by the computer.

Many visualization techniques, including animation and visual reality, are suitable for helping to construct and revise process models, particularly where they are complex and involve crossing functional or geographic boundaries, and permit the support of visual workflows or workflows with visual components. Visualization tools, including virtual reality tools, allow workflow processes to be simulated or visualized in one place as they occur in multiple physical locations. This permits central management of geographical disbursed (and possibly physically hazardous) tasks. It also permits the headquarters' disbursement of resources and the reassignment of work to balance workloads and ensure that deadlines are met and customer satisfaction goals are achieved.

In the workflow world of the late 20th century, a sales representative in a remote location in China or Africa would be able to tap into the actual work-in-progress data for a plant anywhere in the world and show the customer the visualization of a product being built right on the screen of his portable computer.

Early visualization tools will be somewhat limited in scope; as time goes on they will portray more realistic scenarios, based on photorealism. Animation, and elaborate computer image recognition. This will permit workflow builders and users to see not just representations of the workflow, but an actual, movie-like dramatization, complete with appropriate backgrounds and characters (your home office and the boss).

The point of any collection of technologies—and before we reach the end of this century, the ones we have selected to mention here will inevitably be joined by many others as yet unpredicted—is to support human efforts. These technologies seem to offer a substantially enhanced potential for supporting more complex work and, at the same time, providing better input to human decisions, when such human input is required or desired. It is, after all, not the role of any technology to replace humans, but rather to replace the work that is tedious and repetitive, leaving for human minds and hands that which requires human intellect, creativity and a sense of joy.

Appendix A

About the Contributors

Bair, James H.

Research Director
Gartner Group
5201 Great America Parkway
Santa Clara CA 95054
Tel: 1 408-970-0270
Fax: 408450-4501

James H. Bair, Research Director with Gartner Group Company, has 27 years experience in the computer industry. Prior to joining Gartner Group, Mr. Bair founded Cooperative Systems Consulting after being Manager, Advanced Solutions, for Xerox's Integrated Office Systems Division. Before Xerox, he was Manager, Advanced Functions, for Hewlett-Packard's Information Systems Group focusing on R&D in workgroup computing. He came to HP from Bell-Northern Research, Inc., where he was Manager of Information Systems Research, conducting user needs studies on large corporations. During the 1970s, he was a Senior Scientist at Stanford Research Institute helping to develop the first office system. He has seventy-three publications in research and trade journals, and three books including *The Office of the Future*.

Mr. Bair holds a B.S. degree from Utah State University, an M.A. degree and Ph.D. work from Pennsylvania State University.

Bell, R. Kraft

President
RKB Limited and
Executive Consultant, Prism Performance Systems
37000 Grand River Suite 230
Farmington Hills MI 48335
1-810-474-8855 Fax: 810-474 1116

Dr. Bell has over 20 years of management and consulting experience in Turnarounds, Workflow Redesign, Strategic Planning, and Large Scale Change. He lead successful efforts at Ford and Dow Corning with dramatic time, quality, and cost results. In 1988 Dr. Bell founded RKB, Ltd. where he has integrated a consulting and computer-augmented teamwork approach that expedites dramatic change through reengineering and capability development.

Bruss, Lois R.

Co-founder and Principal
HDA Consulting
7 Kendall Road
Lexington, MA 02173
Tel: 1 617-861-8933
Fax: 1-617-863-1681

Based in Lexington, MA, Ms. Bruss is recognized as an expert in the human and organizational impact of imaging. She consults to organizations on the management of technological change, organization and team effectiveness and work redesign. Her clients include State governments, insurance companies, pharmaceutical companies and manufacturing companies. Currently, Ms. Bruss is the Chair of the AIIM Standards Committee on Human and Organizational Issues Impacting Imaging Success.

Burns, Nina

President
Creative Networks, Inc.
480 Lytton Avenue, Suite 6
Palo Alto, CA 94305
Tel: 1 415 326-9926
Fax: 1 415 326-4014

Nina Burns, President and CEO of Creative Networks, is a leading expert in workflow automation. She works with end-user organizations in planning workflow infrastructures, defining requirements and selecting products and technologies. She works with workflow vendors on product planning and market development. She has published numerous articles for leading trade publications, teaches a two-day tutorial on workflow automation at Interop and speaks frequently at premier conferences and industry events.

Boyd, Stowe

Founder, President, Managing Director
Work Media
209 Eldon Street, Suite 202
Herndon, VA 22070
Tel: 703-708-9050   Fax: 703-708-9055

Internet: workmedia@workmedia.com

Stowe Boyd is president of Work Media, a consulting and market research firm focused on the work software industry, a term coined by Boyd to refer to the covergence of BPR tools, workflow and groupware technologies.

Subsequent to founding the company in 1994, Boyd established the DC chapter of WARIA and serves upon WARIA's national advisory board; he serves as Technical Editor of Enterprise Reengineering, the national publication for BPR; he was program chair for the *Tools and Methods for Business Engineering* conference '95 and serves on the advisory board for the National BPR '95 conference.

Boyd has published numerous papers on software, management, and business engineering; frequently serves as invited speaker diverse forums. He was formerly senior vice president of engineering for Verdix and previously president of Meridian Software Systems; both compaines were leaders in software tools. He holds and MS degree in Computer Science from Boston University and a BS degree from the University of Massachusetts, Amherst.

Byles, Torrey

Director of Electronic Commerce
BIS Strategic Decisions
500 Chiquita Street, Suite 9
Mountain View CA 94041
Tel: 1 415-962-9544
E-mail: torrey@scruznet.com
Compuserve: 73517, 2011

Torrey Byles is the Director of Electronic Commerce at BIS Strategic Decisions, a strategic planning consultancy. Mr. Byles advises companies in the development and deployment of electronic commerce systems. Mr. Byles brings close to 15 years experience in the communications industry both as a user and provider of information technologies.

Mr. Byles has a bachelors degree in economics from the University of California, San Diego; he has conducted graduate work in education at California State University, Los Angeles; and he has completed university and intensive language programs in Taiwan and Mexico.

Cruse, Dean

Vice President, Marketing
Recognition International Inc.
PO Box 660204
Dallas, TX 75266-0204
Tel.: 1 214-579-6000
Fax: 1 214-579-6400

Cruse joined Recognition in 1987 as a product manager and has evolved through the product management and marketing ranks to his current position. Cruse has been involved with the company's imaging and workflow software products since their inception and has been a key developer of marketing vision for the company's workflow products and direction. His current responsibilities include strategic product and marketing planning, market development, market research and requirements definition and product marketing for the Plexus software products.

Prior to Recognition, Cruse held various product marketing positions at Cable and Wireless, a telecommunications company. He earned a Bachelor of Arts degree in marketing at Texas A & M University and has taken graduate studies in marketing and competitiveness at Harvard and Stanford Universities.

Denning, Peter J.

Associate Dean for Computing
Chair, Computer Science Department
George Mason University
School of Information Technology and Engineering
4400 University Drive
Science & Tech II, Room 430
Fairfax, VA 22030-4444
Tel: 1 703-993-1525
Fax: 1 703-993-3729

Professor Denning is also director of the Center for the New Engineer, which he founded at George Mason University. He was formerly the founding director of the Research Institute for Advanced Computer Science at the NASA Ames Research Center, was co-founder of CSNET, and was head of the computer science department at Purdue. He received a Ph.D. from MIT and BEE from Manhattan College. He was president of the Association for Computing Machinery a decade ago and is now chair of the ACM publications board. He has published three books and several hundred articles on computers, networks, and their operating systems, and is working on two more books. He holds two honorary degrees, three professional society fellowships, two best-paper awards, and two distinguished service awards.

Fischer, Layna

President and Chief Executive Officer
Future Strategies Inc.
3640 N. Federal Highway
Lighthouse Point, FL 33064
Tel: +1 305-782-3376
Fax: +1 305-782-6365
Internet: waria@gate.net

Ms. Fischer held the position of conference co-director of BIS' *Business Process and Workflow Conference* and was the director of the *Workflow '94 Boston* conference and *The Workflow Conference on Business Process Technology*, of which her company, Future Strategies, was the joint producer. She also currently heads up WARIA, the Workflow And Reengineering International Association she founded in 1994.

Her experience in the computer industry includes being the president and CEO of a high technology export company for seven years. Ms. Fischer was also a senior editor of a leading computer publication for four years and has been involved in international computer journalism and publishing for over 12 years. She was a founding director of the U.S. Computer Press Association in 1985.

Her company, Future Strategies, a consulting and publishing firm based in South Florida, provides strategic consulting and business process training through its wide network of qualified and experienced business partners, thus ensuring a tailor-made match between client and consultant.

Founded in 1992, the company offers services to both user and vendor organizations and specializes in the research and dissemination of information on workflow technology and business process reengineering.

Howard, Michael K.

Vice-President, Marketing
Xerox Corporation
290 Woodcliff Drive
Fairport, NY 14450
Tel: 1 716-383-7864
Fax: 716-383-7228

Mr. Howard has more than 18 years of experience in the information technology (IT) industry. At Xerox, Mr. Howard is responsible for product portfolio direction and management. Joining Xerox in late 1994, he is charged with the responsibility of moving Xerox 's office equipment systems into the digital world. In 1989 he introduced Gartner Group's document imaging and workflow software practices under the OIS service umbrella. Over the past four years, he has helped hundreds of clients develop and execute strategies in these application arenas. He joined Gartner Group's consulting practice in 1987 where he managed more than 25 custom projects focusing on corporate IT strategies.

Prior to joining Gartner Group, he was vice president of marketing for a turnkey system firm specializing in distribution solutions. He served as a manager and senior consultant in Price Waterhouse's Management Consulting Services for four years focusing on financial and manufacturing applications. Mr. Howard received an artium baccalaureus in economics from Princeton University. He is a graduate of GE's Financial Management Program.

Imparato, Nicholas

Professor of Marketing and Management
University of San Francisco.
McLaren School of Business
2130 Fulton Street
San Francisco, CA 94117
Tel: 1 415-666-6740
Fax: 1 415-666-2502

Co-author of *Jumping the Curve*, Imparato has been a visiting Scholar at Stanford University and a Visiting Professor of Computer Sciences at Boston College. During a series of special leaves from the University, he obtained "hands-on experience" as the Chief Operating Officer for Coit Companies and as Senior Vice President and Ford Liaison at First Nationwide Bank. He also worked as a seminar leader and speaker for the Tom Peters Group. Additionally Nicholas has served as a director for both privately and publicly held companies, including Voicemail International, and as a member of the board of advisors for several IBM marketing organizations, Park City Group and other firms. He has won numerous teaching honors, including the University's Distinguished Teacher Award.

Libit, Jordan, M.

Vice President Marketing
FileNet Corporation
3565 Harbor Blvd.
Costa Mesa, CA 92626
Tel: 1 714-966-3575

Fax: 1 714-966-3490

Mr. Libit is responsible for strategic planning, product marketing, industry marketing, corporate communications, documentation and education for File-Net's family of document imaging and workflow software products and services. Mr. Libit has more than 20 years' experience in the computer industry. He joined FileNet as Director of Product Marketing and was promoted to Vice President in 1992. He previously spent 18 years at IBM. Mr. Libit holds a Bachelor of Science Degree in mathematics and computer science from the University of Illinois.

Lockwood, Rose

Director,
ITALICS
45A Oseney Crescent
London, NW5 2BE ENGLAND
Tel: 1 071-284-4951
Fax: 1 071-267-6504
Compuserve: 100436,232

Rose Lockwood is a consultant and analyst specialising in the application of information and communication technologies to office work. She is a leading expert in markets for natural language processing. Dr. Lockwood is co-founder of the *International Trade and Language Industries Consortium* (*ITALICS*), a Netherlands-based foundation which promotes awareness of the significance of language in global business. Ms. Lockwood is program director for the *ITALICS* annual conference, and provides consultancy to both users and suppliers of language-based technologies and solutions.

Ms. Lockwood is author of a number of published studies in various areas of office technology, and has conducted many custom studies for clients in both Europe and the US.

Ms Lockwood is also Executive Editor of *The LISA Showcase* - a CD-ROM information resource developed by the Localisation Industry Standards Association in Geneva. The CD covers products and suppliers of localisation and translation, methods and processes, industry views and standards.

Ms Lockwood holds an MA and PhD in Social and Economic History from Tufts University, and a BA in Social Studies from Bennington College and has done postgraduate studies in Business Studies from Harvard University.

Marshak, Ronni T.

Vice President, Editor-in-Chief Workgroup Computing Report

Patricia Seybold Group
148 State Street 7th Floor
Boston, MA 02109
Tel: 1 617-742-5200
Fax: 1 617-742-1028

Ronni T. Marshak, vice president of the Patricia Seybold Group, has worked in the computing industry for over 12 years, 11 of which have been with the Patricia Seybold Group. She specializes in workgroup issues and products including interface design, compound document editors, workflow automation, and document management systems. Marshak is the editor-in-chief of the *Office Computing Report: Guide to Workgroup Computing*, a monthly research newsletter, now in its 15th year, that explores the issues, technologies, products and vendors that surround organizational computing, specifically at the departmental level. She also acts as senior editor for *Open Information Systems* and *Distributed Computing Monitor*. She holds a BA from the University of Massachusetts and a Master's degree from Northeastern University.

Medina-Mora, Raúl

Senior Vice President and Chief Scientist
Action Technologies, Inc.
1301 Marina Village Parkway, Suite 100
Alameda, CA 94501
Tel: 1 510-521-6190
Fax: 1 510-769-0596

Dr. Raúl Medina-Mora was born in Mexico City. He received his B.S. degree in Mathematics from the National University of Mexico in 1976. He received his M.Sc. degree in Computer Science in 1979 and his Ph.D. degree in Computer Science in 1982, both from Carnegie-Mellon University.

He was a research assistant at the Computer Science Department, Carnegie-Mellon University from 1976 to 1982 and an Associate Professor at the National University of Mexico from 1982 to 1984.

Since 1984 he has been associated with Action Technologies, Inc., leading teams in the development of electronic communication and management systems; MHS by Action Technologies, The Coordinator Software and Action-Workflow Technology. He is Chief Architect of the ActionWorkflow Technology.

Opper, Susanna

President

Susanna Opper & Associates
388 West Road
Alford, MA 01266
Tel: 1 413-528-6513
Fax: 1 413-528-0734

Susanna Opper heads the consulting firm she founded in 1983 to help organizations use networked computers to achieve competitiveness and improve profitability. Clients include major U.S. and multinational companies, associations, consulting firm and small businesses. She is co-author of *Technology For Teams: Enhancing Productivity in Networked Organizations*, published by Van Nostrand Reinhold in 1992.

Parry, Michael F.

Vice President, Strategic Alliances
Integris,
Technology Park, 2 Wall Street MA02/113N
Billerica, MA 01821
Tel: 1.800-291-6975
Fax: 1 508-294-7901

Michael F. Parry is Vice President of Strategic Alliances for Integris, a Boston area work management company. He is responsible for creating strategic client and technology partner relationships and driving the firm's work management and consulting business areas.

Before joining Integris, Mr. Parry was Vice President of Regional Operations for GTE Vantage Solutions where he managed delivery of reengineering, systems design, and systems integration projects for Fortune 1000 clients. Mr. Parry has also served as the Manager of Workflow Solutions at TASC, a renowned systems engineering and integration firm where he was responsible for strategy, development and sales of workflow management and simulation products. He has held senior management positions with Digital Equipment Corporation and Honeywell Information Systems.

Mr. Parry holds an M.S. in Engineering Management from Northeastern University, and a B.A. in Mathematics from New York University.

Rose, Louis C.

System Architect
Logicon, Inc.
Strategic and Information Systems Division
2100 Washington Boulevard

Arlington, VA 22204
Tel: 1 703-486-3500
Fax: 1 703-979-0268

Louis C. Rose is a system architect for the Information Systems Engineering Department of Logicon, Inc. Rose is the principal investigator responsible for the design and implementation of the LOGICORE Software Engineering Environment.

Roos, Helene T.

Co-founder and Principal
HDA Consulting
4059 26th Street
San Francisco, CA 94131
Tel: 1.415-826-5700
Fax: 1 415-826-1456

HDA specializes in the management of technological change. Based in San Francisco, California. Dr. Roos is a frequent conference speaker, seminar and workshop leader and consultant to numerous organizations. Over the past 11 years, she has conducted numerous projects in the change management area, including Technology Assimilation Assessments, in-house training on developing change management skills, team building and work redesign.

Silver, Bruce

Principal
Bruce Silver Associates
260 Glen Road
Weston, MA 02193
Tel 617-237-6879   Fax 617-237-1641
Email 75213.2033@compuserve.com

Dr. Bruce Silver is Principal at Bruce Silver Associates, a Boston-based consultancy specializing in workflow and document management, and Senior Consulting Partner at BIS Strategic Decisions, a market research and consulting company. Before starting his own company he was Vice President at BIS Strategic Decisions, where he advised most of the leading vendors of workflow and document management software, as well as workflow and imaging buyers. He is the author of BIS's recently published Workflow Market Opportunity Report, and is currently in the process of developing the 1995 BIS Guide to Workflow Software.

Prior to his five years at BIS, Dr. Silver was a principal developer of Wang Laboratories' WIIS document imaging system, and prior to that held a variety of positions in R&D and business planning at Polaroid. He holds degrees in Physics from Princeton and MIT, and has 4 US patents in document imaging and digital photography.

Soles, Dr. Stanley

Professor of Information Systems and Sciences
Fairleigh Dickinson University
21 Ardmore Rd
Scarsdale, NY 10583-7113
Tel: 1 914-725-5468
Fax: 1 914-723-5668

Dr. Soles is an ex-Californian, who graduated from USC and earned a doctorate from Stanford. He taught at San Francisco State, Fordham and elsewhere before joining Fairleigh Dickinson University, Rutherford, NJ, where he is currently a Professor. He has held management positions in San Francisco and New York in both the public and private sectors. Dr. Soles has over 30 publications. He is director of OPUS, Scarsdale NY, a consulting firm.

Keith Swenson

Architect
Fujitsu OSSI
3055 Orchard Dr.
San Jose, CA, 95134
Voice: +1 408 456-7667
Fax: +1 408 456-7050
Internet: kswenson@ossi.com

Keith D. Swenson is currently at Fujitsu Open Systems Solutions, Inc. in California developing coordination and collaboration software known as Regatta Technology, a next-generation workflow support tool that allows groups of people to collaboratively define the processes that they are involved in, while performing their normal work tasks.

He is active in the ACM SIG for Office Information Systems, including founding a Silicon Valley local chapter this year to provide a forum for Groupware discussions. He is an active participant of the Workflow Management Coalition, chairing a working group on the Process Definition Interface. He is known for giving presentations and lectures on the future of workflow and how such technology can be made to better support human interaction.

He has an M.Sc. in Computer Science with a specialization in public hypertext information systems. He has lead teams in the past for the development of several popular integrated application programs for personal computers at Software Products International and at Ashton-Tate. He can be reached at kswenson@ossi.com.

Wohl, Amy D.

President
Wohl Associates
915 Montgomery Ave, Suite 309
Narberth, PA 19072
Tel: 1 215-667-4842
Fax: 1 215-667-3081

Amy Wohl is president of Wohl Associates, a consulting and market research firm that follows the intersection of technology and office work. The firm provides services on strategic planning, system design and evaluation, marketing strategy, marketing research, and training to manufacturers of office information systems and personal computer hardware and software, as well as to user organizations. Ms. Wohl is a monthly columnist in *Computer Shopper, Beyond Computing* and *The OS/2 Magazine*. Ms. Wohl publishes the monthly *TrendsLetter* newsletter and is the Technology Editor of *Perspectives.*

Appendix B

Business Process Reengineering and Workflow Organizations

The IOPT Club

for the Introduction of Process Technology
c/o Tim Huckvale
Praxis plc
20 Manvers Street
Bath
BA 1 1PX
England
Tel: +44 225-444-700
Fax: +44 225-465-205
Email: iopt@praxis.co.uk

The IOPT Club for the Introduction of Process Technology is a forum for discussion of BPR, with the emphasis on practical tecniques and tools that support the Business Process Engineering lifecycyle. It is run as a service for members by Praxis plc, the Software Engineering Company of Touche Ross Management Consultants.

WARIA

Workflow And Reengineering International Association
3640 North Federal Highway,
Lighthouse Point, FL 33064
Tel: 305-782-3376   Fax: 305-782-6365
E-mail: waria@gate.net

WARIA Charter

The charter of this organization is to identify and clarify issues that are common to all users of workflow and/or those who are in the process of reengineering their organizations. The group facilitates opportunities for members to discuss and share both good and bad experiences freely.

WARIA's mission is to make sense of what's happening in BPR and workflow and reach clarity through sharing experiences, product evalutions, networking between users and vendors, education and training.

As the organization continues to grow, focus groups will be defined to examine specific areas of interest to members. These focus groups will give members an excellent opportunity to shape the future of this burgeoning industry, define goals and ensure that users' needs are heard.

WARIA offers a Fax-on-Demand system called 1-800-GROUPWARE (800-476-8792) providing information on vendors, products and services in workgroup, business process reengineering and workflow technology. For more details see end of the Vendor Directory.

Workflow Management Coalition (WfMC)

Workflow Management Coalition
Avenue Marcel Thiry 204
1200 Brussels, Belgium
Tel: +32 2 774 96 33   Fax: +32 2 774 96 90
100113.1555@compuserve.com

The Workflow Management Coalition, founded in August 1993, is a non-profit, international organization of workflow vendors, users and analysts. The Coalition's mission is to promote the use of workflow through the establishment of standards for software terminology, interoperability and connectivity between workflow products. Consisting of over 100 members, the Coalition has quickly become established as the primary standards body for this rapidly expanding software market.

Mission Statement

- Increase the value of customers' investments with workflow technology
- Decrease the risk of using workflow products
- Expand the workflow market through increasing awareness for workflow

Framework

The Coalition has proposed a framework for the establishment of workflow standards. This framework includes five categories of interoperability and communication standards that will allow multiple workflow products to coexist and interoperate within a user's environment. Technical details are included in the white paper titled The Work of the Coalition (see also chapter entitled *Workflow Management Standards and Interoperability* by Keith Swenson).

Appendix C
Vendor Directory

This directory is intended as a resource for both users and vendors. If you seek products, services or vendors not listed here, please see the 1-800 GROUPWARE Fax-on-Demand system and World Wide Web Homepage details at the end of this directory.

ACT Business Systems

Technology House
Maylands Avenue, Hemel Hempstead
Hertfordshire HP2 7DF, United Kingdom
+44 1 442 242277 Fax: +44 1 442 69475

Vendor independent workflow consultancy and implementation services specialising in integration with existing applications, hardware and software. Hands-on experience of both ProcessIT and Staffware with systems implemented using both products. Customer profile covers Financial, Insurance, Utilities, Commercial, Government and Defense.

Action Technologies Inc.

1301 Marina Village Parkway, Suite 100
Alameda, CA 94501
1 510-521-6190 1-800-WORKFLOW
Fax: 510-769-0596

- Product(s): ActionWorkflow Analyst, ActionWorkflow Application Builder, ActionWorkflow Workflow Manager

Action offers a full suite of client/server based software tools for the analysis, automation and management of business processes. Through the use of these tools and supported by its educational and consulting offerings, Action clients have experienced significant reductions in cycle time, resources utilized, cost and customer satisfaction of their business processes.

Action has a two-prong approach for the sale of its tools. It enters into partnerships with other companies, who offer Action's tools as part of their product offerings. Action also sells its tools through systems integrators and value-added resellers.

Action has developed a set of application programming interfaces (APIs) that allow for the integration of existing applications from mainframe-based to PC-centric into its workflow system.

Antley Business Systems, Inc.

5217 Wayzata Blvd., Suite 213
Minneapolis, MN 55416
1 612-542-9651 Fax: 612-549-9665

- Products(s): ABSI-Docs
  ABSI-Docs is an electronic workflow system that will manage all aspects of a project using the latest Macintosh client/server technology. ABSI-Docs links together individual Macintosh computers so that everyone is able to work together as a team. You can track customers and projects, make assignments to workgroups or individuals on the network and stay informed about the status of a project and all its components. ABSI-Docs is also a database. You can store and track entire documents (files) and access them and work on them within the database. ABSI-Docs is a networked document management system. You can create, store, retrieve, compress, share, tract and work on documents in any Macintosh application on your desktop, whether it is work processing, graphic design, publishing, CAD or a spreadsheet. ABSI-Docs can compress and decompress documents on-the-fly as they are moved in and out of the database.

AT&T Global Information Solutions

3245 Platt Springs Road
West Columbia, SC 29170
1 803-939-7950 Fax: 803-939-7745

- Product(s): ProcessIT
  ProcessIT—a new management solution that helps implement, manage, and control mission-critical work processes. NCR ProcessIT, information technology for work and process management is based on NCR's open cooperative computing strategy. ProcessIT provides the ability to implement solutions that coordinate and evolve individual and group activities into enterprise work processes to achieve organizational objectives.

Banyan Systems

17 New England Executive Park
Burlington, MA 01803
1 508-898-1000 Fax: 617-229-1114

- Product(s): BeyondMail

BeyondMail is a LAN based e-mail system offering state of the art messaging functionality. BeyondMail offers e-mail users and entire organizations the ability to automate their workflow through BeyondRules. Release 2.0 of BeyondMail includes the following additional features: automated routing slip, enhanced rule language, third party forms integration, database access and image-enabled mail through the Watermark Explorer Edition.

Blueridge Technologies

PO Box 430
Flint Hill Square
Flint Hill, VA 22627
1 703-675-3015 Fax: 703-675-3130

- Product(s): Optix Workflow

Optix WorkFlow is cross-platform workflow for the Macintosh and Windows-based PCs that is designated to work as part of a complete Electronic Document Management System, integrating seamlessly with other Optix cross-platform applications including: Document Imaging, Text Search, OCR, Archival/Retrieval, and Fax Server. Optix Workflow allows businesses to move electronic documents automatically along a user-defined routing path, from one workstation to the next, around both local area networks and wide area networks. Macintosh and Windows workstation clients on the Optix Workflow Route access the UNIX server (Apple Workgroup Server running A/UX or an RS6000 running A/IX) via TCP/IP

Bull HN Information Systems, Inc.

2 Wall Street Technology Park
M.S. MA02-301S
Billerica, MA 01821
1 508-294-4911 Fax: 508-294-6109

- Product(s): FlowPATH IMAGEWorks

FlowPATH can act as a stand-alone workflow application, or be integrated with IMAGEWorks Classic document management systems. FlowPATH has a graphics flow editor, Mobile Graphical Editor, that also provides simulator capability.

Centre-file Ltd

UK: 75 Leman Street, London E1 8EX
Tel: 44-171-410-3000 Fax: 44-171-410-3434
US VAR: Timeline Inc.
3055 112th Avenue North East, Suite 106,
Bellevue, WA 98004

- Product(s): WinWork

  WinWork is a workflow tool kit providing a core task processing engine and a number of optional modules which may be integrated with the engine. The product is targeted at large business with high volume throughput and/or large numbers of users.

Cimage Corporation

3885 Research Park Drive
Ann Arbor, MI 48108
1 313-761-6550 Fax: 313-761-6551

- Product(s): ImageMaster, Engineering Workflow System, Document Manager

  Cimage Engineering Workflow improves engineering cycle time for time-critical processes. It ensures all jobs and related information get where they are needed quickly and accurately. Management control is improved by providing visibility and information on the status of outstanding jobs. Engineering Workflow integration with Document Manager and ImageMaster gives you the tools necessary for a concurrent engineering environment.

Computron Technologies

301 Route 17 North
Rutherford, NJ 07070
1 201-935-3400 Fax: 201-935-6355

- Product(s): EPIC

  EPIC transfers your documents into computer images and controls how they are routed throughout your organization. You simply enter your unique routing and decision rules. EPIC automatically presents the document image and the necessary decisions to each person. Workers can make electronics notes on documents, print them, Fax them and reroute them to others. Supervisors monitor performance and are alerted to bottlenecks before they occur. Comprehensive reporting capabilities allow management to analyze results and suggest changes.

Delrina Corporation

895 Don Mills Road
500-2 Park Center
Toronto, ONT. M3C 1W3
1 416-441-3676 Fax: 416-441-0333

- Product(s): FormFlow

Delrina FormFlow integrates e-mail and database technology with forms processing capabilities to develop workflow automation solutions.

Digital Equipment Corporation

529 Bryant Street
Palo Alto, CA 94301
1 415-617-3619 Fax: 415-617-3655

- Product(s): LinkWorks TeamLinks
LinkWorks includes workflow as a crucial component. TeamLinks contains as a critical component TeamLinks Routing which is software for adhoc workflow.

DST Systems Inc.

1055 Broadway
Kansas City, MO 64105
1 816-435-1000 Fax: 816-435-4550

- Product(s): AWD (Automated Work Distributor) POWERSCAN POWERSTORE
DST has been providing service and software solutions to the insurance, banking, financial services, and pharmaceutical industries for more than 20 years. In 1989 DST continued its tradition by developing a product called the Automated Work Distributor (AWD).

AWD is an image-enabled intelligent work management system that electronically routes work associated with documents, phone calls, faxes, and other sources through an organization. AWD was engineered by DST to enhance control of workflow, particularly in complex clerical operations, and to integrate with any existing line-of-business applications.

Dun & Bradstreet Software Services, Inc.

3449 Peachtree Road, N.E.
Atlanta, GA 30326
1 404-239-INFO Fax: 404-239-2404

- Product(s): SmartStream®
The SmartStream® platform is the vehicle by which D&B Software provides automated workflow management for its enterprise-wide business applications. Through automated workflow technology embedded in SmartStream, users have the flexibility to streamline business transaction processes by intelligently filtering and electronically routing information among related business activities and users throughout the organization. With client-defined agents, users personalize their interaction with the application workflow process, wholly

automating selected tasks, filtering documents into To-Do lists and distributing information to appropriate channels. This is marked contrast to traditional software applications that are reactive by design and simply track business activity or automate localized activities. SmartStream's ability to automate workflow processing enterprise-wide dramatically reduces the time spent locating, evaluating and acting on needed information to gain a competitive advantage.

Edify Corporation

2840 San Tomas Expressway
Santa Clara, CA 95051
1 408-982-2000 Fax: 408-982-0777

- Product(s): The Electronic Workforce
  The Electronic Workforce is a next generation automation software product that uses advanced software agent technology to automate information handling and communications. It uses all information delivery media and provides access to both host and client/server information systems. Using the product's object-oriented applications generator, a wide variety of applications can be quickly generated without a single line of script or code being written. Its standards-based software architecture provide maximum flexibility for selecting and integrating hardware components.

Elf Technologies Inc.

9423 South East 36th Street, Suite 202
Mercer Island, WA 98040
1 206-232-7808 Fax: 206-236-1586

- Product(s): ELF Legal Services
  ELF Legal Services are designed to improve the working relationship between law firms and their clients. These services use Lotus Notes as their primary technology platform, and include the ability to integrate and make visible the information from a variety of disparate systems and applications. The set of services offered by ELF are orchestrated by Elfs, intelligent and programmable agents that manage the collection, organization, and distribution of information required by attorneys to manage their caseload. They also allow for sharing of key case information with clients.

Excalibur Technologies Corporation

9255 Towne Centre Drive, 9th Floor
San Diego, CA   92121
1 619-625-7900 Fax: 619-625-7901

- Product(s): Excalibur EFS™ Electronic Filing Software

Based on a scaleable client/server architecture, Excalibur EFS helps organizations manage their electronic documents in office automation and administrative applications, from document capture, scanning and correction-free OCR to pattern-based retrieval and printing. The key differentiator of Excalibur EFS is its automatic full-content indexing and Adaptive Pattern Recognition based fuzzy-searching. EFS is the only document imaging software that indexes information content without costly and time-consuming manual set-up and pre-processing of data. Excalibur EFS operates on IBM RISC System/6000, Sun Sparcstations, Digital Ultrix, VAX/VMS and Alpha computers, and HP 9000 Series workstations. In client/server environments, Excalibur EFS supports personal computers running Microsoft Windows and Apple Macintoshes.

F3 Software Corp.

6365 NW 6th Way #320
Fort Lauderdale, FL   33309
1 305-489-3200 Fax: 305-489-3220
Internet: f3@f3forms.com

- Product(s): F3 Forms Automation System
    The F3 Forms Automation System allows users to fill out forms on-screen and route them electronically over e-mail, local and wide-area networks. The F3 WYSIWYG forms filler is cross-platform, running on DOS, Windows, and Macintosh, and has the best security available on the market. It has extensive connectivity to over 55 back-end databases and a powerful programming language for specifying form logic. F3 Pro Designer is the standard used by paper forms manufacturers to design complex preprinted forms.

FileNet Corporation

3565 Harbor Blvd.
Costa Mesa, CA 92626
1.800-FILENET Fax: 714-966-3490

- Product(s): WorkFlo Business System
    WorkFlo Business System is a fully integrated set of tools to automate and intelligently manage the flow of images, data, text and other information throughout an enterprise. FileNet WorkFlo software currently supports Microsoft Windows and OS/2 environments. FileNet has provided industry-standard client/server software products for document imaging and workflow management for more than ten years.

Fischer International Systems Corporation

4073 Mercantile Avenue
Naples, FL 33942

1 800-237-4510 Fax: 813-643-3772

- Product(s): WorkFlow.2000, WorkFlow.2020
   WorkFlow.2000 provides programmable forms that mirror business processes. Designed to operate on platforms from mainframes to midranges to micros, WorkFlow.2000 intelligently collects, moves and distributes information and data among an unlimited number of platforms. It provides flexible electronic form display, uses REXX as its logic/control language, uses TeX as the pattern to define forms, provides full digital signature support for security and is EDI integrated. WorkFlow.2000 can be integrated with virtually any application. WorkFlow.2000 collects data from various users and systems, processes it as needed, and distributes the final result as desired.

Fleet & Partners, Inc.

   P.O. Box 373
   Richford, VT 05476
   Tel: 1 905-855-9095 Fax: 905-855-9661

- Product(s): BenchMarker Plus
   Benchmaker Plus is tool oriented toward the capture, storage and analysis of cost and time based information. Based on this data the user is provided a variety of mechanisms for analysing and extracting information - with around 20 different charting tools, a report generator and the automatic generation of process flow diagrams. The product can be used for calculating the Total Work Hours, Total Costs and Staff Capacity Utilisation. Data may be imported directly from a variety of flow diagramming products including ABC FlowCharter/Toolkit and Visio.

Fujitsu Open Systems Solutions Inc.

   3055 Orchard Drive,
   San Jose CA 95134
   1 408-456-7864 Fax 408-456-7667

- Product(s) Regatta
   Fujitsu OSSI aggressively pursues software product development and sales to the open systems marketplace. Futjitsu's Regatta workflow technology, partnered after Black & White Software, enables developers to benefit from workflow application development supported by UIM/X features and cross platform GUI development capability. .

Hewlett Packard, Work Management Operation

3404 East Harmony Road, Mail Stop 110
Fort Collins, Colorado 80525
1 303-229-4206 Fax: 303-229-7182

- Product(s): HP Workmanager
  Product data management and workflow solutions for engineering and manufacturing. Workflow solutions can be purchased separate from WorkManager to cover a broad range of industry needs, including both ad hoc and structured workflows.

High Performance Systems

45 Lyme Road Suite 300
Hanover, NH 03755
1 603-643-9636 Fax: 603-643-9502

- Product(s): i-think
  i-think is one of the most widely used simulation environments in use within BPR initiatives. The product is based on the concept of feedback systems and is a deterministic modeling environment. A graphical modeling approach is used to create the simulation equations automatically. A high level mapping layer allows the user to build a 'management flight simulator'. The tool has traditionally been available on Apple Macintosh computers but has recently been ported to the MS-Windows interface.

HOLOSOFX Inc

(Formerly Virtual Management Inc.)
111 N. Sepulveda blvd., Suite 150
Manhattan Beach, CA 90266
1 310-798-2425 Fax: 310-798-2365

- Product(s): Workflow•BPR
  Workflow•BPR introduces a new paradigm for generating and evaluating business process alternatives—or cases—that can result from specified business conditions. This innovative process design tool captures, defines, and analyzes all alternative possibilities for a particular business process. It then generates process maps that provide a graphical depiction of what is going on—or could go on—in an organization, including detailed information about the time, cost, and value of each step in a business process.

I Levy & Associates Inc.

1633 Des Peres Road, Suite 300
St. Louis, MO 63131-1821

1 314-822-0810 Fax: 314-822-0309

- Product(s): Navigator 2000/Document Management Systems Navigator 2000/Workflow

  Navigator 2000/Document Management System allows users to electronically store, retrieve and manage multiple object types such as images, word processing files, spreadsheets, data processing files, voice, etc. Navigator 2000/Workflow is an optional component of the Navigator 2000/DMS that incorporates powerful facilities to automatically integrate, move, process and manage information among individuals and work groups throughout an organization.

IBM Corporation

Old Orchard Road
Armonk, NY 10504
1 914-765-1900 Fax: 914-766-9147

- Product(s): IBM SAA ImagePlus IBM FlowMark

  The work management builder of the IBM SAA ImagePlus Workfolder Application Facility/400 provides a versatile, easy-to-use graphical tool for a business professional to handle work management-defining and optimizing the work process of a workgroup, department or enterprise. By using icons, a user can construct a comprehensive, yet easy-to-understand diagram of how work is to flow through the organization.

  FlowMark is IBM's offering to optimize your business processes with a workflow management tool. You use FlowMark to design, refine, document, and control your business processes. Your company can focus on the work at hand while FlowMark operates your processes. FlowMark assists you in daily operations, in planning and management, and in the design of applications tailored to your business.

ICL (International Computers Limited)

Lovelace Rd Bracknell
Berkshire RG12 8SN, ENGLAND
44 34-447-3815 Fax: 34-447-3000

- Product(s): PowerFlow TeamFlow ProcessWise

  PowerFlow is the workflow procedure processing option for OfficePower, ICL's UNIX-based office information System. Based on Staffware, it provides facilities for modeling an organization's office procedures and for managing information as it flows through procedures. It is particularly suitable for managing CASE-based, well-defined procedures, such as benefit claims processing, help desk, property purchase/sale, sales order processing. When used with the

Staffware Windows client, PowerFlow applications can operate In a client/server environment.

TeamFlow is a workflow option for TeamOffice, ICL's client/server office information system. It utilizes TeamMAIL as its communications medium, and uses SQL-based options from TeamTOOLS for managing information such as audit trails..

ProcessWise incorporates a set of products and services to provide a comprehensive business process planning and enactment capability. It comprises two major elements, ProcessWise Workbench and ProcessWise Integrator; these are both freestanding products that may be used in conjunction with a variety of standard industry infrastructure and office software.

IdentiTech, Inc.

100 Rialto Place, Suite 800
Melbourne, FL 32901
1 407-951-9503 Fax: 407-951-9505

• Product(s): FYI Workflow

IdentiTech takes a different approach to the implementation of workflow capabilities by integrating Workflow into its FYI software package. FYI is an open architecture, multimedia imaging and information management package with integrated Workflow that provides immediate access to any file, in any digital format, anywhere across an entire computing network. FYI's Workflow is intuitive and menu-driven; users do not need to learn complex workflow languages that require mastery of lower-level programming to use FYI Workflow.

Image Business Systems

417 5th Avenue
New York, NY 10016
1 212-696-2500 Fax: 212-696-5299

• Product(s): IBS Workflow Manager

IBS Workflow Manager is designed to let both end users and MIS professionals precisely tailor workflow operations and processes to meet business objectives. IBS Workflow Manager is an automated client/server workflow management system that controls and automates information and document flow based upon specific requirements. It employs easy-to-construct business rules to enable users to design customized work management applications. Image Business Systems Corp. (IBS) markets a family of document and workflow management software products and services. IBS, an IBM business partner, provides document and workflow management solutions for many Fortune 1000 companies spanning a variety of applications and industries. IBS software runs on a RISC System/6000 server and multiple desktop platforms.

Image Fast Software Systems Inc.

7926 Jones Branch Drive, Suite 260
McLean, VA 22102
1 703-893-1934 Fax: 703-893-7499

- Product(s): ImageFast, WorkFast

WorkFast is a Windows-based, database-enabled workflow routing and messaging package. Users can initiate workflow along pre-defined routes or can perform direct person-to-person routing of drawers, folders, multi-page documents, images and other work objects, with optional return receipts. All received objects and images can be launched or viewed with a simple double click.

WorkFast workflow task logging provides comprehensive and detailed management information for determining productivity patterns and bottleneck areas through real-time data logging. E-Mail functionality in workflow is possible with a built-in word processor, allowing users to create, send, edit, forward and respond to electronic notes from any user, with the same tracking capabilities as workflow tasks.

WorkFast is fully integrated with ImageFast, a software system for the complete desktop organization of all electronic information and services. ImageFast users can easily set up their own flexible indexing format with Database Design Wizards, and can use Action! Icons to create new documents directly within ImageFast folders.

Infologistik

1950 Stemmons Frwy.
Suite 2017
Dallas, TX 75207
Phone: 214-746-4680 FAX: 214-746-4015

- Products(s): WORKlogikTM

WORKlogik is a client/server production oriented workflow product which offers businesses the ability to graphically capture, improve and manage the flow of work and information through cross-functional areas. It is particularly well suited for complex environments which require the incorporation of an organization 's business rules into the process model. WORKlogik uses a combination of statistical based heuristics, sophisticated load leveling algorithms and tight adherence to the workflow Management Coalition's international workflow interface standard. WORKlogik integrates an organization's existing disparate applications. It is data type independent allowing documents, data and multimedia to all be handled from within the same environment.

WORKlogik is open, modular and ODBC compliant. It supports most popular database engines, server platforms and network environments. WORKlogik is an ideal integration point for the often heterogeneous systems and processes that exist within organizations today.

Intelus

9210 Corporate Boulevard, 4th Floor
Rockville, MD 20850
1 301-990-6363 Fax: 301-990-6011

- Product(s): ProcessFlo

ProcessFlo is a multimedia workflow and document management system that combines document imaging, digitized voice, text, data, and hard copy paperwork management functions with extensive business process reengineering tools. In addition, the system is designed to facilitate customization, extension, and integration with legacy systems and other applications.

Incorporating both graphical and table driven set-up tools, ProcessFlo allows a complete application to be defined and implemented on a rapid prototype basis in hours with no custom code. The system accommodates both passive (next step controlled by software) and active (next step controlled by user) work methods and allows routing to any combination of person, work group, and step (as opposed to hierarchical user within role within activity routing). Work can be organized according to either a one-queue/one-worker model, a one-queue/many-workers model, or a mixture of the two models. Object-oriented design is at the heart of ProcessFlo.

Jetform Corporation

Waterfall Center 800 South Street, Suite 305
Waltham, MA 02154
1 617-647-7700 Fax: 617-647-4121

- Product(s): Jetform E-Mail

Jetform E-Mail allows users to send, receive and track all their business forms via cc: Mail, Microsoft Mail, Windows for Workgroups, HP Open Mail, Higgins and other e-mail systems.

JTS Limited

5090 Orbitor Drive Suite 100,
Mississauga, Ontario, CANADA L4W 5B5
1 905-602-5678 Fax: 1 905-602-6594

- Product(s): Open Image

Open Image is primarily a document management system based on extensions to the Sybase RDBMS. It allows the direct integration of business systems with any associated documents. The product uses SQL Stored Procedures which permit the developer to contemplate integrating the document management functionality with virtually any third party application.

Keyfile Corporation

22 Cotton Road
Nashua, NH 03063
1 603-883-3800 Fax: 603-889-9259

- Product(s): Keyfile 2.2
  Keyfile is an integrated document management software that allows users to handle every office document—paper and electronic, spreadsheet or word processed memo, graphic illustration or bill of materials. File, retrieve, share, distribute, automate, Fax, print, create, mark-up, revise, and archive documents using industry standard devices and networks. Key features include: JobMaker, Keyfile's revolutionary workflow tool for ad hoc and systematic routing and tracking of tasks and documents; full client and server support for Microsoft's Dynamic Data Exchange (DDE) and Object Linking and Embedding (OLE) protocols which allow users to document-enable any DDE or OLE-compliant application; TIFF-protocols that allow users to document-enable any DDE or OLE-compliant application; TIFF-IT technology that automatically converts any electronic application file to a tiff image for printing, faxing, and annotating (even if you do not have the application) and enhanced display features. Keyfile also features a Windows-based desktop environment featuring "smart icons" that represent familiar office objects; "drag and drop" mouse movements; an intuitive, easy-to-use interface; and full text indexing; voice, typed, text, and Type-MATIC (text on forms).

Knowledge Based Systems, Inc.

1 BKSI Place
1408 University Drive
College Station TX 77840
Tel: 1 409-260-5274 Fax: 409-260-1965

- Product(s) PROSIM Process Modeling Software
  The ProSim tool has been developed especially for the business practitioner and allows process descriptions to be animated and simulated through the AT&T Istel simulation oackage, WITNESS. ProSim generates a fuly functional witness model from the process description.

LaserData

300 Vesper Park
Tyngboro, MA 01879

1 508-649-4600 Fax: 508-649-4436

- Product(s): DocuFlow
LaserData's DocuFlow software provides production-capable workflow services. It is also a robust environment for integrating document management functions with workflow capabilities in applications that manage complex business process. DocuFlow uses the ActionWorkflow System as its workflow engine.

Lotus Development Corporation

55 Cambridge Parkway
Cambridge, MA 02142
1 617-577-8500 Fax: 617-693-5562

- Product(s): Notes Lotus Notes Document Imaging
Lotus Notes is the leading platform for building LAN-based client/server applications. These applications are used on the workgroup and enterprise level, and include distributed document management, information sharing, process tracking, and workflow. Notes services include document and database management, replication, and a full client/server store-and-forward messaging system. Notes Mail is currently being used to support workgroup and enterprise messaging requirements.

Meta Software Corporation

125 Cambridge Park Drive
Cambridge, MA 02140
1-617-576-6920 Fax: 617-661-2008

- Product(s): WorkFlow Analyzer
The WorkFlow Analyzer allows you to study a proposed process redesign and see in advance how it would work. The WorkFlow Analyzer is designed specifically for analyzing workflow problems that involve exceptions and ambiguities. Meta's WorkFlow Analyzer does not require programming skills.. Workflow models are created with an easy-to-use graphical modeler. The WorkFlow Analyzer will analyze workflows that include concurrent processes.

Metafile Information Systems

421 First Avenue, S.W.
Rochester, MN 55902
1 507-286-9232 Fax: 507-286-9065

- Product(s): Metaview FOLDERS

Metaview FOLDERS is a windows-based document imaging and workflow solution. Customizable turnkey application designed to store, retrieve, display and route folders of scanned images, host reports, faxes, word processing files, spreadsheets, even voice and video. Integrate other software and databases using OLE 2.0 (object linking and embedding), ODBC (open database connectivity), DDE and APIs.

Metaphase Technology, Inc.

4201 Lexington Avenue North
Arden Hills, MN 55126-6198
1 612-482-4219 Fax: 612-482-4348

- Product(s): Metaphase 2.0

Metaphase 2.0 is an object management system with comprehensive workflow capabilities ranging from simple informal routing to enterprise-wide distribution and workflow processing. Workflow capabilities include calendar-based events, electronic signoffs, serial and parallel processes, and decision-based processing. Additional modules provide product structure, configuration management, and image view and markup features. Based on open systems standards, Metaphase is available on UNIX platforms from Sun, HP, SGI, IBM and DEC as well as PCs and Macintoshes. Metaphase 2.0 is available through a network of systems integrators and value added resellers worldwide.

Microsoft Corporation

One Microsoft Way
Redmond, WA 98052-6399
1 206-882-8080 Fax: 206-936-7329

- Product(s): Electronic Forms Designer 1.0

Electronic Forms Designer allows programmers to use the Microsoft Visual Basic programming system to create electronic forms for users of Microsoft Mail for Windows. Forms produced with the Electronic Forms Designer are integrated with the mail system and can be integrated with other applications to create workgroup solutions.

Mondas Information Technology

16-17 Springfield Lane
Weybridge, Surrey, KT13 8AW ENGLAND
+44 1-932-828-822 Fax: 1932-828-992

- Product(s): radica!

radica! is a product which seeks an holistic approach to work management systems, incorporating the ability to capture all information flowing through the company. The most interesting feature within the product is that it does much more than move work around the office - the developers have included the concepts of performance management and the transactions of the business directly within the work management environment.

Odesta Systems Corporation

4084 Commercial
Northbrook, IL 60062
1 708-498-5615 Fax: 708-498-9917

- Product(s): ODMS

Odesta Document Management Systems (Open ODMS) is a client/server software environment for industrial-strength workflow and document management. Open ODMS supports entering, storing, retrieving, routing and distributing documents across the network. Open ODMS automatically tracks the status of all documents and projects, and can manage any desktop document from any source, including word processing documents, spreadsheets, images and graphics. Open ODMS provides the ability to modify ODMS applications through its ODMS Toolkit, a graphical object-based development environment. Open ODMS also provides access to a customer's information systems with its Application Programming Interface (API). Open ODMS supported clients are MS-Windows PCs, Macintoshes and Motif workstations. Open ODMS supported databases are Oracle, Sybase and Digital Equipment Corporation's Rdb, and supported servers include any server the before mentioned databases run on, including (but not limited to) Sun Sparc, IBM RS/6000, HP, DEC VAXs, Intel and Power PC-based machines.

Olivetti & Co, SpA

Via Jervis
10015 Ivrea, Italy
39.125-529-189 Fax: 39.125-521-385

- Product(s): X_Workflow, IBIsys

Olivetti sells a full range of hardware products; software products include operating systems, development tools, desktop applications, vertical applications, and the Integrated Business Information System, known as IBIsys.

X_Workflow is an optional component of IBIsys and was developed internally by Olivetti. X_Workflow contains four modules. An authoring environment is used for defining procedures. The maintenance module installs the previously defined procedures and defines the user directory and roles. The user module is the environment in which users initiate and execute steps of the procedure, and the auditing module monitors, audits and reports on process activities.

Optika Imaging Systems

5755 Mark Dabling Blvd., Suite 100
Colorado Springs, CO 80919
1 719-548-9800 Fax: 719-531-7915

- Product(s): FilePower
  Optika's FilePower product line is comprised of a family of software modules, each optimized to an imaging task and all operating under the latest version of Microsoft Windows. The result is a seamlessly integrated and robust set of software tools that provides the ability to store, route, access and print millions of document images, faxes and report pages.

Portfolio Technologies Inc.

5600 Mowry School Road, Suite 100
Newark, CA 94560
1 510-226-5600 Fax: 510-226-8182

- Product(s): Office.IQ
  Office.IQ collaborative software is an intelligent workgroup product designed to package diverse information types by project or task, for distribution among workgroups. Among the features that enable Office.IQ to process work so effectively are its graphical workflow, concurrent and referential sharing capabilities, user-definable search fields, annotation tools and document security features. Office.IQ "workgroup" enables virtually all Windows application documents including annotated voice files, spreadsheets, text and graphics files, and compound documents such as faxed or scanned images. Office.IQ runs on PCs running Windows in a Novell NetWare environment. The most important thing Office.IQ provides is the ability for people to organize, share and process the information they use in a manner best suited to the way they work, rather than forcing them to conform their work processes to the constraints of the software.

Premenos Corporation

1000 Burnett Avenue, Second Floor
Concord, CA 94520
1 510-602-2000 Fax: 510-602-2024

- Product(s): EDI/400, EDI/38, EDI/36, EDI/e QMail
  These products are widely used midrange Electronic Data Interchange (EDI) translators. QMail is an electronic mail and workflow management messaging system for the IBM AS/400.

Quality Decision Management, Inc.

200 Sutton Street Suite 225
North Andover, MA 01845
1 508-688-8266 Fax: 508-688-5181

- Product(s): Quality at Work, Version 2.0
  Quality *At Work*—The Bridge from Communication to Coordination. Quality *At Work* is an add-on product for Lotus Notes that uses workflow technology to help you effectively manage change and proactively create the changes that are shaping the direction of business today. While groupware operates on the assumption that information is only useful when shared, workflow-enabled groupware is based on the notion that shared information is only useful when it fosters and facilitates timely, effective action. Groupware disseminates information, workflow-enabled groupware incites action.

Reach Software Corporation

872 Hermosa Drive
Sunnyvale, CA 94086
1 408-733-8685 Fax: 408-733-9265

- Product(s): WorkMAN
  WorkMAN is a workflow platform that leverages the directory services and connectivity of e-mail. WorkMAN actively manages the flow and processing of information between people, departments, or across the enterprise. WorkMAN automates business processing by using WorkMAN Tools, a visual development environment. Business processes are automated and information and process status are tracked.

Recognition International Inc.

Software Division
1310 Chesapeake Terrace
Sunnyvale, CA 94089
1 408-743-4300 Fax: 408-747-1245

- Product(s): Plexus FloWare
  FloWare is a client/server workflow application which coordinates the interaction of an organization's documents, data, tasks and people, making them more effective, efficient and adaptable. FloWare enables users to graphically build, monitor, analyze and interactively manage business process aplications, allowing organizations to reengineer and streamline business processes that span multiple application programs. Through its open, scalable arichitecture, FloWare software provides a proven basis for enabling best-of-breed application solutions

requiring enterprise-wide workflow services. Originally introduced in 1992, FloWare software is installed in some of the largest production systems in the world.

Remedy Corporation

1505 Salador Dr.
Mountain View, CA 94043
1 415-903-5200 Fax: 415-903-9001

Contact: Lawrence Garlick, Chairman and Chief Executive Officer

- Product(s): Action Request System
  Action Request System is a foundation application that is the "spreadsheet" analog for any organization that provides support or service. The Action Request (AR) System manages the timely resolution of problems and support requests. It is a client/server system in which clients can be both the support staff and the end user being supported. It suggests a flexible, tailorable workflow process for the support staff and end users that reduces the time and cost to resolve day-to-day requests. It automatically captures an experience database to give leverage to the support staff in solving future requests. It can be customized to meet the precise needs of all the roles in the support process.

RKB Limited/Prism Performance Systems

37000 Grand River Suite 230
Farmington Hills MI 48335
1-810-474-8855 Fax: 810-474 1116

- Product(s): RKB WorkFrame
  RKB, Ltd. has developed a behavioral and computer technology that supports broader and deeper change. RKB continues to successfully utilize Integrative Strategic Change but now enhances it with the RKB WorkFrame Strategic Change; WorkFlow and TeamWork business solutions to enable clients to cost-effectively internalize crucial change capabilities. Marketing and distribution is handled by Prism Performance Systems.

Saros Corporation

10900 NE 8th Street 700 Plaza
Bellevue, WA 98004
1 206-462-1066 Fax: 206-462-0879

- Product(s): Saros Document Manager Saros Mezzanine
No information submitted

Scopus Technology, Inc.

1900 Powell Street, Suite 700, 7th Floor
Emeryville, CA 94608
1 510-428-0500 Fax: 510-428-1027

- Products(s)
Founded in 1990, Scopus Technology, Inc. is a provider of workflow automation tools for customer-centric information systems. Scopus' customizable products enable companies to record, access and manage all available customer and product information. The company's diverse customer base includes organizations in finance, telecommunications, CAD/CAM petrochemicals, hardware systems and companies supporting both shrink-wrap and customizable software products.

Siemens-Nixdorf Information Systems

33094 Paderborn
Riemekestrasse 160, Germany
49 896-36-40325 Fax: 896-36-49940

- Product(s): WorkParty
Siemens Nixdorf supports the control of office activities involving many users within the framework of the OCIS (Office Communication & Information Systems) office concept by means of WorkParty workflow management. Workflows consist of individual flow steps that can be made up of manual or programmable actions. WorkParty allows these actions to be performed by the user or via programs or program segments.

Sigma Imaging Systems

622 Third Avenue
New York, NY 10017
1 212-476-3000 Fax: 212-986-0175

- Product(s): Route Builder OmniDesk
Sigma Imaging Systems develops state-of-the-art imaging system software for paper-intensive businesses including insurance, banking, finance, utilities, and the public sector. Sigma's OmniDesk software provides tools with which users can develop and maintain complex workflows without custom programming. Sigma is pioneer in the development of graphical workflow software for business process reengineering.

Staffware Ltd

70 Walnut Street
Wellesley, MA 02181

1 617-239-8221 Fax: 617-239-8223
and
46 Chagford Street
London, NW1 6EB, U.K.
44 71-262-1021 Fax: 44 71-262-3956

- Product(s): Staffware
Staffware is procedure processing software that automates the execution and control of routine procedures. It automatically requests and passes the necessary documents and information among the individuals involved to ensure that a procedure is completed on time without relying on each individual to initiate successive stages.

Sterling Software Inc

3340 Peachtree Road, NE
Atlanta, GA 30326
1 404-231-8575 Fax: 1 404-231-3510

- Product(s): MAXIM
MAXIM is a flow and organisational diagramming tool which links processes to the organisational units (roles) which have responsibility for undertaking the work. The products and documents which the process utilises or produces can also be linked into the model. The Organisational Flow Diagrammer shows the way in which work traverses organisational units and the hierarchical nature of most organisational structures. User-defined process measures may be stored within the repository. The product supports both OLE 2.0 and DDE.

Tandem Document Management System

10210 NE Points Drive, Suite 300
Kirkland, WA 98033
1 206-828-8704 Fax: 206-822-8022

- Product(s): Product & Process Document Management
Tandem's Product and Process Document Management (PPDM) system supports enterprises that demand mission-critical Non-Stop document availability and comprehensive workflow change control in complex document environments. PPDM clients run on PCs, UNIX, and Macintosh workstations that are LAN connected to the Tandem file and workflow server. PPDM takes advantage of Tandem's linear expandability and distributed processing features to support growth from few to thousands of users at multiple sites.

TASC Image System Integration Division

55 Walkers Brook Drive
Reading, MA 01857
1 617-942-2000 Fax: 617-942-7100

Product(s): TASC-Flow (No information submitted)

TeamWARE

800 Central Expressway, MS 34-10
Santa Clara CA 95052
1-800-240-8326

- Product(s) TeamWARE Office

TeamWARE Office provides a total solution, including e-mail, group scheduling, document management, conferencing/bulletin board, workflow and remote access. TeamWARE Office is modular; the products can be used ind-pendently, or together as a fully integrated solution sharing a common directory.. The product allows you to integrate or create custom applications.

Technology Economics Inc.

11212 Stephanie Lane
Rockville, Md 20852
1 301-984-1334 Fax: 1 301-984-0816

- Product(s): BPSimulator Template, Business Process Analyzer

The BPSimulator (BPS) is one facet of the BPR tool set developed by Technology Economics Inc.. The BPS is one of a family of templates available that sit on top of the ARENA simulation environment. The product comprises a collection of customised modules that may be combined to describe complex business processes.

The Business Process Analyzer (BPA) is a repository based product in-tended for use throughout the life-cycle of a BPR initiative. It records informa-tion about many facets of the business and does not restrict itself to process con-cepts.

Texas Instruments Inc., AIM Division

6620 Chase Oaks Boulevard, MS 8502
Plano, TX 75023
1 800-336-5236 Fax: 1 214-995-2067

- Product(s): BDF & PowerGrAF

The BDF has been designed for use by BPR practitioners to assist in the capture, modelling and analysis of information for a BPR project. The associated PowerGrAF product can be used to provide the modeller with a method of visualising data - this will likely be stored within the BDF repository or may come from external spreadsheet data.

The Vantive Corporation

1890 North Shoreline Boulevard
Mountain View, CA 94043
1 415-691-1500 Fax: 415-691-1515

- Product(s): The Vantive System
  The Vantive System comprises five integrated applications that automate and integrate customer support, help desk, quality assurance/engineering, sales, remote customers and suppliers. These applications share a common enterprise database collectively, all the data from multiple departments about a company's customers, its products, and how customers use those products. All applications feature extensive problem-solving help, workflow management, and reporting functionality. The Vantive System is based on a client/server architecture for high OLTP performance and is highly portable and scaleable across popular platforms.

Timephaser Corporation

9171 Towne Centre Drive #555
San Diego, CA 92122
1 619-490-3636 Fax: 619-554-1028

- Product(s): TimePhaser Global Work Scheduler
  TimePhaser Global Work Scheduler provides management at all levels of the organization with the ability to measure and track the performance o fhuman resources, facilities, production and finances from an integrated and global perspective. TimePhaser's interference engine technology delivers automation tools that are capable of measuring and tracking work in a real-time, enterprise-wide framework.

UES, Inc.

5162 Blazer Memorial Parkway
Dublin, OH 43017
1 614-792-9993 Fax: 614-792-0998

- Product(s): K1 Shell
  K1 Shell is a workflow process modeling and enactment system. It is available across multiple platforms and supports heterogeneous workflow clients.

Unisys Corporation

Township Line and Union Meeting Roads
PO Box 500 M/S B260
Blue Bell PA 19422-0500
Tel: 1 215-986-4183 fax: 215 986-2558
- Product(s) InfoImage Solutions, Event Manager II

InfoImage is a high production workflow software application.

Verimation

50 Tice Boulevard
Woodcliff Lake, NJ 07675
1 201-391-2888 Fax: 201-391-2039
- Product(s): Memo

Verimation develops, markets and supports electronic mail and office automation software for multiple platforms including mainframe, midrange, LAN and PC workstations. Workflow capabilities are included in the products to improve efficiency and productivity.

ViewStar Corporation

5820 Shellmound Street, Suite 600
Emeryville, CA 94608-1912
1 510-652-7827 Fax: 510-653-9926

- Product(s): ViewStar

The ViewStar System is a client/server software system for document management and workflow processing. This product facilitates the automation of paper-intensive business functions within large corporations. The ViewStar System includes a wide range of functionality for processing and manipulating image, text and other format documents over local and wide-area networks and includes functions for document capture, storage, management, display, annotation, editing, routing, distribution and output. In addition, ViewStar provides an advanced application development toolkit with an object-oriented programming language for customization and extension of the system to address customer-specific application needs.

Vision Software

505 14th Street
Oakland CA 94612
1 510-258-4100 Fax: 510-238-4101

- Product(s): Image Application Workbench (IAW)

IAW allows you to develop new imaging and workflow systems. It eliminates tedious script language programming. It is an object oriented, GUI toolset.

Wang Laboratories Inc.

One Industrial Avenue
Lowell, MA 01851
1 508-967-7682 Fax: 508-967-1105

- Product(s): OPEN/workflow

  OPEN/workflow bring graphical development technology to the automation of business procedures by allowing non-programmers in work groups and departments to quickly create and modify applications that automate their work processes, including those portions that might previously have been hard coded or not automated at all.

  It includes a graphical tool for describing a series of tasks and business rules and a runtime system that routes and tracks work packages, integrates applications and services needed to accomplish the process. Beyond automation of business procedures, OPEN/workflow also captures measurement information (both time and cost) for planning, work management, and as the basis for continual improvement.

WordPerfect, Novell Applications Division

1555 North Technology Way
Orem, UT 84057
1 801-225-5000 Fax: 801-222-5077

- Product(s): Informs 1.0b, GroupWise 4.1 (formerly Office), and SoftSolutions 4.0

  The Novell GroupWare products offer a complete solution to your workgroup needs. They can also be used individually, and will work within your current system.
- InForms creates forms, distribute them through any mail package, fills them in, and saves the records to any database.

  GroupWise is an advanced electronic messaging program, integrating e-mail, calendaring and scheduling, and task management from within one product.

  SoftSolutions creates an environment for managing your documents and other files, and is the #1 Document Management program on the market.

WorkFlow Incorporated

7181 No. Austin Avenue
Niles, IL 60714
1 708-647-0444 Fax: 708-647-0895

- Product(s): DOC-FLOW

DOC-FLOW creates, organizes, displays, prints, transmits, and monitors character-based documents. DOC-FLOW is a general-purpose systems and is adapted by our application engineers to specific application.

Workflow, Inc.

P.O. Box 896
Concordville, PA 19331
1 610-459-9487 Fax: 610 459-7895

- Product(s): FlowMaker

FlowMaker - The workflow solution for Notes - meets the challenges of coding parallel approvals, negotiations, pooling, reminders and more, with less programming and no run times. You won't need to make any excuses when automating purchase requisition, program review, engineering change request or personnel appraisel workflows in Notes.

Workgroup Technology

81 Hartwell Avenue
Lexington, MA 02173
1 617-674-7655 Fax: 617-674-0034

- Product(s): CMS/Workflow

CM/Workflow is a member of the CMS family of Product Data Management (PDM) solutions. CMS manages all product related data, regardless of the source, throughout the entire product life cycle. CMS ensures that product data is accurate, organized, accessible, and where appropriate, modifiable.

CMS/Workflow, an add-on module to CMS, is a dynamic tool for re-engineering, and automating business processes and procedures. As a result, CMS is helping organizations worldwide to improve their time to market, reduce their cycle times and maximize product quality.

XSoft, A Division of Xerox

Four Cambridge Center
Cambridge, MA 02142-1494
1 800-626-6775 Fax: 617-499-4409

- Product(s): InConcert

InConcert, from XSoft, is fully featured workflow management software that models and coordinates the components of a work process—the people, procedures and information for the management of business processes. InConcert integrates sophisticated, object-oriented workflow technology with powerful document management services. Add this to an innovative job-based model for collaborative processing, and the result is a superior collection of tools for automating and maintaining business process.

1-800-GROUPWARE Fax-on-Demand
(1-800-476-8792)

WARIA, the Workflow And Reengineering International Association, in conjunction with Future Strategies Inc., offers a Fax-on-Demand service on which the vendor directory will be kept updated. This free information service also includes conference events, analyst reports, white papers, press releases, product technical support etc.

To access:

In the USA, dial-1-800-GROUPWARE (800-476-8792) from any touch-tone phone and key in your fax number to download the menu of available documents. Follow the easy instructions.

Non-USA callers should dial 1-415-637-2600 from a fax machine to have information faxed directly back to them.

The World Wide Web 1-800-GROUPWARE homepage is under construction at time of going to press. Details on how to access it will be available on the 1-800-GROUPWARE Fax-on-Demand system.

To be listed:

If vendor or consulting organizations would like their product information, updates, press releases or services included in the next edition of the book, on 1-800-GROUPWARE or the World Wide Web, please contact the editor, Layna Fischer, at 305-782-3376, fax 305-782-6365 or waria@gate.net.

INDEX

—V—

value chains, 282
Verimation, 231
ViewStar, 186, 190, 192, 193
Vision Software, 339
Visual Basic, 194, 271
voice, 290, 291, 293, 294, 298
voice recognition, 290, 291

—W—

Wal-Mart, 123
Wang, 117, 192, 193
WARIA, 117, 303, 305
Winograd, Terry, 59, 73, 119, 137, 138
WinWork, 318
Wohl, Amy, 312
Wohl, Amy D., 289
WordPerfect, 117, 253
Work Media, 15
workflow
  definition, 88, 219
workflow analysis, 88, 96, 182

Workflow And Reengineering International Association, 11, 117, 305
Workflow Automation, 269
Workflow Conference, 272
Workflow Management Coalition, 25, 121
Workflow, Inc., 341
Workflow.BPR, 323
workgroup architecture, 249, 266
WorkMAN, 222, 229
WorkParty, 265
World Wide Web, 279
Wright, Frank Lloyd, 294

—X—

XDP, 216
Xerox Corporation, 114, 129
XSoft Corporation, 229

—Y—

Young and Rubicam, 79, 80, 188

ORDER FORM

To order additional copies of this book please fill out and mail the coupon
below to: **Future Strategies, 3640 N. Federal Highway, Pompano Beach, FL
33064.** For faster service you can fax your order to (305) 782-6365 **OR** E-Mail
Internet: waria@gate.net.

SHIPPING INFO:

Name: _____

Title/Occupation: _____

Company: _____

Address: _____

_____

Phone: _____ Fax: _____

PAYMENT INFO: *(Sorry, no orders shipped COD.)*

☐ Check in US $ (payable to Future Strategies, Inc.)

☐ Diner's Club ☐ Visa ☐ MasterCard ☐ AMEX

Credit Card No. : _____

Expiration Date: _____

Signature: _____

(We must have signature to process your order.)

US Airmail Shipping/Handling Charges are PER BOOK*:

* USA Priority Mail $3.50 * Canada/Mexico $5.50 * UK/Europe $9.50 *
Pacific Rim $12.50 * Africa/South America $14.50.

**Quantity and Educational Discounts Available. Shipping charges
accordingly.**